DATE DUE

FEB 2 8 '79		
OCT 3 1 '79		
NOV 7 '79		
NOV 21 '79		
OCT ? ? '80		
FEB 4 '81		
JAN 2 6 '89		

Please Touch

Jane Howard

PLEASE TOUCH

A Guided Tour of the
Human Potential Movement

McGRAW-HILL BOOK COMPANY
New York   St. Louis   San Francisco
Dusseldorf   Mexico   Panama   Toronto

For

JOHN AND SARAH

and

HENRY AND TOM

and

TWO SMALL JANES

and

ALL THEIR PARENTS

Preface

❡ Since I came across it in some forgotten English class in the 1950s I have had an abiding fondness for the stanza from W. H. Auden's poem "Under Which Lyre—A Revolutionary Tract for the Times," which advises:

> Thou shalt not answer questionnaires
> Or quizzes upon World-Affairs,
>   Nor with compliance
> Take any test. Thou shalt not sit
> With statisticians, nor commit
>   A social science.

My regard for these sentiments is such that for years I took pains to avoid all forms and practitioners of social science. But lately, in a paradoxical about-face, I have spent nearly all my time in their midst. I have done so because of some other lines, even more deeply embedded in my consciousness, from the Book of Isaiah: "Then shall the eyes of the blind be opened and the ears of the deaf unstopped. Then shall the lame man leap as an hart, and the tongue of the dumb shall sing."

This book tells of a year of my life. It is about my reactions to the efforts of some social scientists (and a good many other people as well) to provide us all with new ways to see and hear and leap and sing—and, in several senses of the word, to touch one another.

Acknowledgments

For chancing to steer me in the direction of this book in the first place, and for giving me many more months' leave of absence than anyone thought it would take, I am grateful to *Life* magazine.

For pointing out the way, and for any number of helpful kindnesses, I am indebted to all the group leaders and theorists of the human potential movement quoted on these pages, and to many others whose names are not mentioned. Kenneth Benne, Betty Berzon, Leland Bradford, Robert Driver, Abraham Maslow, Michael Murphy, William Schutz, Bob and Lennie Schwartz, Charles Seashore and John and Joyce Weir were particularly helpful.

For letting me be part of their groups, on the grounds that I appeared to be a human being as well as an emissary from the dread "media," I owe thanks to an even longer list of people, most of whose identities are here deliberately disguised.

For assembling some of the list of human potential organizations I am indebted to Ann Hoadley, and for typing part of the manuscript to Sylvia Seefurth Jaynes.

Acknowledgments

For weeks of space, peace and solitude without which I could never have made sense out of my chaotic mounds of notes I thank Ellen and Ben Bloom.

For enduring me at my unsettled worst, and for making me laugh when nothing seemed funny, I am grateful to my friends from the "real world," especially to Julius Goldstein, Kathy and Steve Jacobs, Bill and Beth McPherson, and Virginia Sadler. I also thank Anne Murphy, for sympathetic editing, and Frank Taylor, for the vision that got me off crutches and into print.

For encouragement in this and in many other projects I owe more than I can say to Dave Scherman. He made me laugh, too.

ꭤ

Contents

xi

Contents

"Lots of people with no symptoms at all are dying."

—A member of a weekend encounter group

Please Touch

Whatever Possessed Me

(The number I have dialed, it often seems to me, is not a working number. Much of what I see and read and smell and hear offends me. I hate inhaling smog, listening to jack-hammers, watching high-rise geometric slabs dominate landscapes, and needing to know the phone number of the Air Pollution Complaint office. I grieve for birds drowned in oil slick, lakes ruined by garbage, and sheep dead of nerve gas, not to say boys dead of Vietnam. I sigh at the look of banners festooning gas stations next to franchised trading stamp redemption centers next to franchised finger-lickin' chicken takeout stands. I wince when I think of the California schoolteacher who was fired for assigning his first graders the words LOVE and PEACE as a penmanship exercise. "There's too much of that stuff around already," his boss was quoted in a newspaper article.

Another newspaper article I chanced to see told how the Air Force needed German Shepherd puppies. The puppies, the story said, could "look forward to serving until they are around nine years old, when they will be put to sleep. They are too dangerous, after their training, to be loosed again on the civilian world. 'There is nothing more beautiful than seeing a dog flush out a man and run him down,' said Sergeant Riley."

The thought of Sergeant Riley, whoever he may be, haunts me. I wonder what else he thinks is beautiful. I'll bet he will be the first to cheer when supersonic transports streak 330 passengers to their destinations, disturbing the sleep of 3 billion other people below. I'll bet he takes his transistor radio with him to national parks, and keeps the volume up good and loud. But I credit him with redeeming features. I'll bet he's a nice daddy, who obliges when his children pester him for presents, like miniature tricycle license plates with names on them.

Those tricycle license plates transfix me. Sometimes I stand looking at revolving racks of them by the cash registers of highway restaurants, thinking how many kids must exist to justify each name on them. ALAN. BOBBIE. BRETT. CANDY. CHIP. DENISE. DWAYNE. ELAINE. ERNEST. GWEN. GLENN. JENNIFER. KEVIN. LORIE. MARC. MARK. MELODY. MINDY. PATTI. RICK. ROD. SCOTT. SHERRI. SHERRY. TODD. TONI. VICKI. I think how soon all those Sherris and Marcs will graduate from tricycles to two-wheelers to each other, and of all the children they will have. I think of estimates that by the year 2000 (if such a year comes) there will be 7.4 billion of us—twice as many as we are now, twice as crowded as we are now. And, because crowdedness has been proven to beget alienation, they will be twice as alienated as we are now.

We are in plenty of trouble as it is. In treading on the moon we have fulfilled Marshall McLuhan's prophecy and become a Global Village. Hypocrisy no longer suits us; we need candor. Shoving and pushing and slaughtering do not suit us; we need trust. Alienation does not suit us; we need intimacy. And so it is a curious fact that now, in the final third of our century, many among us are attempting to program candor and trust and intimacy, the same way others program voyages to space. An epidemic of such programs, reminiscent at once of systems analysis and social science and snake oil, is all around us. These programs, usually called sensitivity training, T-groups, or encounter groups, are as much a part of our time as lunar modules, acid rock and assassinations. A Bengal Indian I chanced to meet on a commuter train to Grand Central Station said oh yes, he'd been to several encounter groups. My mother's cousin Chuck, near Los Angeles, said oh yes, he had thought of leading groups himself. A pair of bearded guitarists on a Caribbean beach said oh yes, they had hitchhiked most of the way down from New Hampshire to be in a twelve-day encounter. But people still ask, sometimes, what an encounter group is. I, by an odd series of circumstances, am in a position to give them a pretty good composite idea.

An encounter group is a gathering, for a few hours or a few days, of twelve or eighteen personable, responsible, certifiably normal and temporarily smelly people. Their destination is intimacy, trust and awareness of why they behave as they do in groups; their vehicle is candor. Exhorted to "get in touch with their feelings" and to "live in the here-and-now," they sprawl on the floor of a smoky room littered with styrofoam coffee cups, half-empty Kleenex boxes and overflowing ashtrays. As they grow tired they rest their heads on rolled-up sweaters or corners of cot mattresses or each other's laps.

In many instances they have never even met before, but, like the proverbial strangers on a train, quickly talk of their deepest emotions. Sometimes they use gadgets and exercises and props; sometimes they don't. Some of them shout, seethe,

3

sob, attack and eventually embrace each other. All of them survive long spells of silence. In fact they become connoisseurs of different qualities of silence—awkward, peaceful, Quaker, pregnant, painful, comfortable.

Each group is a microcosm of society, but no two groups are ever alike. All are part of a loosely organized force which resists labeling but which for the sake of convenience is often called the human potential movement. The movement is many things. It is a business, a means of recreation, a subculture, a counterculture, a form of theatre, a philosophy of education, a kind of psychotherapy, and an underground religion, with its own synods, sects, prophets, schisms and heretics. Depending on who is assessing it, it is also a passing fad, a godsend, a silly collection of parlor games or a menace.

The people who keep the movement moving are as prone as any others to backbiting and misunderstanding. They have converged from many disciplines. The majority were trained in education, theology, business, dance, psychology, sociology or social work. Some of them don't even know who the others are. They all, however, share an unwritten credo. They all believe that you don't have to be sick to get better, that you needn't stop growing just because you are chronologically an adult, and that the best place to achieve growth is among other people also engaged in growing. They all believe, in short, in encounter groups, which are known vernacularly as a kind of "therapy for normal people." Encounters, one leader of the movement says, "teach intimacy, which gives life a whole new dimension. It makes life different, rich, exciting and scary. Encounter groups kick open whole new doors you might not even have known were there."

Some groups try to kick doors open for organizations instead of individuals, shedding light on problems overlooked or created by some of our most entrenched social institutions: churches, schools, marriages, universities, police forces, families, business, even governments. Threatening as they do to

4

impose change on all these institutions, the groups raise end-
less questions. Are they a Communist plot, an invasion of privacy, a form of brainwashing? Are they really therapeutic?
Should they be? Who screens their members? Who leads them?
Who needs them? Are we not all, with the exception of the odd
wolf-child here and there, members of ready-made groups?
Why then should we join artificial ones? Should we not get on
with the work of the world, rather than preoccupying ourselves with "interpersonal relationships?" (As opposed to
what, by the way, our relationships with pepper mills and gi-
raffes and carburetors?) Where did this so-called "movement"
come from, and where is it bound?

And who appointed me to reckon with these questions?

I did, for several reasons. Not because of any infatuation
with the "behavioral sciences," but rather because the movement is a curiosity, and if there is one thing I am it is temper-
amentally, professionally and all but pathologically curious.
The only way I have ever earned a living is to write about
things that make me wonder. Most things do. For several
years, as I kept writing magazine articles and leading a fragmented life, I had wondered how it would be to try something
longer. I had turned down several suggested book topics when
I encountered, quite by chance, the human potential movement. The scope of its ambitions impressed me, and so did the
idealism of its people. Naive and silly and even dangerous
though some of them might be, I sensed a gallantry in their efforts to change the world.

Almost nothing had been written for laymen about the
movement or the several distinct types of encounter groups
through which it hopes to bring about change. I thought a
valid device might be to subject my own psyche—or at least
the defenses that cover it—to a sampling of such groups. I
thought that by so doing I could learn something worth writ-

5

ing about, as well as something about myself. My life, I thought, was as much in need as anyone's of "a whole new dimension." My strengths, it seemed to me, could well use bolstering, and my frailties could profit by being exposed. How could it hurt to find out how I came across to other people, to kick open new doors, and (to use group jargon) to "enhance my self-image"? And so I set forth, resolving to cover as much ground, geographically and otherwise, as time and sanity would allow.

When they learned what I was up to, my friends thought I was crazy.

"If you were married to *me*," one of them declared, "I'd absolutely forbid you to do something so outrageous."

"I wouldn't go to one of those groups if you *paid* me to," many others said.

"You realize what you're taking on, of course," a leader of the movement said. "You're trying to be a journalist, poet, critic, scientist, and anthropologist, all at once."

"Don't you think," another wondered, "that going from group to group to group will be like going to a wine-tasting without stopping for coffee to clear your palate between the wines?"

That sounded right, but I wouldn't have time for coffee. I have sampled, to continue the analogy, many kinds of wine: sweet, dry, nutty, fruity, insouciant, rotgut, presumptuous and noble. I've been high and I've been hung over, and I have felt like the only sober person at a party full of drunks. I have been angry and nervous and bored and scared. Often I have dozed off, nudged awake by neighbors contemptuous of my fatigue. (In no groups does anybody get much rest and in some, known as marathons, sleep is explicitly forbidden.)

Generalizing about the groups I have been in is hard. One had five people, and one had eight hundred. One lasted an afternoon, one eight days and nights. In one it was considered risqué to take off so much as a loafer; in another nobody wore anything at all. Some cost nothing, others charged upward of $50 a day. Some gathered in windowless rooms in the middle of dismal cities, others in secluded and splendid wilderness resorts. In breaks between group sessions some members listened to the Doors and Feliciano, and some gathered around out-of-tune upright pianos for old favorites like "Her Mother Never Told Her." Some of their leaders read aloud from Rod McKuen and Kahlil Gibran, but others favored William Blake. Some of my fellow group members wore granny glasses and body paint, but a good many had class rings and crewcuts, and expressed their pleasure by exclaiming not "Out of sight!" but "Copasetic!"

In no group did I deny that in addition to harboring at least as many anxieties, hypocrisies and shortcomings as the next supposedly "normal" person, I was also there as a writer. As a result, my presence was nearly always the first heated topic of group discussion. I grew deeply weary of explaining myself and apologizing. Many of the memories I accumulated are woeful. I recall one dawn when I stopped for a solitary cup of coffee at a desolate all-night cafe, after a marathon that left me too tired and troubled to sleep. I remember the long drive home from another group, when I confided my stream-of-consciousness impressions to a tape recorder. (People in nearby cars looked at me queerly.) I think of the man who told me, as we danced during a recess in another marathon, "You know what? I'm attracted to you, but I'm not getting any *vibes* from you."

"Tough," I wish I had told that man, "because I'm getting *too many* from you."

There were other times, though, when I felt genuine love for people who a few hours or days earlier had struck me as monumentally dull. There were times when I felt profoundly moved to watch the changes in people's faces, which at odd moments looked as I fancied they must have in infancy, and would on their deathbeds. I went to no movies in this period.

Please Touch

I didn't need to. The groups were more theatrical than any drama, more affecting than a sunrise and more disturbing than the funeral of a child.

I have interrelated on the Sunset Strip and in northern New England and in many places in between, under eucalyptuses and flaming maples and naked oaks and unflattering fluorescent lights. But by no means did I go to nearly all the places or meet nearly all the people I was told I should. I doubt that any chronicler of the movement ever can, because the movement grows faster than presses print books. For all I know I will learn tomorrow that the President and the astronauts and the Pope are planning a weekend sensitivity workshop, or that my Aunt Janet has started a T-group on the family farm in Iowa.

Artichokes
and a Massive
Trauma

❦ I had never heard of any of this until a little before January 27, 1968, when *Life* magazine sent me to Big Sur, California, to take part in and report on a five-day "Advanced Encounter Workshop" at the Esalen Institute. To that assignment I brought a lot of innocent ignorance, some cultural skepticism and very little background knowledge. Most of my previous stories had been about specific individuals, not sweeping ideas. I had never heard of an "Advanced Encounter Workshop," much less been to an elementary one, nor had I even much idea of what one was. But I had done risky things before. Had I not skipped fifth grade, bypassing the good Miss McKay altogether and going straight from Miss Lamb's room to Miss

Please Touch

Olson's? Had I not on one foolhardy occasion leaped from a plane with a parachute? Perhaps now, with a similar combination of luck and *chutzpah,* I could fake it and "encounter"— whatever encountering was—in a passably advanced manner.

From San Francisco I drove with the photographer assigned to illustrate the story four or five hours down the coast. We stopped only at Castroville, which banners proclaimed to be the World Artichoke Capital. Now I have a penchant for any world capital—of Tangerines, Whips, Riboflavin, Soybeans, Ice Hockey, what have you—and although I'm not so partial to artichokes as, say, my cousin Kathleen, I did feel obliged to pay homage. The real reason for the stop, though, was arrant procrastination. I was apprehensive about what Esalen would prove to be the capital of. Its brochure, cataloguing approximately a semester's worth of seminars and workshops, called it "a center to explore those trends in the behavioral sciences, religion and philosophy that emphasize the potentialities and values of human existence."

Its resident staff was reported to possess "a tool kit of nonverbal and sensory experiences" to help Esalen's ever-changing stream of visitors "know what it is to be human." Somebody had called Esalen "a spiritual colony, an opportunity, a symbol like the German Bauhaus." What it symbolized, presumably, was the merit of raw—not secondhand or vicarious —experience. What would overwhelm me about Esalen, I had heard, was its undiluted candor, its aversion to the common Prufrockian obsession with preparing faces to meet faces, and its demand that visitors risk revealing their unmasked, vulnerable selves. Esalen, it was rumored, did not hold with masks or facades. Esalen did not see life as a poker game. Esalen, furthermore and therefore, could be rough going. "You'll probably cry," somebody who had been there before told me, "and you might have an out-and-out ecstatic experience. You surely won't be bored."

I wasn't.

Artichokes and a Massive Trauma

On the way down I noticed a spot on my coat, and asked the photographer if there was a dry cleaner near Esalen. He just laughed, and soon I found out why. The nine-acre institute, a short drive seaward off U.S. 1 in the middle of the Big Sur wilderness, isn't near anything civilized. No dry cleaners, no newsstands, no library, no stores, no beauty shops, not a hint of franchised urban sprawl. Instead there are mountains, wildflowers, butterflies, canyons, conifers, rocks the size of rooms leading 200 feet down to the surf, hot sulphur springs, flute music and the smell of homemade bread. The permanent residents, most of whom dress hippie, look rinsed and radiant and in possession of some secret knowledge. They sleep, as visitors also do, in unimposing wooden houses and cabins connected by random dirt paths. The paths converge at a sprawling lodge where people eat, drink beer or wine if they like, sit before an enormous stone fireplace, watch the Pacific and dance. No scene has ever dazzled me more. I didn't even mind that fog, which I usually wish would go away, blanketed Esalen entirely my first two days there. When the sun broke through on the third morning, I felt as if I were witnessing Creation.

Anywhere else, even elsewhere in the militantly liberated state of California, people might have thought the twelve of us from the Advanced Encounter Workshop were crazy, or so I thought at the time. On that third morning we weren't following our scripts at all. We were supposed to be indoors interpersonally relating, interacting, honing and venting our feelings about one another, psychically unmasking ourselves and one another, and equipping one another with generous doses of what to me was a new currency: the gift of seeing ourselves as others see us, technically known as feedback. ("You seem a *little* less uptight and Eastern than you did yesterday" is a sample of the kind of feedback I kept getting.)

But we had thrown our schedules, along with our inhibitions, to the gentle Big Sur winds. There were otters and a

11

whale within sight in the Pacific, and I thought of some lines of John Berryman's:

> Hard on the land wears the strong sea,
> And empty grows every bed.

Esalen, like Berryman, heightened one's sense of mortality and the passage of time. To waste so spectacular a morning indoors would somehow have been obscene. So instead, before we knew it and without ever really planning it, we formed a little circle outside the main lodge and began to devise individual, impromptu dances.

"Let whatever wants to happen happen!" cried Josie, the only real dancer among us. "Stay with the feeling! Make whatever noises you want to make, in time with your heartbeat! Flow!"

Flow we did, or tried to. Staying with our fugitive feelings, we swung, swooped, soared and flailed, shouting rhythmic nonsense words. My word made me wonder if I might have some secret knack for glossolalia. It came out sounding like a balloon caption from some mock-Paleolithic comic strip.

"FROONGA!," I found myself shouting. "FROONG-*GA!*"

We doubtless looked as if we were rehearsing for the finale of Act II of *Marat/Sade,* but nobody around us seemed puzzled at all. The other people on the premises (who had come for other workshops) just smiled absently and went about their business, which, like ours, was to be spontaneous. As serenity is prized at a geriatric home, so is spontaneity at Esalen, which incidentally is pronounced to rhyme with wrestlin' and not, as some have guessed, "East Salem," or, more commonly, "Essalon." The place is named for an Indian tribe said to have interrelated, long ago, on the same grounds.

The twelve of us who flowed and shouted in the open air had first met one another, and the Advanced Encounter's two dozen other members, the previous Sunday night. After dinner all thirty-six of us had gathered in one big room, vacant except for our bodies and some cot mattresses. The room was named Maslow in honor of the psychologist Dr. Abraham Maslow, an early Esalen supporter who had blessed the place by pronouncing it "potentially one of the most important educational institutions in the world." On opening night each of us was supposed to give a thumbnail sketch of whatever problem he had come to "work on." Unprepared, I decided when my turn came that I would "work on" a pathological and chronic disinclination to say no. Others present confessed to maladies that ranged from "celebrityitis" (the affliction plaguing our leader, Dr. William Schutz, whose book *Joy* had just been published) to alcoholism.

The next morning we reassembled in Maslow for a long, tedious discussion of whether or not we ought to split into smaller, more workable units. I was annoyed at our leaders for not helping us make this trivial decision. Was this not supposed to be their life work? Were they not accredited—indeed, eminent—psychologists? Ought they not to be able to puzzle out such a simple matter as whether or not we should subdivide, and let us get down to work? But then came my first insight about encountering. Making such decisions, and enduring all the attendant anxiety and discomfort, was our work. That first anxiety came back to me later when I read that encounter groups are deliberately designed as "social vacuums" whose members are given a rare chance to be "tossed, figuratively, from the sky to face the necessity of hacking their way collaboratively out of the social jungle." We decided, at length, to form three subdivisions: Group One, Group Two and Group Nine.

For me, the five days that followed were filled with uneasiness. I was disturbed, first of all, that people sat around at and between the meetings draped all over one another, leaning against one another with their arms around one another, giving backrubs sometimes to people they didn't even know. But as the days went on I changed. Regretting my own chronic

13

undemonstrativeness, I did some draping and became a drapee myself.

"It's all right to touch," an elderly man kept assuring me.

On the drive down from San Francisco the photographer had said something about the Esalen bathhouse, where hot sulphur spring water flowed into giant tubs in which everybody communally soaked.

"I guess I won't be able to do that," I said, "because I didn't think to bring a bathing suit along."

"Nobody *wears* bathing suits," he said. That gave me pause. Except for a couple of furtive midnight skinny-dips I had never taken my clothes off in public and I wasn't eager to now. Not for three days did I venture to the three-sided bathhouse, halfway down a cliff overlooking the ocean. When I undressed and slipped into a tub with five or six other people I thought I might choke from self-conscious embarrassment. But that feeling passed. I found that no matter who else was around, or how they or I looked, it was far more peaceful than prurient to soak there and watch the waves break out at sea.

Salt water appeared on our cheeks, too. "Tears," I was to hear later and believe, "are a necessary stopping point on the path from emotional rigidity to joy." An unspoken Esalen motto seemed to be "I hurt, therefore I am." Crying was encouraged, but not indiscriminately. Everybody was exasperated with one woman who was a human fountain of racking sobs, her face a constant mask of Tragedy or Grief. Any mildly poignant anecdote could touch off a new fit of her weeping. In my journey through the human potential movement I was to see many more of her kind—copious sobbers who first evoked kindly pats on the shoulder and murmurs of "there, there," but who eventually were ordered to shut up.

My own first public tears concerned a handsome if inscrutable young man named Steve, quite a bit taller than I with a Tom Sawyerish lock of blond hair hanging in his face. We were

14

in a session called a "Microlab," divided at random into subgroups of five. Each quintet was to select the two people in it who knew each other the least. My group chose Steve and me. We were instructed to stand at opposite corners of the room and advance slowly, diagonally toward each other. When we met in the middle we were to express our reactions to each other however we liked, so long as what we did was nonverbal. (Nonverbalness, I was beginning to catch on, was locally akin to godliness.)

Well, I figured, Steve was certainly appealing, but I wasn't going to give him what I'd already heard described, derisively, as the "all-purpose, cop-out Esalen hug." With such hugs people known as "glib touchers" or, worse, "sensual pedants" were wont to greet the world at large. Instead I'd pat him on the cheek—friendly, a bit California, yet dignified—smile agreeably and move on. Only that wasn't the way it worked out. When Steve and I met he suddenly and quite forcefully shoved me back to the corner of the room where I'd come from. He seemed as surprised as I was, and a trifle ashamed. I pretended with mock cheer that it didn't matter.

"*Well,*" I said as we resumed our places in the group, "I guess I ought to be afraid of *you.*" I attempted the sort of smile that had been encouraged in the classrooms and gymnasia of yesteryear, when "good sportsmanship" was more valued even than good grooming.

"What are you smiling for?" asked Steve. "Do you think that what happened was funny?" As a matter of fact, I didn't think so at all. I couldn't recall ever having felt so utterly, classically rejected. Besides, as a girl named Pamela observed, my chin was a-tremble and a-quiver, so why didn't I just go ahead and cry? Well, I did, in unlovely sobs that must have looked like sideways figure eights. Doing so made me feel better and the others like me better, too. They liked me because I was exposing and expressing my real feelings, not the ones I thought were expected of me. I was being authentic and congruent and in touch with myself, and living in the Here and Now. It felt exhilarating.

A few times in the course of those five days I wished I had stayed back in Castroville with the artichokes. All that attention to candor could be absurd. Once I asked a waitress to bring me a glass of wine, "when you have time."

"You don't mean that," said the man next to me. "You mean she should bring it *right now*. Why don't you say so?"

During another dinner I mentioned somebody I thought was "a superior person."

"I don't know what you mean by *that*," said a doctor of philosophy who I was quite sure knew exactly what I meant. All told, though, I was so affected by the place and its inhabitants that the thought crossed my mind, for a few seconds anyway, just to chuck it all and stay on at Esalen as a waitress. After the Advanced Encounter I was persuaded easily to remain for the weekend.

"You'll find out a lot more about Esalen if you stay," I was promised. There were to be two attractions: a conference of teachers reporting on how they were using a Ford Foundation grant (administered through Esalen) to study new methods of education, and a whole new seminar called a Quest for Love. Okay, I decided. I'll stay the weekend, learn more, fly straight back to New York, write the story and then get on with something else.

The teachers, experimenting with something they called the Affective Domain of learning, really were worth meeting. I found them inspired and inspiring both as they told how children once dismissed as unreachable had blossomed in their experimental classrooms. The Quest for Love, abetted by tape-recorded instructions, was also a success; the questers ended up leaping in nonverbal delight all over the sunny greensward. When it was over somebody mentioned a gathering down the coastline, where Esalen people would meet others from the Big Sur community to talk and hear some drum music. I liked that idea, and thought it too might be part of my story, so I joined three others for the drive down the coast.

We never got there. Our car collided, head on, with another. Miraculously, nobody was killed, but of the six passengers involved three of us were rather seriously injured. The journey I made, therefore, was not by jet to Kennedy Airport but by wailing ambulance to a hospital in Carmel. There, to my lugubrious satisfaction, I was pronounced to have suffered a "massive trauma," in the form of several contusions and fractures. My worst wound was a severely broken left heel bone.

I spent nearly three weeks in a pretty room overlooking a forest full of quail and butterflies. I didn't feel so much cursed to be injured as euphoric to have survived, especially in the province of so cheerful a hospital. I got lots of get-well cards. "Wave to the pine trees," my Aunt Frances wrote me, "they always wave back." Awash in such solicitude and unaccustomed time for reflection, I looked through my Esalen notes and the reading matter some of my less hawkishly nonverbal new friends brought. As my bones knit and bruises faded, I began to get the idea that there was a lot more to all this Esalen business than we back in New York had suspected.

Convalescence

(After physical therapy sessions in which I felt like one of the valiant patients in an old movie about Sister Kenny, I learned to lurch along on cast and crutches. The hospital dismissed me with good wishes and a phone bill in three figures. I flew for a period of convalescence to Tucson, near which live my cousin Kathleen (the one with the artichoke fetish) and her family. For three weeks there I studied cactuses, children, mountain shadows and more books about the human potential movement.

The movement, I gathered, is closely allied with an equally amorphous phenomenon called humanistic psychology. Humanistic psychology differs from regular orthodox psychology in that it studies man as a feeling, thinking subject, capable of

18

heights as well as depths, rather than as a programmable object. Humanistic psychology envisions "a new and enhanced image of man." Its province is not sickness, not health even, but transcendence. It rejects Freud's preoccupation with the murky recesses of the id. It rejects the inroads technology has made on our sanity. It rejects the lament of traditional Christianity that "there is no health in us."

Balderdash, the humanistic psychologists don't say but might as well: there is plenty of health in us, more than we ever suspected. Within us all are deep, untapped reserves of decency and strength and good. What ails us is that we block the pathways that could lead us to these reserves. We spend so much energy concealing the depths of our personalities that we suppress a lot of the good along with the questionable.

Having achieved giant technological leaps, we are not merely free now but obligated now to turn from what we can do to what we should do. We are ready for a revolution regarding man's view of his place on this globe in this solar system in this universe—a revolution some think may rank in historical importance along with the discovery of the wheel, or of agriculture, or of outer space.

I came across several references to a description by Aldous Huxley of man as a "multiple amphibian," obliged to live at once in many worlds—biological, social, spiritual, emotional, cerebral—but guilty, after several centuries' obsession with technology, of neglecting most of these worlds. Much of our potential, Huxley said and others agreed, has atrophied. All of us might be much more than we are.

I found many allusions to and quotes from Dr. Carl Rogers, the eminent psychologist who pioneered in "non-directive counseling." He believes that "the best solution to any problem is the people who have the problem." Rogers also wrote that "intensive group experiences," such as I had at Esalen, were "perhaps the most significant social invention of this century," teaching us as they purport to that "security resides

19

not in hiding oneself, but in being more fully known." If you confess to me some fear or apprehension that you have had for years, it might make me not hate you but love you, or at least comprehend you. If I tell you of my doubts, you might tell me that they are your doubts, too. What is most private is most universal.

To paraphrase further the books I read, the groups—composed not of "patients" but of "clients"—can help their members to become what Maslow calls "self-actualizing" people, capable of "peak experiences." People who "peak" can transcend the mundane and feel ecstatically fulfilled. The stimulus for that ecstasy is as hard to guess as next week's weather, but its quality, Maslow wrote, is unmistakable. I tried to recall what my own peak experiences had been: a picnic one afternoon in Maine with white wine and lobsterolles and a paperback Gerard Manley Hopkins? An evening of banjo music and song right there in Tucson? Another evening when five friends and I almost finished reading *Antony and Cleopatra,* taking turns reading each speech instead of casting parts? An interlude on the boulders of a stream in the White Mountains? Had those been Peaks? Could Science, for all its wisdom, program such feelings? I doubted it. But I read on.

The human potential groups were striving to reacquaint us with the "affective domain," and to help us be less "cognitive." They aimed to remind us that we have bodies below our necks, and senses other than sight. The groups were planned to help us quit weaving tangled webs of polite, diplomatic, but corrosive dishonesty. In them we were meant to risk showing each other what we really think and really feel, even when our exposed thoughts and feelings might displease.

The groups that practice and teach these theories represent a continuum with two extremes. One extreme, which for reasons more emotional than political might be called the left, is represented by fifty or so "Growth Centers," of which Esalen is the oldest and by far the best known. Growth Centers are concerned with self-knowledge and with reducing people's inhibitions. They do not primarily care, as people do at the other end of the continuum, about what happens to organizations and institutions and systems. They figure that the way to change systems is to start by changing people. The right-wing end of the continuum has the opposite notion: that if a system is changed the individuals in it automatically will change too.

Growth Centers began as a West Coast phenomenon. The more conservative groups originated much earlier in the East. Esalen, which attracts 25,000 people a year, is the spiritual vortex of the radical end of the continuum, and its right-wing counterpart is at Bethel, Maine, on the campus of a boys' preparatory school called the Gould Academy. For more than twenty summers the academy and much of the town of Bethel have been taken over by a formidable organization formidably called the National Training Laboratories Institute for Applied Behavioral Science. Since 1947 the NTL has been conducting "T-groups" (T for training), akin in format and spirit to their distant cousins and descendants, the encounter groups. NTL laboratories are held in many places throughout the United States and elsewhere, but the magic word is Bethel.

Between Bethel and Esalen, geographically and otherwise, the human potential movement has hundreds of other establishments. If the movement were envisioned as a triangle instead of as a linear continuum, the third side might be Synanon, a much-imitated "therapeutic community" whose self-help groups (called "Games" and originally meant just for drug addicts) are now popular in some cities among the general public. Costing only one cent a month and available to many more people than high-priced, esoteric workshops, the Games too have been influential in spreading the movement.

All my reading made me feel more confused, instead of less so. I plainly had much more to learn. As I got more agile on crutches, and added to my wardrobe a splendidly ugly pair of red orthopedic shoes, I developed a plot. If I was to under-

21

stand Esalen better, should I not go back to gather more impressions of it? Besides, New York in March was too cold and slushy for a plaster-casted leg. My sympathetic employers agreed to send me back for another workshop, called "Encounter and Meditation."

Meditation had caught my fancy in the course of an earlier assignment involving the then still voguish Maharishi Mahesh Yogi. I had met the tiny, giggling benevolence himself, and run across more swamis and gurus than I would ever have thought New York contained. In the course of learning about *mantras* and being mesmerized by the Hare Krishna chant, I had become envious of those who could control their streams of consciousness. Would it not be fine, I thought, to experience "the bow being pulled back just before the arrow is released"? Transcendental meditation was supposed to make you feel there was just such a bow, at such a moment, inside your own skull. It was supposed to feel like being "bathed in bliss"—a tempting image for one who could not bathe totally even in water. Besides, I was clinically curious about what so lone a practice as meditation might have to do with something so necessarily social as encounter.

The journey back, with several stops, was melodramatic. I might have been headed for Lourdes. I held my crossed crutches on my lap like some rich and aging British eccentric, as porters rolled me down airport corridors in wheelchairs, and special hydraulic platforms elevated me to the doors of planes. It was good to see the ocean again, and to have my meal ticket punched by long-skirted, long-haired waitresses bringing fine brown homemade bread. But I didn't immediately like my second workshop. In our opening session we were all told to feel each other's faces, which for some reason made me uncomfortable. Then the sexes were to stand on opposite sides of the room, with the men coming across to choose partners. There were two extra women, and I was one of the two not chosen. But otherwise the men of Esalen were

22

kind and strong. They would carry me in their arms (and I am not petite) up and down the winding muddy paths.

In meditation sessions I sat in my own plaster-cast version of the Full Lotus Position, in quest of what was variously described as the White Light, the Black Void and the Blue Line. I can't say I experienced bliss, exactly, but after forty minutes' immobile effort to banish mundane thoughts, I did get a sense of the bow being pulled back in the head. Even more vividly I got an image of a candle burning and glowing within my skull, as if I were a Hallowe'en pumpkin. That was something, anyway. Wasn't it?

"Hmmm," agreed Michael Murphy, Esalen's founder and president and the co-leader (with Schutz) of this workshop. "That's an interesting picture."

My skull was also crammed with more new impressions and information than I could digest. During one workshop session a divorced couple shrieked out their repressed grievances at each other until the cords on both their necks stood out in taut relief.

"You never wrote a single thank-you note to anybody all the time we were married!" accused the man.

"That's all you give a damn about, isn't it?" shouted his ex-wife. "Why don't you go to work for Hallmark greeting cards if you care so much about etiquette?"

For the sin of using too many syllables, three other verbose people and I were relegated to something we called the Pedants' Corner. Trying to get more in touch with my subcerebral self, I spent one evening mindlessly pounding bongo drums in an impromptu music session before an open fire. Later I felt emboldened to debate Schutz himself. I took issue with his idea that a young man who goes to an Army surplus store to buy a colonel's shirt has "hangups about authority figures." I argued that maybe the man just liked the shirt.

Feeling more liberated all the time, I was moved one afternoon to a curious terpsichorean feat. On my crutches I did

23

what somebody called "The Dance of the Spider Lady." Since nudity no longer fazed me, and since after six weeks of near immobility I was in sorry physical shape, I signed up for an Esalen massage, which people said would be not only good for my muscle tone but a mystical experience. At the hands of the magnificently bearded Seymour Carter, it was. Even now, hundreds of human potential people later, Seymour remains one of my favorites. As an issue of the Esalen catalogue says, he "claims to be or to have been a drug user, village idiot, thief, madman, carney, masseur and shaman." Seymour, who comes from Opportunity, Washington, also knows how to bake bread and eat fire. He used to live at Synanon after he gave up drugs. He told me, memorably enough, that "your fingers should feel like hot fudge." At times they do.

But where, I wondered, did Seymour fit in with the Harvard University Department of Psychology, where other Esalen leaders had been trained? What had Synanon to do with all of this? How influential were other elements of the movement I kept hearing about?

In March 1968 Esalen had only one public telephone, conspicuously located. It didn't do to be seen too often talking to someone out There of Then, whether Then meant past or future. But I risked such scorn, calling New York several times to report how the movement was turning out to be even more complex than I had thought. I suggested that maybe my story should expand beyond just Esalen.

Funny you should mention that, said the people at the office. They had been thinking that my story could incorporate two other related sets of pictures. The newer ones, which had come in just the other week, concerned a weekend of "Nude Encounter Therapy," run in some swimming pool near Los Angeles by a therapist whose efforts had received the provisional blessing of Dr. Maslow. The other pictures had been

Convalescence

waiting around, good but unused, for two years. They showed a Basic Encounter Workshop at the Western Behavioral Sciences Institute in La Jolla, conducted by Dr. Carl Rogers.*

Maslow and Rogers being the most prestigious of the movement's founders, it seemed sensible for the story to include ideas they espoused. So I was assigned to go ahead and do whatever I physically could to find out more about their ideas, as well as more about Esalen. I couldn't very well go swimming, nude or otherwise, but there was plenty I could do. Feeling a little like both of the kids in Father Flanagan's Boys' Town poster that reads "He ain't heavy, Fadder, he's me brudder," I set forth. I went to see Dr. Rogers and his staff in La Jolla. I watched a first-grade classroom near Santa Barbara practice sensitivity techniques its teacher had learned as part of the Ford Foundation project at Esalen. I stopped in Atlanta to sit in on a school superintendents' workshop. When the New York slush melted I returned home to consult, by phone if not in person, still more specialists and experts and evangelists and critics of the movement. Finally I wrote the story.

Headlined "Inhibitions Thrown to the Gentle Winds," the story appeared in the *Life* issue of July 12, 1968. In it I happened to mention that one technique some encounter groups use is fasting. On the cover of that issue was a picture of some starving Biafran children. Such ironies did not escape readers. What more objected to, though, in a tidal wave of hate mail and canceled subscriptions, was the several prominent pictures of people who weren't wearing any clothes. "Jane Howard and the people who let her do this story *must* be sluts," one correspondent wrote. "You should have made the headline read 'Genital,' not 'Gentle.' Don't you realize we have *children?*"

But not all the outrage came from the pious Bible Belt.

* A movie of that same WBSI group, entitled *Journey to the Center of the Self,* won an Academy Award as Best Documentary of 1968.

25

Please Touch

Pained objections poured in from people within the human potential movement, who said the pictures of naked people had scared away their financial supporters. The movement depends greatly on the kindness of foundations; foundations are hard to interest in psychic frontiers or the literal removal of facades. "How does it make you feel that you lost us our grant?" I was asked more than once. One of the most eminent leaders in all the movement, several times quoted in the article, told me a couple of months later that the nude pictures had so disheartened him that he never had bothered to read the words.

But some of the response—"feedback," I should say—was more thoughtful. One result was a contract to write this book.

Cattle Barons
and Kleptomaniacs

❡ Cynthia and George live in the same comfortable old Victorian house Cynthia's father had built back in the days when craftsmen took a little pride in their handiwork. The house, on a bluff overlooking the Mississippi River, is spacious and grand, but a little lonely now that the three children who grew up in it are gone. It is also a little tense, because the doubts Cynthia and George suppressed about each other all along are becoming more pronounced.

They are both fifty-two now, but she looks five years older and he twelve years younger. He is interested, more than idly, in other women, but also in holding on to the comforts to which life in Cynthia's house has accustomed him. On his teacher's salary he could never duplicate those comforts.

Please Touch

Cynthia does all she can to look young. She wears Marimekko dresses and has her hair cut modishly by Gregory at Louis Guy'D when she is in New York. George has a goatee. Many men in their town have beards now—more even than during the Centennial, a few years back—because many, following Cynthia's and George's example, have been to Esalen. Cynthia and George started going there a couple of years ago, when they gave up on their therapist. Now they go there, or to Oasis (in Chicago) or Aureon (in New York) or Kairos (in San Diego), for a workshop every month or six weeks or so. They are literally "working," in those workshops, on their marriage.

"It does cost us pretty much," Cynthia admitted during an Aureon workshop, "to keep flying to San Diego or San Francisco or here just for the weekend, and then pay another $200 or so for the workshops.

"But the way we look at it, it's *still* less than Dr. Seaman, the therapist, used to charge us. And sometimes," she said as her eyes darted around the room looking for her husband, "sometimes we even think maybe we're getting somewhere. Oh, I know where George is; he's up in our room doing his Yoga." Remembering this, she looked a little happier.

Even if Cynthia and George aren't "getting anywhere," at least they're having scenic and theatrical weekends. At least they're together. And the glimpses they get of other people's troubles may provide at least vicarious insights into their own. They're starting their own "Tuesday-evening ongoing leaderless encounter group," too.

"What's your favorite fairy tale?" Virginia Satir asked an intense and sorrowful-looking man who was one of the thirty people gathered for one of her weekend marathons in last year's circuit.

"King Arthur, I guess," the man said.

Cattle Barons and Kleptomaniacs

"All right," she told him, *"be* King Arthur. Give everybody in this room a title." She handed him a pile of stacked-together styrofoam coffee cups. He used this like a sword, touching people's shoulders as he conferred titles on them. The titles were based on his first impressions of us: Third Minister to Scotland, Queen of the Court, Lord of Law and Order, Lady Lonelystreets (that was me), Lord Treasurer, and, in the case of a meek-looking woman whose voice was barely audible, Lady Notary Public.

"But how could you have known?" the lady said with wistful disbelief. "I really *am* a Notary Public."

"What's the matter?" the man wondered. "Don't you like that title? What sort of title would you rather have?"

"Well," said the woman, "maybe something a little more like Lady Romantic?"

"You? Are you kidding?" said another, much brasher woman, already marked as the group gadfly. "Do you realize that means taking *chances,* taking *risks?* Do you remember that poem 'The Highwayman?' *That* girl was romantic. She sat there and got shot through the breast for a man. Would *you* be willing to do something like that?"

It turned out Lady Notary Public probably wouldn't. She was my partner in an exercise called the Blind Walk, in which we took turns guiding each other blindfolded around the lobby of our rococo hotel. We were supposed to join hands and introduce each other to the widest possible variety of tactile experiences. The idea was to *"feel* the world, for a change, instead of seeing it," and in the process to sense how it was to be dependent. I guided Lady Notary Public to smooth marble table tops, prickly horsehair upholstery, offensive plastic plants, tinkly crystal lamp pendants and a trunk hidden away in the storage room. She barely touched any of these surfaces, reaching out tentatively and quickly withdrawing her clear-polished fingertips.

She was fifty, Lady Notary Public eventually told us, although she looked a good deal younger in a bland, lashless way. She wore plastic-rimmed harlequin glasses and had a jeweled clasp for her cardigan sweater. It had been ten years since she had had so much as a plain, old-fashioned, regular *good time*. That good time transpired one evening when she and some of her pals from the office went to a neighborhood bar. It wasn't New Year's Eve or anybody's birthday or anything. They just went to this bar and had a few drinks and a few laughs and that was that, "and now that bar's all torn down and everyone in that crowd is married and they all sit home watching television." Had she in the space of an entire decade found no other bars, no other people congenial enough to join for a spontaneous drink? No men to go out with?

"Well," said Lady Notary Public, "I *did* have a blind date three or four months ago, but he was just like all the others, if you know what I mean. He was only interested in *one thing*. Besides, he was so stupid. He actually *believed* in Adam and Eve." All of us shuddered to think of the 3600 evenings that had passed since that woman's last good time.

Not long afterward, continuing my rounds of groups, I met a woman of about thirty with quite another story to tell. Hers, too, provoked shudders, and she too spoke in italics. "I've just about given *up* on the Sexual Freedom League," she said, "because there you can't be sure *who* you're going to run into. I've heard a lot of talk about VD. I think the regular sex club parties are a *lot* nicer, and a lot safer too."

Neither of these two living American females was overtly sick or abnormal, or more neurotic than anyone else you might scoop up at random off La Cienega Boulevard or Massachusetts Avenue or West Randolph Street. Neither were Cynthia and George. But they all made me think of something I had heard the psychologist Richard Farson say at the Western Behavioral Science Institute, that "many ostensibly normal people go through life without knowing the security of a single deep or significant relationship on which they can depend for support and understanding, sharing problems and feelings, and in which they can be truly and simply themselves, without fear or facade."

The debate about who is normal and who is not occupies the movement's thinkers endlessly. Am I normal, even though I eat chocolate ice cream and parsnips for breakfast and fall asleep in movies? Are you, even though you are fifty-one and heterosexual and a bachelor? Is she, even though she has nothing but sixty-watt light bulbs in her whole house? Where is the line to be drawn between amusing eccentricity and alarming neurosis? Does sanity consist of being responsible, of putting one foot in front of the other, of holding down a gainful job and doing what's expected? If so, then many of us qualify. Does it mean polluting the environment and authorizing the slaughter of distant babies and the destruction of distant cities? Then few of us can. Which is normal: adjustment to an absurd world or fury at its absurdities?

Normal or not, the people who go to encounter groups represent an almost cornily wide spectrum of humanity, like a latter-day *Canterbury Tales,* and they speak in a cornily wide variety of vernaculars. Since candor is so highly prized in these circles, one often hears language that would offend, say, a Congregationalist ladies' group in Wisconsin. On the other hand, though, some of these people are Congregationalist ladies from Wisconsin. After one T-group, a story has it, a man went to his office on Monday morning feeling so wondrously liberated that he boasted: "Why, now I can even say 'shit' to M-O-T-H-E-R!"

Some groups I took part in reminded me of English Department faculty parties I once used to go to in a small college town in New England. People there were kind, literate and witty, but in a rather desperate way. Other groups made me think of the comfortable Chicago suburb where I grew up, filled with people so stridently upright and prosperous that one wondered what emotional price had been paid for all their success. But many groups reminded me of nothing I had known anywhere or ever. My fellow members included cattle barons, clinical psychologists, wife-swappers, black militants, associate professors, movie stars, a professional poker player, computer programmers, publishers, insurance adjustors, engineers, dancers, ex-convicts, stockbrokers, the idle rich, the embittered poor, the halt, the lame, the blind, the blond, the bland, the blunt and young ladies who I guess you could say were That Cosmopolitan Girl. I met not a few men and women of the cloth, many on the point of leaping, or who had leapt already, over the wall to a secular life. (The fathers and brothers are hard to spot when they aren't wearing their turned-around collars, but somehow the nuns are easier to tell. They tend to have more innocent faces and longer skirts than other women, and they often wear what look like 1952 models of Ship 'n' Shore blouses.)

The groups in which these people are shuffled together have many different labels and designs. In conversations, and by browsing through the catalogues of the various growth centers (a literary genre worthy of study just for itself), I have learned of labs and workshops especially planned for kleptomaniacs, bisexuals, dentists, ambassadors, myopes, admirals, corporation presidents, their secretaries, stewardesses and Episcopalian young people. There are "Cousin Labs," for people who do the same sort of work in different hierarchies, and "Stranger Labs," which are what they sound like. Some groups are "task-oriented"; many are concerned not with jobs but with psyches. There are Alumni Labs (for veterans of prerequisite ones), Nonverbal Labs, Conflict Management Labs, Creative Divorce Workshops, Consultations Skills Seminars and Risk-Taking Labs. Some are Instrumented Labs, with charts and paraphernalia. Some are meant to span the gaps between polarized opposites, confronting Junior Leaguers with ghetto children, policemen with criminals, whites with blacks, architects with their clients or, as they say in the branch of the movement called Gestalt Therapy, your own Top Dog with your own Under Dog.

Some people attend these sessions in the same spirit others bring to bars and parties.

"Have you heard what's happened to Terry?" one friend of mine said of another. "She's hitting groups—the way other people hit the bottle." Such zealots are known to group leaders, a little ruefully, as "lab hounds," "group freaks" or "sensitivity heads." The hounds, freaks and heads don't seem to have much of a social life outside the groups. They live, as it is possible to do especially in California, from one group-generated spell of euphoria to the next, savoring the "instant intimacy" some groups are famous for providing. For these people it is old hat to leave matters of friendship, affection and love to chance and chemistry. Not for them the anxious waits for unseen gears to shift from Interest to Like to Love; for them there are shortcuts. A shoulder to weep on, a face to kiss and a body to embrace need be no further away than the next scheduled encounter. These people might say they "grow" a little every time they are in a group, but the Los Angeles psychologist Frederick Stoller, for one, says he doubts such claims.

"They don't get 'weller and weller' with each group," says Stoller. "They just get a maintenance dose of intimacy."

But not all group enthusiasts lead such arid lives. Most are sensible enough to let time lapse between group experiences, so they can accumulate what Stoller calls "barnacles" for the groups to scrape off "in dry dock." Most people enroll in groups simply because they want to change, even if the change only lasts a short time.

"There is no monolithic way for human beings to change," says the NTL's president-elect Warren Bennis. "There is no sacredness to anything, including encounter." Many leaders think that any technique people have faith in will work.

Please Touch

"They can commit themselves to a leader, or a tape recorder or anything else," Farson told me. "Maybe they could commit themselves just as effectively to a rock pile." For some the critical step is just submitting to the scrutiny of an encounter group in the first place, even if when they get there they never advance to what is known as the "hot seat." Lady Notary Public appalled us with her timidity, but the truly amazing thing is that she was there at all.

Group leaders are always debating whether what they accomplish is therapy, and trading definitions of encounter workshops versus therapeutic groups. Encounter and T-groups differ from therapy groups, some say, in that the latter are concerned with the historical roots of behavior patterns— "personal archeology and museum pieces," as somebody put it—rather than with the immediate here and now. Encounter groups don't ask how come you happen to be the way you are, but what you're planning to do about it.

Therapy reconstructs, it is said, and encounter groups educate. Therapy is for the sick (which is to say those who in one way or another cannot function), and encounter groups treat the well. Therapy goes on indefinitely; encounters are typically compressed into an explosive weekend, or, at the longest, a fortnight. Therapy relieves discomfort and teaches adjustment; encounter groups assume equilibrium and build to transcendence.

"It's very unhealthy," says the psychologist Rollo May, "to worship mere health. We mustn't produce adjustment at the expense of sensitivity and other things we ought to value more."

"Many of us," says Dr. Carl Rogers, "live in a kind of precarious balance. We have learned to get along with ourselves and our world in some way, and the possibility that this balance might be upset is always threatening."

Cattle Barons and Kleptomaniacs

Some people probably shouldn't go to T-groups or encounters at all. NTL's former president Leland Bradford thinks groups are contraindicated "for people who are so fragile or neurotic they spend a lot of their waking hours trying to keep in one piece—but the ratio of these to those who *can* benefit is 4 or 5 to 300."

Richard Beckhard, described to me as "the world champion consultant on training groups," says groups can be not only pointless but actually harmful for "people, for instance, who are latent homosexuals. It isn't doing them any favor to tell them of their condition and then just leave them."

When I visited NTL's Bethel encampment, Dr. Al Powell, then the physician-in-residence, said he didn't think groups should accept people who sought to solve certain specific problems in their personal lives.

"If you come here with a life crisis," he said, "you're likely to end up with *more* crises. If you're in a crisis at home, then your defenses will crumble under attack."

"Any important crisis in your life," the California group leader Dr. Everett Shostrom wrote in *Psychology Today*, "has been a long time in preparation, and deserves reflection. If you are sanely suspicious of your grasp on reality, be doubly cautious. A trained person responsible for a meaningful session would not throw precariously balanced persons into a good encounter group. Nor would he allow persons who are diabolically experienced in the ways of group dynamics to form a group. If you find yourself in a group in which everybody talks jargon, simply walk out."

But no early warning system has yet been devised to weed out unlikely or disruptive group members in advance. The UCLA professor James V. Clark, who has led many groups with his wife Frances, said "at first we went through an elaborate screening process. We'd use questionnaires about mental illness, advance interviews and so on. But we don't do that

35

any more. Either way, with or without the screening, we seem to get about the same percentage of people we wish we didn't have."

The very word "therapy" exasperates the Clarks, who in a joint paper wrote "Does *anybody* know what it means any more?"

Some human potential people don't even bother to question that groups are a form of therapy. "Sure they are," said one devotee of encounter groups. "I quit my shrink because more happened to me in four days with Bill Schutz than in four years of therapy." Schutz, who delights in such compliments and gets them often, scratches his beard and agrees.

"Therapy," he says, "is creating conditions under which people grow. The reason people stay in analysis for eight or nine years is that there they never have to confront anything. Nobody ever pushes them. I experienced this in my own 600-hour analysis. I was so clever I just didn't get much out of it. Some people should be supported and made comfortable, sure, but others need to be pushed. You have to use your own fallible judgment as to which people are which. But one thing I won't do any more is individual work. Groups are more efficient."

Sometimes T-groups and encounters and traditional analysis turn out to be supplementary, not mutually exclusive. "Groups don't replace analysts," Richard Farson told me as we sat in a restaurant in La Jolla. "They make work for them. But as an answer to the needs of all the people, individual therapy is hopeless."

"Therapy must start at home," said Dr. Jacob L. Moreno in his own home near the Hudson River. "It's too expensive otherwise."

"Face-to-face therapy is a luxury," said Dr. Maslow in the house he used to live in on the Charles River near Boston. "It's too slow and too expensive. It's not the right answer if you think, as I shamelessly do, in terms of changing the whole

36

world. We need more shortcuts. We have to teach everyone to be a therapist. A lot more people might be therapeutic than might think they have it in them to be."

So saying, Dr. Maslow excused himself and left for an appointment with his regular Freudian analyst.

The Circuit
Riders

⟨ "Take off your glasses," I was told.

"I'd rather not," I said. "I really need them. They're not just an affectation. They're not emotional armor. I really do have lousy eyes." The other pairs of eyes in the room looked skeptical.

"You're not going to be reading *here,* this afternoon, are you?"

"I guess not," I said. Hardly, at my first Esalen workshop.

"Well then, hand the glasses over. Don't you trust us?"

"I think I trust you," I said as I handed them over.

"You *think?* Who aren't you sure you trust?"

I squinted around the room. "Him," I said, pointing at a man named Michael Kahn, who somehow resembled both

Abraham Lincoln and Michelangelo's David. "He doesn't look all that trustworthy."

"Don't tell me," said William Schutz, "tell him."

"You don't look all that trustworthy," I told Kahn, who was not only Schutz' co-leader for the week but, I later learned, his former student at Harvard, where Kahn had earned his doctorate.

Kahn frowned. "Why not?" he asked, his voice exuding baritone concern.

"It's your looks, a lot," I said. "You're too good looking. I tend to like people who have some sort of tragic flaw, like a misshapen nose or pockmarked skin or being too short or something. You have nothing like that. You're perfect looking, and I'm afraid of you. Besides, you have a phony voice. The way you go around leading us all humming 'OM' all the time is too show-businessy for me. Your voice sounds to me as if you stayed home and practiced on it."

Schutz broke in. "Would you like to try something?" he asked me.

"Okay," I said. He directed me to stand about four feet from Kahn, facing away. I was to fall backward, trusting that Kahn would catch me. He did. Although I wondered what else in the name of professional ethics and human charity he could have done, I did come to trust him more thereafter. I even got to like him, because he turned out to be not only attractive but funny. And I was right about his show-business background: he actually had been a television cowboy—"probably the first Jewish one in history," he told a carful of us who went along when Schutz drove him to the Monterey airport after the workshop. His departure was fittingly romantic. Unlike the suited, necktied, vested and pathetically rigid-looking "real people" who awaited prosaic commercial planes, Kahn vanished into the night like a Saint-Exupéry hero, flying off in his own tiny plane over the mountains and desert toward, of all places, the University of Texas.

Please Touch

His path and mine were destined to cross and re-cross. Six months later I saw him again at Bethel, where he was co-leading an Advanced Personal Growth Laboratory. His hair was two inches longer, his avuncular and nonverbal hug thirty seconds more protracted, and his new name, for the two-week duration of the lab, was T'Ai, which devotees of the *I Ching* in his group advised me meant "Peace." He was, as they said, very much into mysticism. Addressing his group one night he spoke, winningly I thought, of "the quiet heart, at peace despite the vicissitudes of the world. That's where I'd *like* to be, but I'd be lying in my teeth if I claimed to be there now."

A month after that I saw Kahn again outside the Fairmont Hotel in San Francisco, where he and 1400 other members of the American Association of Humanistic Psychology were disporting and convening. And a couple of months after that I spent eight days myself in a lab he helped lead near Boston. (Maybe my Aunt Janet will hire him for the T-group on the farm.)

Kahn and hundreds of men and women like him are today's circuit riders. In the spiritual life of this century they occupy a niche similar to that of itinerant preachers in the last. They travel by jet instead of horseback, covering a nation instead of a county, but their message is not much different. The kingdom of heaven, they say in their various jargons, is within: within you and within me and within us all. They are gossiped about, denigrated, praised and received in some quarters with the degree of adulation usually reserved for Mary Poppins, Johnny Appleseed and the Easter Bunny.

Their schedules are chilling to contemplate, for those of us who aren't running for national office. Pasadena today, Boston tomorrow, Houston after that—why not? A trainer thrives on a challenge. "Trainers" is what the circuit riders are often called, usually by members and followers of the NTL; in the Far West and some other places, people who do the same work are referred to as leaders or "facilitators." Semantic ex-

40

actitude is no strength of the human potential movement, but one might safely generalize that *trainers* lead *laboratories,* which tend to be more structured than *workshops,* which are conducted by *facilitators* or just *leaders.* People from each school of thought tend to sniff at mention of the other.

"I'm not sure 'trainer' is the proper word," a leading facilitator says. "It's pretty much of a misnomer."

"Facilitators," says a prominent trainer, "ought to be called 'greasers.' All they have to do is be nice and good. They need no special skills so long as they can grease the way."

By whatever name they are called, the circuit riders make their rounds with great style, at times resembling alchemists and tribal witch doctors. Behavioral science notwithstanding, their rituals seem mysterious and primitive. They are engaged, sometimes quite literally, in the laying on of hands and the exorcism of devils. Their heady mission is to open people, free them from inhibitions and help them ease up to and beyond their limits. They must perceive what the peak emotion in a group is at any given time, and work with it. They must be mindful, as Charles Seashore of the NTL has put it, that "the peak emotion is not necessarily the one that's being expressed." They must try to sense what everybody in a room is saying or not saying. Their sense of timing must be superior.

A trainer also needs what Dr. Seashore calls a special set of eyes and ears. "He must be able to tell when people are in cages, and when to intervene. You don't always move 100 percent on target when you make a comment to a person. Sometimes people need to use their defenses. Everybody isn't always ready for a bombshell of a revelation. It's more important to build support than to be the deliverer of an insight.

"You have to learn oblique intervention, too, and develop a repertoire of fantasies, analogies and games to provide people with ways to experience directly things that aren't intellectual." At least one circuit rider, Dr. Goodwin Watson, has cod-

41

ified a repertoire of 48 exercises and games.* But some trainers' personalities matter more than their techniques.

"I'm getting clearer about why some of the things I do work," says Peter Caffentzis of New York City, one of the busiest trainers in the East. "It's not the design, but the way *I* am. The best design in the world won't work if the guy has a squeaky voice." Circuit riders must indeed have unabrasive voices, showmanship, finesse and infinite tact. Their work is at once an art and a craft, a business and a science.

"I look on myself as a symphony conductor," Virginia Satir confided after the first night of a weekend marathon in the Midwest. "The symphony is written as I go along." Mrs. Satir is an exceptionally colorful group leader. On a recent birthday some of her well-wishers at Big Sur granted her a long-standing wish: to bathe in a giant Esalen tub filled with jelled Jell-O.

The styles of trainers and leaders are as distinctive as those of mezzosopranos, abstract painters or skiers. Some are so restrained as to seem almost stuffy, venturing little, and in the judgment of their rivals, not gaining much either. But some prefer top-volume noise, primary colors and maximum risk. Of these the most conspicuous is Schutz.

"The further you go toward violence, sexuality and loneliness," he once told a hotel ballroom full of people, "the better trainer you are, almost linearly." Schutz might be called the Father Wallenda of the encounter world. He has trained what he calls a "Flying Circus" of younger leaders who draw big crowds at growth centers around the country, leading workshops his way. Like him they have what one calls "a need to be central and important," and like him they often get things rolling by asking random people in their groups who in the room they'd most like to sleep with. Schutz dislikes secrets the way gardeners dislike weeds. He has professed to see no seri-

---

* His list may be ordered from the Laboratory of Applied Behavioral Sciences at Newark State College, Union, New Jersey.

The Circuit Riders

ous harm in a leader's sleeping with one of his own group members, provided it was for her own good and provided the leader didn't make a secret of it.

"I'd never do that myself," Schutz went on, "unless I told the whole group about it the next day." Not one to shrink from novelty or extremes, Schutz asked men in one of his workshops to urinate in front of each other.

"My shtick," he says, "is synthesis. A leader makes his own synthesis from dance, dramatic arts, oriental philosophy and whatever else he knows. You find whatever combination best helps you to help others expand their self-concepts."

What criteria, somebody asked, would Schutz use to disqualify potential leaders?

"If they're no good."

And how to tell if they're any good or not?

"Vibrations," he answered, "are very important. At Esalen we take people we're interested in, regardless of their background. Leadership requires three things: a good training program, surveillance and evaluation. NTL's training program can lead to what I call trained incapacity."

Still, Schutz himself belongs to NTL's prestigious network of 340 fellows, affiliates and professional members, which so far is alone in undertaking to certify group leaders on any large scale. NTL does not claim that its people are the only good leaders. It does guarantee, however, that they have all had at least a six-week internship followed by a year's supervised training, or the equivalent. Most of them also have advanced degrees in psychology, sociology, social work or business administration.

Not many leaders, NTL or otherwise, spend all their time with groups. Group leading can be profitable. Leaders are paid $15 per weekend per head. The big names, some of whom are said to have annual incomes of well over $80,000, can earn up to $400 a day. But most are primarily occupied otherwise.

43

Few circuit riders are prosaic, but some look it. Wilbert McGaw could probably still pass for what he used to be: a specialist in astronautics missiles. In that capacity he brainstormed 157 ways for people to communicate, scheduled a role-playing session for 211 managers and became, he says, "the only nonpsychiatrist involved in role-playing in all San Diego." Gradually he drifted into work with small groups, which he says was "no less bizarre than if I had become a deep-sea diver." He and his wife Audrey led the marriage workshop I went to. He also produced WBSI's documentary film "Journey to the Center of the Self," and pioneered in sensitivity training for churches.

Other trainers have backgrounds in dance, weight-lifting, bartending and publishing, as well as in more obviously relevant professions. One enthusiast who has thought of leading workshops herself is a veteran member of many encounter groups: the actress Jennifer Jones Selznick. Her guest house in Los Angeles is often used for groups and marathons and informal human potential meetings. Once when I was at Esalen for a workshop (the "Quest for Love"), she was there too. At first I didn't recognize her, and could only think "Gee, whoever she is she looks so *clean:* she's so much more well-groomed than the rest of us."

Most group leaders in fact are good looking, or at least they look exceptionally fulfilled. They radiate a contagious zest. For my own taste some of them are a little presumptuous, assuring you they know just how you feel before you even know yourself, but the good ones are restrained. All are earnest. It is their lot—an occupational hazard, you might say (like jet lag)—to talk a good bit in groups about their own personal lives. They do so to show they aren't the usual aloof authority figures, and to encourage group members to reveal more about themselves. The best leaders are thought to be those who have most thoroughly examined their own psyches, and who hesitate least to share the full range of their own experience.

"I come across as a human being," says Frank Jasinski of TRW Systems in California, who has a doctorate in anthropology from Yale and who often leads groups of businessmen. "I admit my own inadequacies and also my own strengths. There's too much *mea culpa, mea culpa, mea magna culpa* in this business. For me to cast the first stone on me is to tell you my limits, beyond which you can't go. I separate psyche-ego-personality—whatever you want to call it—from behavior. It's easier to get change that way. I can't change the whole next twenty years of my life, but I can change the next twenty minutes.

"At one workshop," Jasinski recalled, "there was a guy who behaved like a tense, coiled bastard. It turned out he really was a warm, sweet, accepting person, who had learned that supervisors were supposed to be hardnosed. He felt that was how he had to be too, before the group. But at the end of the week he walked relaxed and cool. His face looked entirely different, because he didn't have to spend all that energy maintaining a false front."

Some circuit riders are blissfully married, but seldom for the first time. "The behavioral scientist who's still happy with his first wife," I heard the second wife of one observe, "is as hard to find as Diogenes' honest man." Some circuit riders have husbands instead of wives. "Female trainers are better," asserts Dr. Jacob L. Moreno, who looks like a giant blue frog, younger than his eighty years, and who founded the much-used technique of psychodrama. "They're more aggressive and vigorous than men are." His own wife Zerka, a one-armed lady who often conducts group psychodrama sessions, is not to be faulted on grounds of either vigor or aggression. Feminist crusaders need not trouble themselves about this most

45

avant garde of professions. The only worry I heard expressed about women trainers came from Dr. Jerome I. Berlin, a sometime facilitator who looks like an astronaut and founded a Bell & Howell company in Atlanta called the Human Development Institute.

"Women trainers," Berlin said, "can get to be masculine and matriarchal."

In some apparently idyllic instances women co-train with their husbands. The McGaws, and James and Elizabeth Bugental, and John and Joyce Weir are notable examples. So are James and Frances Clark, whose weekend groups (usually for married couples) are held not oftener than every two months.

"We tried it at two-week intervals," Clark said, "but it got to be too much of a drain. What we try to do is dive into the moment, the depth of the here and now. That's exhausting."

"The input of insights," said Clark's wife, "is such that you feel like a snake who has swallowed a pig. Pigs take a long time to digest."

"The only way to do this work without exhaustion," said Dr. Frederick Stoller, who co-invented the "marathon" technique, "is to really be in it. The more I'm in it, the more turned on and exhilarated I get, and the more I get out of it. If you really *use* yourself, you get new insights, new directions and a sense of power."

But not all group leaders are so candid. "Those of us who train for a living," one told me, "are especially uptight in our own groups. Skilled sensitivity trainers tend to become the most cool, defensive, manipulative people of all. We have to form special groups to keep ourselves honest, because we know the jargon and how to fake it, the agony and dangers and how to avoid them."

Some people in the movement think leaders need not matter so much. Robert Allen, who profitably runs Scientific Resources, Inc., in New Jersey, and leads many groups himself, thinks that a carefully designed laboratory can be led by "any

The Circuit Riders

well-intentioned, random, relatively inexperienced person. Unless the design has a superlative structure," Allen says, "you need a person to help keep the group out of the way of danger and to provide alternatives. We spend two or three weeks working on a design for a one-day program. By the time that design comes off, I could give it to my youngster to handle."

Robert Blake, whose firm * has headquarters in Austin, Texas, and 125 employees around the world, says that "in our view it's a very wasteful thing for people to flounder around in labs trying to decide *what* to learn, when they're there to learn something, and designs for them to learn it do exist."

Many think that groups can thrive without any leaders at all. Richard Farson, who oversaw the early days of the WBSI in La Jolla, told one audience that "it is overwhelmingly clear that self-directed groups are almost indistinguishable, in every important way, from professionally directed ones."

Farson's associate Betty Berzon, who used to be among other things a dealer in rare books, spent eight years at WBSI perfecting a "program of interpersonal exercises for self-directed small groups" called Encountertapes. Now marketed for $300 a set through the Human Development Institute, Encountertapes come in a series of ten sessions, each lasting an hour and a half. In a much-discussed Walter Cronkite television program on Easter Sunday 1969, they were dramatically used by a roomful of college students. Groups of from six to twelve people who use them are urged to focus on their here-and-now feelings, and on their strengths instead of weaknesses. Further series are being planned for vocational education and biracial action groups.

The tapes seem Orwellian to some critics, but as Miss Berzon once told her colleagues, "We need to package more of what we've learned, and make it available to more people in less esoteric situations. It's too easy to be too precious about our techniques. Nonleader groups have a very central place.

* Described further on page 182.

47

They're a good way to get people into the tent and teach them to build on their own strengths so they can become more who they want to be in the world."

Not all leaderless groups use technological aids. A group of college professors has been meeting once a week, two hours at a time, every week for seven years.

"We're all colleagues," one of the professors told me, "and we all care a lot about each other. It's a model of people building a mutual, ongoing home support group." When I mentioned to one trainer that I belonged to no such ongoing group at home in New York, he seemed surprised and a little pitying.

"How can you get along without a group?" he asked me. "You must be very lonely."

Maybe he was being prophetic. Maybe a time will come when everybody will naturally fall into some such leaderless, mutually supportive group. Led groups, however, are not likely to vanish from the behavioral horizon. Richard Beckhard told me that "the closer you get to inter- and intra-personal work, the more advisable it is to have a trainer on hand." Besides, the rewards of circuit riding in any of its manifestations are heady indeed. It amused me when Charles Dederich, Synanon's formidable creator, said how good he thought it was that psychiatrists were losing their status as a priestly class "because we don't need priests any more." Maybe we don't, but Dederich himself is as much of a priest as anybody I've met in this business—perhaps even a cardinal. It wouldn't surprise me to learn that newcomers at Synanon save his fingernail parings as relics.

A more relevant comment on circuit riding came from John Weir, one of the most gifted trainers I have run across, when I mused in his hearing that "it must be great to be treated almost like a deity."

"What do you mean, *almost?*" he said, and he wasn't entirely kidding.

Transparent
by Midnight

❡ "Well, you see, Doctor," I said on the phone, in my most covered-bridge, Louisa May Alcott sort of voice, "I'm not sure that would be right, because I live in New York, and New York is pretty much where my social life is. Do you understand what I mean?" Three thousand miles away in Beverly Hills, George R. Bach, Ph.D., was suggesting that for the sake of my research I attend one of his marathon workshops in "Fight Training for Couples and Lovers," with the proviso that I bring a mate. I was explaining that I wasn't married to anybody anywhere and had only casual friends in the West.

"That's okay," said the doctor, "just bring somebody you're sleeping with. After all, how long does it take to screw a guy?" The way he said it, it sounded like "scrgew." The doctor came to this country from Latvia, which probably has something to do with the insinuating way he fondles his words. He is one of the most controversial men in the human potential movement. People think him sweetly elfin, or malevolent, or absurd, or a saint, or an important pioneer in the group dynamics movement, or all of the above. He wrote an early textbook about group relations, teaches a course at U.C.L.A. in "Creative Aggression" and recently published a book (with his ideas and Peter Wyden's prose) called *The Intimate Enemy*. Like the Institute for Group Psychotherapy which Dr. Bach runs in Beverly Hills, the book attempts to teach people to express their aggressions. One of his favorite methods is to have people fight more and sleep less, in the course of marathons that go on for twenty-four and sometimes thirty-six hours. Dr. Bach and his colleague Frederick Stoller were among the first in the movement to discover that tired people are truthful people.

I did not choose to stage a peccadillo just for the sake of a Bach marathon. When I got to California, however, I visited his suite of offices where, as befits a champion of aggressiveness, he grows cactuses, talks of his German shepherds and observes the aggression patterns not, alas, of hawks but of doves. He had good news for me. Coming up on his calendar was a weekend of "Aggressive Dating." All you had to be to get in was single (which for most Californians over the age of fifteen means divorced) and fed up with traditional, hypocritical patterns of courtship. Having spent who knows how many hundred evenings in the absurd act of "dating," I signed up.

The workshop began on Valentine's Day, in the growth center called Kairos, outside San Diego. Of the thirty-eight of us fed-up daters, one had come from Chicago just for the weekend, and another, even more flatteringly to Dr. Bach, all the way from New York. Before I could sign in somebody yanked me by the wrist and pulled me into a room with a sign on the door that said FEMALE GENDER CLUB. I was issued a box of Crayolas and told to draw a self-portrait.

I produced one that showed my face in the middle of the page, with a puzzled expression, surrounded with symbols of the confusions of my life. To the far left was a huge, florid, Steinbergian "W" for West, done in warm earth tones with psychedelically drooping edges. From the "W" extended a little cartoon hand, with a finger beckoning me thither. On the right was a sturdy, three-dimensional "E" for East, in tasteful dark stripes. It had a dangling anchor, and was also adorned with a beckoning finger. In between and all around were Crayola representations of suitcases, hearts, keys, a jangling telephone and (get it, folks?) an empty baby carriage. The symbols of my life, I thought, and rather poignantly done, too.

As I finished Dr. Bach came up and asked me to write how many "A-jams" I had received while doing the portrait. *"A-jams,"* he repeated impatiently, as if it were a household word. "Anti-joy Messages."

"But I *liked* doing it," I told him.

"You did? All right, then, write how many Pro-jams." Obediently I wrote "Pro-jams: 3."

We were told to use our self-portraits in the next exercise, in which one at a time we would leave our Gender Club and go introduce ourselves to a roomful of the opposite sex. We had ninety seconds in which to introduce ourselves, and they had another ninety to comment on what we said. When my turn came the men told me I didn't seem as nervous as I claimed to feel. Of the male presentations the most interesting came from a boy in his early twenties, who strode forth and just said: "I'm Tim, and here's what I drew."

He had drawn a pair of lines made with the sides of a purple and a gray Crayola, running parallel a while and then diverging off the page. Tim sat there holding his "self-portrait" for a full minute and a half, not saying a syllable. The roomful of women was perplexed.

"Schizoid!" one accused.

"Phony!"

"Arrogant!"

"What is he, stoned?"

Later, after a good steak supper (and at $85 for the weekend it should have been), the sexes sat down together to hear some of Dr. Bach's theories.

"This is not a matchmaking weekend," he said, "but a time to learn the skills of intimate communications. It's not a matter of hooking a stranger across a crowded room, but finding ways to be when you *do* hook one. Normally, the minute you have the hots for somebody you become phony, you collude, you accommodate. This is wrong! Instead, you should check on your real selves by starting to fight shortly after you become interested in each other.

"Successful couples never stop fighting. Realistic romance depends on letting your partner know exactly what and who you are and what are your expectations. What we're concerned with here is real intimacy, which is being of central importance to someone who is centrally important to you. The real task of any individual in this world is not to be alone. It is intolerable to confess 'I belong to no one.'

"The art is to let somebody get to know you, rather than playing hide and seek. We're against Puebloism—sneaking, snooping, trying to find out 'where is he at, what does he like, does he like me?' You should know who you are and where he is, *especially* in the early stages of your dating. Illusions should be kept as close to reality as possible. There's so much artificial 'nice-making.' What we're here to do is to learn the art of elegance in fighting."

I thought of something William Schutz had told another group. "Temporary relationships," he said, "should be less fraught with guilt and other pain than they are. Our whole society is set up to make you think 'marry him or it's a waste of time,' but temporary relationships are what suit some people. The key, no matter how long it lasts, is to enjoy it, be honest, and not deceive each other."

"Tomorrow," Bach went on, "we will have a twelve-hour 'mini-marathon.' Fatigue makes people transparent. That will be our goal: transparent by midnight. We will all learn to fight together, because the best time to fight is when other people are present. Modern etiquette is so neurotically preoccupied with privacy!"

I felt neurotically wistful about privacy the next morning. Out on the lawn the doctor was leading an exercise he said he had learned in India, called "nonverbal birth-giving." Couples were writhing around on the grass under bedspreads, looking much less lascivious than embarrassed. I too was expected to lie down on the lawn and pretend to be "giving birth" to some arbitrarily chosen man in the group, so that he could feel re-born.

Birth seemed to me, and still does, a sacred matter, not a subject for parody. I thought of refusing to participate, but I wanted to keep my standing as an inconspicuous group member.

"Keep your knees wide apart," said one of Dr. Bach's assistants as I lay down, "as if you were having a baby. *What?* You've never *had* a baby? So much the better! Relax!" But seldom have I felt less relaxed. An equally tense-looking man who happened along just then was assigned to be my "baby." We both grimaced as he lay down and pressed his head, meant to be my "fetus," on my belly. The assistant covered us both with a bedspread so that all that stuck out was my head. I was supposed to push down on the man's head. He was supposed to resist, but eventually emerge from below the bed-spread. We were both meant to experience wonder, but the whole thing struck me as spurious.

Then each girl was to choose a tree, step twelve paces out

from it, and be pushed back to it by some man. The idea was to see how much resistance women offered. The man who selected me as his pushee wore clear nail polish and did not attract me at all. When I shrank from him involuntarily he exploded.

"I touch you and you pull back—is *that* a *woman?*" I withdrew further. Then each girl had to find a man and "ride" him like a "horse," so the men could test their strength and the girls the clarity of their nonverbal signals. I was glad when this was over. As we went into breakfast, thunder rumbled above.

"Did you hear *that?*" asked Dr. Bach proprietarily. "That's real aggression weather!" While we ate I asked him exactly where in India he had learned about nonverbal birth-giving.

"Actually," he admitted, "I didn't learn it there; I *taught* it there, to the Indians. They loved it. They sensed that I have something to teach them in the aggression department. I emerged from there as a meaningful guru."

Next the meaningful guru taught us two of his "fight techniques," the Vesuvius and the Haircut. A Vesuvius, as the 200 or so regular clients at Bach's Institute know, is a verbal but not necessarily logical or rational unleashing of all one's aggressions. A Haircut (a term the doctor borrowed from Synanon) is a shower of negative feedback, directed by many at one. Each of us was to perform a Vesuvius for a whole roomful of the opposite sex, telling them everything we objected to about their gender in general and them in particular. They would retaliate with a Haircut. The proceedings were to be videotaped.

"Don't be afraid to be a real shrew, a real bitch!" Dr. Bach urged the first girl who went to deliver her Vesuvius. "Get rid of all your pent-up hostilities! Tell them where you're really at! Let it be total, vicious, exaggerated hyperbole!"

In a voice not so much vicious and shrewish as cold with fear, I informed the men when my turn came that they weren't dominating, protective and flexible enough for my taste. In the ensuing Haircut they said "It's your fault, honey, you're the one who's rigid; you're reely, reely rigid. You don't want a man, you want a father."

"Yeah," somebody else said. "Anyone wants a daughter, here's a fine specimen. But who'd want to protect somebody like *you?*"

"Besides," shouted someone else, "you fell *asleep* last night while George was talking to us. Is that the way you show a man how interested you are?"

Chastened and truly shaken, I went back to the Female Gender Club in time for the Vesuvius of the boy who had been mute the night before. He singled out several women, including me, for specific attack. I had a masklike face, he told me, and a nervous, fake smile that scared him. Groovy, I thought. Then a man named Pete accused all the women of "fiscal irresponsibility."

Then we had Fight Training. My fight partner was the man with nail polish who had pushed me to the tree. Every nuance of our confrontation was recorded on scoresheets. We were graded on clarity, candor, humor, fairness and other criteria. I got several points for saying: "You don't interest me as much as I seem to interest you."

"Besides," Bach said, speaking in psychodrama style as my alter ego, "don't say I'm that way with all men just because I'm that way with you."

"Yeah," I said. "For me to have been more responsive to you than I was would have been phony."

"Oh," the man said. He took my hand.

"You don't have to let him keep your hand in his," someone said. I withdrew my hand. He didn't mind. I felt rather pleased: in a tiny, baby-step way I had rejected someone and seen him survive unscathed.

Then our mini-marathon began. We milled around and stood with whatever clusters of people we felt drawn to, thus forming two groups. My group started out with a discussion of how Heather was too pretty. Nobody understood Tim, the kid with the self-portrait, who was attacked for being too non-verbal and too enigmatic. Don, who looked like a Rotarian, asked Tim if he liked fishing.

"You know something?" said Tim, with the first spontaneity he had shown all weekend, "I'd *like* to go fishing with you!" Tim, it developed, was oblique and mysterious because he had studied Zen, and wasn't much into books or words. Allan, a New York publisher, was attacked for being "into" them altogether too much. So was I. Carol was accused of being too reticent, and of always having a phony smile.

"Just see if you can sit for thirty seconds without smiling," someone suggested. She didn't quite make it. I was accused, quite validly, of a tendency to fall asleep. A glum man named Phil, who complained he couldn't find the right girl, was told he was too critical. I thought of something Virginia Satir had told another man at another marathon: "You go around with a hunting knife in one hand and a microscope in the other. You get them, all right, but once you have them you always find something wrong with them. You push and pull at the same time. Right?"

Right, of several of us here in Bach's group, too. Before long, attention focused on me. Could I imagine myself married, someone wondered?

"Sure," I said. "As soon as I so much as have lunch with someone, I start designing the wedding announcements." It was suggested that I could expedite that happy day by getting new glasses—maybe more tilted ones, with jewels on the top? Nearly everyone joined me in groaning at this advice, but they didn't let up on me.

"Maybe the reason you're so stand-offish is fear of rejection?"

"Sure it is," I agreed. "Rejection terrifies me. Getting hurt really hurts." I was asked to choose some man in the room

56

and pretend I had met him for the first time and was interested, "so we can see how you come on." I said that would be false. (Later in another group I was also asked how I showed men I liked them. "I'm too abstract and coy," I said. "I probably just send them some supposedly witty postcard.")

All right, then, if I wouldn't pretend to be flirting with a man in the room, would I read to one of the men a love poem —any love poem—from a paperback anthology? "After all," they said, "it's your *thing*—words and all." I agreed to read a poem, but to the whole room, not just to one man, because no man there captivated me. I chose Shakespeare's 116th Sonnet, the one that starts "Let me not to the marriage of true minds / Admit impediments . . ." Asked to interpret it, I said I guessed it had to do with constancy, which I was looking for more in myself than in others. Dr. Bach announced he had an insight about me.

"You've acted bored here," he said, "and I think it's because you're a leader, and when you're not in the center of attention you *are* bored."

"Maybe you're not really so cold and hard and enigmatic as you seem," someone suggested.

"Well, I *do* have a *few* friends in the world," I said. "There are *some* people who like me, and some people I like very much."

"Who here would you like to date?" they asked.

"I guess maybe Matt," I said, "because even though he's opinionated, he's strong and forceful, and I like his hands."

"Who would you like to date *least?*"

"Joe," I said. Joe looked to me as if he had had a successful lobotomy. "I don't think we'd find much to say to each other."

As lucky fate had it, the next morning Joe turned out to be someone else's partner in an exercise called a Love Feast. We were supposed to caress each other's faces with sprigs of flowering mimosa, and read more love poems aloud. Bach read

Please Touch

Blake's poem that begins "Never seek to tell thy love . . . ,"
which he called "a perfect example of nonverbal communication." Some of the workshop members made dates for when
they got back to Los Angeles. The men served barbecued
hamburgers to the girls. Everybody drifted off unaggressively.

But the most melodramatic part of the weekend had been
the night before, or rather the early hours of that same Sunday. Toward 4 a.m. as the mini-marathon was finishing, we
were told to elect a panel of three judges, who were going to
assess each of us. If we wanted to we could each appoint a
fourth judge when our time came.

The winners were Emily, Heather and Warren. Emily, who
got the most votes, became "Madame Chief Justice," or
"Your Honor" or "Your Highness." As my fourth judge I appointed a man who hadn't said much all along, because I
wondered what he was thinking.

"You ought to loosen up," he told me, "because when the
hard edges come off, you're really attractive, it's really there."

"Your Highness!" Bach intervened. "If I may make a point
of order, Your Highness must reprimand the assistant judge.
This is totally against all the rules of our procedure! You must
produce valid criticism, and not go into gross romanticism in
this court!"

Warren said I seemed enigmatic. Heather didn't think so.

"I see myself in you, as I was not long ago," she said, "and
I hope I'm not presumptuous in saying that I've changed. I see
your rigid control, trying to tempt men but also competing
with them. I used to do that too. I believe sincerely in the
thought that sometimes, just for effect, warmth has to be practiced, even if you don't feel it. It happened to me, that's all I
can say, and I wish you would try it—because it might happen to you, too."

Then it was the Chief Justice's turn.

"It was just perfect that you picked the poem you did," she
told me, "because that's what you want, what Shakespeare

talked about—the impossible. You want it because you'll never get it, and that's perfect because you're not sure you really want it at all, and until you face up to these facts it's going to be the same thing all over again. I believe you when you say how exhausted you get with all that travel, but still, you do live that way, and I'm not convinced of the reasons why you do.

"I think you do it as a kind of copout. I like you very much, and I think you're a very shy and timid person, with all the contradictions and everything else. We're going to pass a very, very severe sentence on you—one that we feel it's in your own best interests to follow. If you don't, the penalty will be severe. Warren, do you want to give her the sentence?"

Warren did. "At least one more, maybe two more intimacy marathons for you," he said.

Little did he know.

The Cap
on the
Toothpaste Tube

¶ Tex reminded me of the young military man at a state funeral who helps fold the flag on the coffin and presents it to the widow. He was crew-cut, correct, acquainted with grief, and quite content to be on the periphery of things. He did nothing to solicit the attention of Bill McGaw, who with his wife Audrey was leading a weekend of sensitivity training at Kairos for seven other couples. But still Tex caught Bill's eye.

"I keep wondering where *you* are, Tex," Bill said after everybody in the circle had explained why he had come. "My needle keeps gravitating to you like north on a compass. I see your face working. I see so much going on there, and I want so much to make myself available to help you. Can I?"

Tex didn't see how anyone could. His wife, Mimi, wanted a

The Cap on the Toothpaste Tube

divorce. She regarded their three years of marriage as a stulti-fying waste—"flustrating," she kept calling it, and nobody even thought of smiling at her mistake. Tex saw the marriage as the most hopeful and beautiful thing that had happened in his twenty-eight years. For him, marriage was the logical sequel to a lesson he had learned for the first time among his comrades in the Marines: that he could care about, and share his feelings with, other human beings. He wanted to teach Mimi the things he had learned, and to build with her a life of looking up together on starry nights from a log cabin in the mountains. He wanted them to comfort each other against the indifferent enormity of the universe.

Mimi didn't feel that way at all. To look at her offhand, you wouldn't know she felt anything. She wore a great deal of makeup but no expression. Her coiffure was piled in an absurd eight-inch heap on top of her head, and she kept taking her wedding band off and twisting it around in her hand, in a gesture easily read by the most psychologically naive observer. After the seventeen of us had sat around in a circle for several hours the first Friday evening we met, Mimi finally summoned the nerve to answer some of the oblique questions people had been putting to her.

"I just married you to get away from my family," she told Tex. "I was *using* you, do you understand? That's terrible, yes, but it's really true. And now I'm flustrated. I'm flustrated because this marriage isn't what I want. It never was. We've lived three years in a house we hate, you doing a job you hate, so you can please your parents (and by the way he hates them too). I want to have fun. I want to be young. I *am* young; I'm only twenty-one, but I feel like I was sixty-five. I don't want to keep house. I'm not good at it and I don't like it, and I don't see why I should have to do it.

"I *do* cheat on you, maybe because you accuse me of it so much I figure I might as well go ahead and prove you right. I cheat on you with Allan. He knows where I'm at. He knows I

61

Please Touch

don't love him, and he doesn't pretend he loves me, either, but we have fun and we're right for each other right now and we give each other something we both need. That's all I want now, that's all I can use, so please go away, I mean please let *me* go away."

The next morning, to everyone's relief, Mimi appeared with her hair still preposterously teased, but at least hanging down. We didn't talk about her and Tex then, but about Kurt and Ginny. Their problem was entirely different. They weren't even married, although Kurt was forty-one and Ginny thirty-three. On three separate occasions they had almost had a wedding, but each time one or the other had backed away. It was getting a little frightening. Ginny wasn't sure how much longer she would be likely to conceive children, which she wanted very much. So she and Kurt had come in desperation all the way from the University of Arizona, where they both taught, to this workshop. They were resolved to decide once and for all whether they were just kidding themselves and wasting each other's time.

Edith and Leonard were in their fifties. Both were social workers, from privileged and educated families. Ostensibly they had come because they wanted to learn to lead similar workshops themselves. But they too had their problems. Edith seemed the most sympathetic and unabrasive of women—the sort who goes to the trouble of finishing your sentences for you.

"Don't let her fool you, though," warned Leonard. "She may look as if she had no temper at all, but you ought to see the coffee stains on our ceiling. My tendency is just to shove everything unpleasant under the rug. But I don't want us to be like my parents. They tortured each other—in a very subtle, polite way, of course—all their married life. But when my father died last month, my mother might as well have died too. That's not what I call living."

62

The Cap on the Toothpaste Tube

Andy and Loretta had been referred to the McGaws by the San Diego Conciliatory Court. Andy was a Navy man who didn't want his wife to get a job. Loretta figured that now, with all four of their children in school, no harm and much good could come of her spending four hours a day in a real-estate office. Andy was too proud to let her.

"I make plenty of money," he said. "You belong at home."

"You just don't want me to grow up," Loretta accused. "You see me as a child, which I was when we were married —I was only eighteen, and to you I'm *still* eighteen. You don't want me to have my own identity at all. Why, our twelve-year-old boy is more mature in a lot of ways than I am."

Sandra felt ignored because Glenn spent all his time and strength trying to finish his doctoral dissertation. Even though she knew he was doing it for her sake and their children's, she felt neglected. The other occupants of their high-rise apartment building seemed to have not only more things but more fun.

"They're always going off water-skiing, always getting new wallpaper, always having new sofas and dishwashers delivered," Sandra complained. "I feel as if there were a banquet going on, and all I get is crumbs. He sits in his den with the door closed and the kids and I have to tiptoe around so he won't be disturbed. I want to enjoy myself *now,* not when we're sixty-five and have a lot of accrued compound quarterly interest, or whatever you call it."

"She may not always be right," said Glenn, very much the wry academic, "but she's never wrong."

When it came Beth's turn to speak her voice was tight and thin. "Our marriage is stable, all right," she said, "but that's all you can say for it, and it's not enough. If we fought it would at least be interesting. We're so *polite* to each other. We never talk of things we really feel. How I really feel, if Tom should ever wonder, is wiped out. But he doesn't ask. He's away at the state legislature about half the time, and that matters much more to him than I do."

"That isn't true," Tom argued. "I just don't have the sort of vocabulary to talk of those things. I can talk about appropriations or rezoning bills or politics, but all my life I've found it very hard to talk about myself and how I really feel. I never knew Beth minded until lately. She always seemed a model politician's wife."

"I do like campaigning," Beth said. "I like to meet people. But it's so superficial. Sometimes I think I'll crack up."

George and Alice were both librarians, and their life too seemed filled with polite hypocrisies.

"Aside from our work," said Alice, "we have so little in common that I don't see how we could have fooled the caseworker who had to okay us before we adopted our children. We live in the same house and we sleep in the same bed, but we might as well live ten miles apart. If we did, I'm not sure I'd even bother to call him up."

"Alice used to be spontaneous and fun," George said. "But now she's so cautious about every little thing that it's painful to watch."

In a time when more than a million Americans are divorced every year, encounter workshops for couples (married and otherwise) are becoming as common as labs for businessmen. Marriages, in fact, have much in common with corporations in the type and extent of their problems.

"The big problem with all long-range systems—marriages, companies, schools, whatever—is that they get boring," I was told by James V. Clark, who also leads couples' workshops. "People often want above all else to be safe, so they get hooked into situations where only predictable things happen, where they can play structured games with each other.

"Most marriages aren't bad, they're just kind of gray, be-

The Cap on the Toothpaste Tube

cause people have shut off so much of themselves from each other. We're bored because parts of our spectrums aren't exposed. If you can expose something in your spectrum that's been concealed, it can't help but enrich the system. Our artfulness, in leading these groups, is to get this to happen in small enough doses so that people can manage the exposure."

Clark and his wife told me they worked privately with one couple for a year and a half before the man and woman ever physically touched each other, and of another couple who wouldn't even *look* at each other.

"They played Mommy and Daddy," Frances Clark said, "or they used their sexuality on the dog. Both of them would stroke that dog all the time. When they finally turned on to each other, and learned that they *could* be intimate after all, a funny thing happened. The dog died."

Marriages lend themselves well to group workshops, the Clarks said, because public revelation can be contagious as well as therapeutic.

"People sometimes say 'you can't change *me* in two days,' " said Clark, "and they're right; we can't. But we can hope to change what goes on between two people. It's the interperson —our 'usness'—that is open to change and growth. We can create the kind of climate that allows people to tell each other, as they never have before, what's really going on with them. Marriage partners are always electrified when they find that they have twenty years of thoughts hidden from each other."

The McGaws, like the Clarks, use a subdued approach that touches only in passing, if at all, on the clinical aspects of sex.

"We're in the business of creating visions," said Audrey McGaw, "not of counting, measuring and evaluating orgasms." That sort of thing is more the province of William Schutz and Pamela Portugal, whose three-year alliance has led to a series of couples' workshops demanding "radical honesty." At these workshops, soon to be described in a book called *The Open Couple,* everyone is obliged to confess publicly to his mate three secrets which might seriously jeopardize the relationship. The secrets usually turn out to be adultery, homosexuality and indifference. Such candor, Schutz insists, results in "a moral monogamy the like of which has seldom been seen in human history."

"We're not trying to make nice people nicer," Schutz says, "but to clarify what a relationship is, and if necessary to change it. The price people pay for not being open with each other is a tremendous deadness. The idea that 'knowing my secret would do you more harm than good' just isn't true. You can't feel good in your body if you're holding something back with your thoughts."

The Clarks say that intimacy, not sex, is the goal of their workshops. "Some of our best friends are sexy," says Frances Clark, "and we have nothing against sex. But we've found that sexual behavior changes automatically as people become more open." Not for them, or for the McGaws, such Schutzian workshop practices as the issuing to men of gynecologist's speculums, the better for them to know their wives' vaginas.

McGaw's style is laconic. He stays relaxed even during twenty-minute silences other people find agonizing. Only once in the weekend I spent at his workshop did he offer what some in the movement would call a "lecturette." It had to do with communication.

"One of the big problems with marriages and all other relationships," he said, "is that nobody listens. We very seldom really register what is said to us. Most of our conversations aren't dialogues but soliloquies." On the blackboard he drew a chart showing six common responses to things people hear. The top three were labeled "I-Messages," and those below "U-Messages" (For "I" and "You").

"I-Messages," said McGaw, "are much groovier. Take the

The Cap on the Toothpaste Tube

matter of the cap on the toothpaste tube. Now a U-Message about that would be 'God damn it, for Christ's sake, why don't you ever remember to put the cap back on? It looks like hell!" An I-Message making the same point would be "Look, honey, it may seem unreasonable to you, but I have a problem. When you don't put the cap back on the toothpaste tube, and the stuff gets all over the porcelain, it makes me very angry. Do you think for my sake you could please cut it out?" McGaw said the former response would be a Minus Two and the latter a Plus One on this scale of communications:

I-Messages	$+3 =$ reflect $+2 =$ understand $+1 =$ question
U-Messages	$-1 =$ evade, joke $-2 =$ attack $-3 =$ withdraw

McGaw also led us in an experiment with fantasy. We all lay down on the floor with closed eyes, silent for five minutes in an effort to clear our heads of all fleeting superficial thoughts. I was almost asleep when a startling noise sounded. It was the clear tap of a fork on a crystal glass, but it might as well have been an oriental gong. For some reason it made me see a rural mailbox surrounded by tulips.* The same sound suggested to Sandra, the woman who thought her academic husband ignored her, a picture of herself standing looking at the ocean. McGaw thereupon told her to "be" the ocean—to speak as if she didn't just see the ocean, but *was* it. She said she'd try.

"I am the ocean," she began, "controlled by the moon. I cover six-sevenths of all the surface of the earth. All the waters of all the continents feed me. I am tranquil sometimes,

* The meaning of fantasy is described on pages 206 and 207.

and turbulent other times. I have vast riches nobody knows about, and hidden depths. I am unexplored. My waves break on beaches where nobody swims. I am cold and warm and serene and stormy and placid and violent. People try, but nobody really can fathom me."

"Did *she* say earlier that *she* felt *dead?*" asked Andy, the career Navy man. Indeed she had. "Well, Sandra, old girl," he said, "you're sure the fieriest corpse *I've* ever seen."

"What you've just given us," said Edith, the woman with the secret temper, "is the best description I've ever heard of the female sex."

It turned out that Glenn, Sandra's husband, had also had a fantasy regarding water. Later in the weekend, somebody suggested that Sandra and Glenn ought to get mad at each other. Glenn answered "but I don't *feel* mad." McGaw had them play a game involving the slapping of each other's hands. They slapped playfully at first, but as time passed, more and more seriously—not painfully, but hard. Sandra suddenly began to weep.

"That's the first time in months that we've really touched each other," she said. Glenn put his arm around her and led her out of the room.

"Where are you two going?" somebody asked.

"To find our ocean," Glenn said.

Tom, the legislator who couldn't talk to his wife, reported that what he had seen in fantasy was a large door—a door to a room, big enough to contain all his inadequacies. Audrey McGaw asked him to go into the room and tell us what he saw there. Tom said he saw many boxes and trunks filled with problems. He said he would like to get into the boxes and look at the problems, but that he couldn't open them without a crowbar.

"Can't you *make* a crowbar?" somebody asked.

"I guess I could," Tom said, "out of that putty over there."

"Okay," said Audrey, "go ahead. Make one." He did, and

opened the boxes. In one of them he found some tarlike substance which he poured over himself. In another were some precious jewels and some unidentifiable glittery stuff, which he also poured onto himself, so that it stuck on the tar. He was directed to go around the room and tell everyone, "Look at me! I'm shining!" Most of us indulgently said, "Of course you are." Audrey and I didn't, though. For us he was still lacklustre.

Kurt and Ginny told of the times in the past when they had almost got married. Audrey asked Ginny who in the world she was closest to. Her sister in Seattle, Ginny said.

"Pretend you're calling up your sister," said Audrey, "and telling her that you've really done it, that at long last you're finally, really married." Ginny tried to pretend, but she couldn't manage. And then, right in front of the assembled company, Kurt proposed to her.

"Let's cut out all this nonsense, Ginny," he said, "and get married as soon as we get back to Tucson." This time he really seemed to mean it—"more than he ever seemed to before," said Ginny. So she agreed. Later I heard that they really had held a wedding.

Most of the couples seemed to benefit somehow or other from the workshop. I doubted that any force, human or otherwise, would ever put asunder Edith and Leonard, the social workers who had their own problems. "We'll never be polite to each other the way my parents were, honey," he said in tones more commanding than inquiring.

"You bet your ass we won't," said the normally dulcet Edith.

Andy finally consented to let Loretta work in the real estate office.

Alice, who had professed such vast indifference to George, changed some too. "You know," she said speculatively to him, "I believe I *would* call you up if you lived ten miles away. I might even ask you over."

But not all the stories ended like Gilbert and Sullivan operettas.

For example, Tex didn't seem any happier Sunday morning than he had Friday night. Mimi's hair was still down, but still backcombed, and she didn't appear to have relented in her determination to leave him. Tex began to look more like the bereaved at the funeral than the folder of the flag. McGaw suggested that we all help Tex break away from the problems he'd been telling us he had. Everyone who felt so inclined could join hands and form a circle, each person representing one of the things Tex had said he feared.

"I'll be What Will the Neighbors Think," Tom said.

"I'll be Despair," said Bill.

"I'll be the tension that will arise if you really lose Mimi," said Audrey.

"I'll be the little boy who never had a chance to be a child," said Sandra.

"I'll be your feeling of worthlessness."

"I'll be your pain."

"I'll be I Want to Blow My Brains Out."

Some of us sat and watched the circle of problems take form. Tex, trapped inside, was ordered to try to break his way out by any method he could think of: shoving, shouldering, pushing, feinting, breaking out from below people's knees. He was very much a strong Marine, but his struggle took a long time. When he did break free, Audrey ordered him to stand in the middle of the room with his arms at his sides. She told us all to go up to him, one by one, and without using words, express whatever feeling we had for him. Tex was ordered not to return any gesture, but just to stand there.

Glenn shook his hand, and Mimi wouldn't go forth at all, but everyone else gave Tex some sort of hug. Tears overflowed from his eyes. "It would have been a lot easier," he said, "if one of you guys had *hit* me." But nobody had or would.

The Cap on the Toothpaste Tube

"I know what you mean," said Audrey. "When a hand comes we duck, because we're so conditioned to expect a slap instead of a pat. But please understand that you don't have to climb a mountain or pay us or thank us for what we've given you. We give you our affection for yourself. It has no fee. It has no price. It's yours."

"See?" said Mimi. "I wanted you to see that you're a person and that you have some worth without me. Now can you see that you don't need me to make it? That there's more to life than just me?"

When we all left on Sunday noon, Mimi's wedding ring was pushed as far back as it would go on Tex's left little finger. Their marriage really was over. His life, however, was not.

Let It All
Hang Out

¶ Some lines from *Hamlet* make me think of Synanon. I mean the part where Hamlet admonishes his weak-willed and lustful mother to:

> Assume a virtue, if you have it not.
> That monster custom, who all sense doth eat,
> Of habits devil, is angel yet in this,
> That to the use of actions fair and good
> He likewise gives a frock or livery
> That aptly is put on . . .

Synanon (pronounced *Sin*-anon and named after an early member's mispronunciation of "seminar") forever demands that its people assume virtues they lack. It is a nonprofit cor-

72

poration that controls $7 million worth of real estate. It has branches in five California cities (Santa Monica, Oakland, San Francisco, Tomales Bay and San Diego), as well as in New York City, Detroit, and San Juan, Puerto Rico. Its "lifestyle," dispensed through 80 groups called Tribes, is based on a kind of encounter group known as the Synanon Game. The Tribes assemble one night each week to play the Game, the only rule of which is that everybody take part, keeping any violence on a verbal level. No topic is barred, everyone expresses his reactions to everyone else's problems and life stories, and the mood quickly shifts from hilarity to rage back to hilarity again.

I asked Chuck Dederich, who founded Synanon, how he thought his gigantic organization fit into the rest of the human potential movement. "We have more fun here than they do at places like Esalen," he said. "We're plugged into a social system. Nothing whatsoever is to be gained by sitting around in a room yelling at your best friend unless doing so is hooked into some system that feeds the human family. Even here, if all they do is play the Game one night a week, they might as well just go to some group therapy session. You can't buy a ticket, a little blood-of-the-lamb to get washed in, if you don't also have some involvement in Synanon's purpose and goals."

A perennial goal is to rid all Synanon members, whether "Dope Fiends" (for whose sake the organization was founded in 1959) or "Squares" (who may be hooked on nothing more lethal than caffein and nicotine), of immature habits. In Synanonese, one of the pithiest dialects in all the movement, Hamlet's advice to his mother is translated into the phrase "act as if." You may not be able to get along without heroin, but act as if you could. You may not be orderly, or honest or industrious, but act as if you were and after a while you'll get so used to it you really will be.

This prescription, which has no conscious connection with the theories of Pavlov and Skinner, applies to all manner of problems. A youth named John, accused of "dressing like a pompous asshole in mailman gray" was told to act as if he wanted to look his age. Another young man was accused of using his harelip to get extra sympathy, and was advised to act as if he had no speech impediment. A matron, who looked like a B. H. Wragge advertisement, had come all the way from Briarcliff Manor to California to try to figure out why her teenage daughter had taken to using drugs. She complained, "I never *have* understood that child." "Act as if you did," they told her, "and then maybe you will."

An ex-monk who now taught in a public high school reported he had had dates with six girls so far but not yet "got down with" (slept with) any of them, much though he longed to, because of his lack of experience. "Act as if you knew how and go ahead," he was told. Do not surmise, however, that Synanon encourages random bedhopping. "You look like a slut, Bianca, and you *are* a slut," a waitress was told. "Take a motion. Write yourself a contract. Lay off *all* men for six months, until you get your head straightened out. Act as if you didn't care about any of them."

Most of this advice was dispensed during the forty-eight hours I spent as an ingredient in Synanon's Perpetual Stew, which is part of the organization's elaborate system of mystiques and rituals. (Despite its name the Stew has since been disbanded, I am assured only temporarily; I therefore refer to it in the present tense.) As its name implies, the Stew bubbles like a pot on an old-fashioned stove nobody ever turns off. New flavorings, in the form of new people, are added all the time. You go out, I come in; you've been there seventy-two hours, I stay for forty-eight. That girl over there may only be booked for four hours, a chunk of time called a "Stew Bit." Intricate logistics are required to choreograph everybody in and out for different cycles.

In February 1969 there were two Perpetual Stews, one in Santa Monica, where Synanon was founded, and one in Oakland, where I sat in. Twenty chairs of various colors were arranged in a circle. A microphone dangled from the ceiling, connected to some expensive-looking electronic equipment so that the proceedings could at any point be tape-recorded. The tape was always switched on when any of the ten members of Synanon's Board of Regents dropped by. Nobody but the regents could sit on the white chairs.

Some of the chairs tilt back, some have flip-out footrests. All are beguilingly comfortable. By five o'clock in the morning, if you've been up thirty or forty hours, it is a real struggle not to fall asleep in them. I often dozed off during my forty-eight hours as a Stew ingredient, but never for long; whoever sat next to me could be depended upon to jab me angrily in the ribs. Falling asleep at Synanon, even at 5 a.m. after two days of no rest, is as much of a *gaffe* as burping at a tea party. For six of my forty-eight hours I was assigned to a cot in the dormitory and told to go nap, but for the other forty-two I was expected to be alert. After all, we were told (in the same tones parents use at mealtimes in reference to the world's starving children), it was a privilege to be in the Stew. To arrive a few minutes late, as I did, for no better reason than having tarried over lunch with a friend, was to get hell.

Of course if you're in the Stew at all you're used to getting hell. They won't let you in unless you're an experienced Game player, which is to say a seasoned member of one of the Tribes. Tribes give their members hell regularly in the course of the Games, which one person said are "like a Zen Koan— they provide pressure from which there is no escape." I qualified for the Stew by spending several weeks as a member of the Thor tribe, which meets promptly at 8 p.m. on Thursdays in Santa Monica. Thor is a Square tribe, which means most of its members know of the horrors of drug addiction only by what they hear from the Dope Fiends.

It is widely but wrongly assumed that Synanon Games consist only of vicious, negative attacks on personalities, at top decibel level and with maximum fury. Such attacks do happen, often and loud, but they are not essentially negative, nor are they the only item on the bill of fare. There is also, for example, Betty's Game, also known as the Virtue Game, invented by and named for the wife of Synanon's founder. In Betty's Game emphasis is on praise, not attack.

"Chuck operates off his intellect, mainly," says Betty Dederich, "and I go by intuition, which in my particular ethnic group we call Mother Wit." Her particular ethnic group, unlike her husband's, is black. "We need a new language of love," Betty says. "We have a great vocabulary for hostility, but we need new ways to say 'I love you.' Receiving affection throws people into more of a crisis than being yelled at. People need both. It's the sound of two hands clapping."

Fads change fast, but in my Synanon period (September 1968 to February 1969) there was quite a lot of talk about two hands clapping, and Ralph Waldo Emerson and Buckminster Fuller. It was also fashionable for men to have all their hair shaved off, and to wear overalls. Tape recordings were another obsession. An invitation to hear a tape by Dederich or Synanon's other leaders was more or less a command performance. I was summoned to hear "Thickened Light," a tape in which Dederich mixed his own ideas with some of Emerson's and Fuller's. Everybody there had to turn in a composition about it by the following Friday.

Professing to be "in the people business," Synanon expects its own people to work, and in return supplies them with everything from Hawaiian Punch to dental care, all "hustled" from well-wishers outside. (Clothes are hustled too. You can determine the status and seniority of residents by what they're wearing.) Synanon also gives its people plenty to think about. All its facilities have Study Halls. Everybody in the Stew, regardless of background, is expected to step forth on no notice and give a "chalk talk" to edify the others. When my turn came I obliged with a reading of Hopkins' "The World Is Charged with the Grandeur of God." Others talked of Indian birth-control methods, the process of offset printing, and the place of plankton in the ecological chain. Synanon also runs a thriving Stew for children, and has an ambitious "Academy" at Tomales Bay, which someday may become an accredited college.

"The average kid goes to college because his father did or didn't," one Academy leader said. "But kids come here because *they* want to." Another thing every Synanon schoolboy knows is that "the best way to learn something is to teach it."

But the Stew isn't all intellect, any more than it is all contumely. For a couple of my forty-eight hours there, before dawn illumined the rainy and abandoned streets of Oakland outside, we just sat there in our plastic easy chairs. Fighting sleep, we listened to music. We heard an odd medley: "Yellow Submarine," a maudlin chorale that had something to do with the founding of Israel, Beethoven's entire Fifth Symphony, some Buffy St. Marie and some Ella Fitzgerald. We had to listen, too. No fair reading, not even from the omnipresent paperback editions of Emerson, but we were permitted to fiddle all we liked with toothpick tetrahedrons, modeled after Fuller's. And we were welcome to all we could stomach of peanut-butter-and-jelly sandwiches and coffee.

We heard a lot, in the Stew, about Synanon's expenses, which come to $200,000 a month, and about projects like the program to work with the adolescents of Oakland.

"The danger," as somebody said while I was there, "is in mimicking the attitude of the bleeding-heart social workers, which is 'what can we do to help these poor black children?' Not us. We don't 'help' the kids, we let them come in as members, which means we make them work, and make them join a Tribe." (There are special Tribes for these children, as there are for parents of Dope Fiends, called Mamas and Papas.) "This is a place for a kid to build himself a character and a future," a Synanon official said of the Oakland facility. "Youngsters are given access to all our educational facilities. The community of Synanon must accept some responsibility for its environment. The Jewish Psychiatrist, the charismatic First Christian, said 'teach by example.' That's what we're trying to do, too."

But Synanon, Dederich assured me, is not interested only in the unfortunate. "We found that the Haves were in as much trouble as the Have Nots, which is to say those who were considered well off if they had underwear. Many people in Synanon were born to the purple. We've got guys who made it twenty years ago, or whose parents made it for them, who since have just vegetated. Synanon provides an outlet for the energies that got them where they are.

"There are millions of people in the world, and a lot of them here, who have never seen a baby born, a man die or a woman go crazy. And there are millions of others who've seen these things plenty of times but who need to learn about manners and customs and civilization. Synanon is where both kinds meet. Everybody brings something in, everybody benefits. We integrate not just racially but economically and chronologically. Nobody, rich or poor, gets a handout here." Dues for the Game Club are $.01 a month, but larger contributions are evangelistically encouraged.

I felt a spurious shame when it came time in the Stew for me to "run my story," which means to summarize my life. How could my story compete for interest with the accounts I had been hearing of anguish, melodrama, crime, punishment and authentic tragedy? My antiseptic memories were not of "sixes" (half-year jail sentences) among "pervo-deevos" and "bull-daggers," or bondsmen or desperation. In haste and with little inflection I recited the facts of my life: two-thirds Midwest, one-third New York City, no marriages, no kids, fond of

words, nature, children, people; many pleasures; many unful-
filled longings; that was about it. Next?

"You look as if you were about to *explode*," somebody said
when I finished. "What are you afraid of? Why don't you give
more of yourself?"

"It's just the way I am," I said. "I don't come on strong at
first. People who know me well sometimes wish I'd shut up,
but it takes me a while to get to that stage. Besides, you all
seem to know each other already. . . ."

"That's just what I thought, too, when I came into the
Stew," said an economics instructor whose time was up. "I
thought everybody here knew each other except me, and that
nothing I could say would interest them. But I was wrong.
You're wrong too. Get in there, mix it up, cut it up, let it all
hang out."

"Yeah," said a black girl named Ontreal, who had ascer-
tained that we were born in the same sign of the Zodiac. "It's
your Stew. Are you gonna *use* it, or not? You probably won't.
You look to me like a disgrace to Taurus."

"I am *not*," I said with the irrational regression that probably meant we were getting somewhere. "*You* are."

"Yeah? Well, tell us, what do *you* ever do that benefits mankind?"

"Well," I said, "I don't make any huge sacrifices. I write
checks to help the Biafrans, and get them to stop tearing
down the redwoods, and send kids to the country and things
like that, but I don't really give in a way that affects me
much. At this point I don't really have time to."

"Yeah," said someone else, "you must be pretty busy with
your jet-set values."

"Me?! *Jet*-set?! Are you kidding?"

"You said you ride a lot of planes, didn't you? They must
be mostly jets, aren't they?"

"I suppose they are, but my God, I'm not like *those* people.
I go a lot of places, but I go there to work, not play."

79

"Maybe you *ought* to play, then," someone said. "Maybe you ought to stay places longer, and not just rush around."

"Maybe so," I said, "but I always have to leave sooner than I want to."

"So you're always saying *bon voyage* prematurely?" Mike Kaiser, Synanon's head public relations man, had stepped into the Stew and was helping to grill me.

"You're not kidding," I said. "All I ever do is say good-bye."

"Isn't there some Country Western song by that name?"

"If there isn't there should be," I said. Somebody hummed a possible tune.

"How come you *do* have so many farewell scenes?" Mike asked.

"I guess it's because I'm afraid to get more involved and be more vulnerable, so I always arrange it so I have to go somewhere else and start something new before I finish what I've started. It's a pattern of my whole life, work and people and everything. I guess it *could* be a good pattern, if I liked it."

"But you don't like it, huh? Because you were raised in the Midwest, and you're expected to be settled by now?"

"That's part of it, all right. What I'd really like, more than anything else, would be a house in the country."

"With a picket fence?"

"Not picket, split rail."

"Can it be," asked Mike, "that you live your whole life in total defiance of your inner nature?"

"That's too simple," I said. "How do I know what my inner nature is? I'm a very complex person."

"We all are."

"I know that sounds pompous and stupid, but it's true. I like tranquility, but I also like whatever you'd call its opposite. I like to rest, but I like to wander. I'm very selfish. All I want is everything, including somebody to tell me what to do

—so long as he orders me to do what I really wanted to do all the while."

"You can't have your cake and eat it too."

"I know, but sometimes for a while I fool myself and I do."

"You talk the talk," said Mike, "but you don't walk the walk. You live in a nonworld of nonexperience. I get the feeling you can't stand anything being too good. If you've got it it's no good, and if you *don't* got it it's no good. You don't like running around all over the place, but still you do it."

"I'll bet you think the world owes you a lot of special privileges," another Synanon man had told me earlier, "because you're a writer. That's probably the real reason you're here. You'd have wanted to come anyway, but without a project you'd never have had the nerve. That's probably why you do a lot of things. You know how I know? Because I'm the same way, and have been since I was a kid, when the big thing to do was go hang around at the Rego Park Jewish Center. I'd go there and look at girls, but I'd be too scared to ask them to dance. Then it occurred to me to go there as a writer. That changed everything. All of a sudden I could go up and say 'Madam, I'm writing an article about the Rego Park Jewish Center,' and from then on everything would be all right."

"Yes, I'm like that too," I admitted. "I'm always pressing my nose to other people's windows. I'd like to have some windows of my own."

"For a start," somebody said inevitably, "you could get some different glasses, preferably contact lenses. The ones you have are *awful.*"

Everyone in the Stew had his moment, or hour, of attention. "Come *on,* Barry," they told one glib square, "cut out that shit and give us a *feeling.*"

Leo's problem was precisely the opposite: he wasn't glib enough.

"I can read okay," he mumbled, "but my writing's not so hot."

"Go to the blackboard and write your name, Leo," they told him. He did, rather well.

"I liked *prison* better than this place," he said. "In prison they let me grow flowers, and I was good at it."

"Maybe you're one of those people who can't tolerate freedom," a Synanon official told him. "How come you haven't grown any flowers for us? Haven't you learned what this place is about? You're all fucked up? Get somebody else out of that bag. You're insecure? Make somebody else secure. But I guess you want to go back to prison again, where you can be creative and disciplined, and Mommy will be proud on visiting day. You don't want to do that here, though, in this society of thieves and drunks and criminals."

"But I *do* want to," said Leo.

"It's true then that we can say, without offending your delicately balanced hearing mechanism, that you are a liar and a fraud?"

Margie, a teenager who had just lately quit using drugs, said she had felt like leaving Synanon and going home.

"For you, going home would be like having cyanide for dessert," she was told. "What if we gave you an alternative to splitting, like say sucking your thumb? Where would you go? You don't want shoes, you poor little Okie, you want combat boots. That cowshit little town you come from! Give one of these rednecks a bath and she thinks she's the queen of England!"

"We can't talk to this girl as if she were an adult," someone said, "because she's sixteen going on twelve. You want to stop being sixteen? Go ahead, try, it's like stopping the sun from coming up in the morning, or telling the ocean 'no more waves.' Why don't you try something *big?* When dealing with ladies of thirty-five and under with spaced teeth who haven't gone through puberty yet, we must listen carefully. Maybe she'd like us to get her some Clearasil. Maybe her acne has backed up and formed a pus pocket where her brain should be."

One boy's parents, who had neglected him for years back in Indiana, had taken lately to pestering him and Synanon both. He was told: "Look, write them that you're all right, that you're in here trying to become a man, which you must do at all costs, and that you've got to get your head straightened out, which you can't do unless they leave you alone for a while. If they don't understand that, have a Chinaman write it and send *that* to them."

A kid who stank was ordered to leave the Stew immediately, in the company of a Synanon staff member, and go take a bath, "a *bubble* bath if you like, but hurry."

A young man who hung around with men five or ten years his senior—"my *role* models," he called them—was told to make friends his own age. "You're eighteen and you did two years in some kiddie joint and you come on like Al Capone," they told him. "But you're not a tough guy at all. You're a sweet, sensitive kid who ought to hang out with kids your own age. That's where it's at. It's a tremendous fix. You really do need to get kicked in the ass by your chronological peers. Cut out that Marlon Brando stuff, and act as if."

"Who's Marlon Brando?" asked the kid. I felt very old.

Then the kid turned the game onto a girl. "Let's examine the hostility you have for me, Linda," he said.

"I do," said Linda. "I really do feel hostile to you. I hate you."

"You know how you act, Linda? You act like some fuckin' latent sex queen. You're gettin' fuckin' out of sight. I'm gettin' fed up with your shit. You're really outfuckinrageous."

("After a while," Dederich had said earlier, "they learn that there is more than one adjective in the language. And we

83

never swear on the floor." At Synanon the "floor" is anywhere outside the Game or Stew. Only in Games and Stews may people "dump" or vent the grievances and grudges that develop on the floor.)

Somebody accused a carpenter named Al of being a phony. "I guess I am," he said. "I guess I project a tough-guy image when I'm really a fuckin' teddy bear. I guess I needed that image in the jungle where I was, but I don't need it here. I'm learning how much I don't know, how ignorant I am. Like I've never even been in a nightclub in my whole life, or up in an airplane."

Cliff, the proprietor of a reducing salon in San Bruno, ran his story. Somebody said "that shirt you have on—you're not wearing it; it's wearing you." He said he had in the past managed a dance studio, supervised a booth where computers analyzed handwriting and been in charge of a juice bar at a health food shop.

"In other words you're a con artist, right?"

"Not an artist," said Cliff, "just a con man."

I liked Synanon for guiding people to such insights. But sometimes its esprit was a little overwhelming. In the Stew a square girl named Donna told how she resented Synanon's encroachments on her husband's time. He was a retired dope fiend, in charge of all the electrical work on the premises, and his work took so much time she didn't see much of him.

"The way I see it," she said, "my responsibility is to my husband, then my home, then the rest of the world, in that order."

"WHAT?" exclaimed several Stew ingredients. "Doesn't the social movement here excite you?"

"No," she said, "it frightens me."

"You look as if it *bored* you," someone said. "You look like a zombie. Don't you see that *Synanon* should be first? Synanon is people, Synanon is you, Synanon is everything. It really lies with you to be anything you want. Synanon is the key."

"Just walk around this whole place someday," another person told her, "and think 'this is mine.' Because it is. This whole fuckin' place is yours, every nook and cranny. You own it. Now, when in the world did *you* ever think *you'd* own a hotel? You do, though. You've got more here than any man could ever offer you. And you've got your own man too, by the way. And you've got happiness at the same time, all labeled Synanon. You stay at Synanon, and you'll grow in your gut. You've got a choice. You can either be sick and poor, or rich and happy. Which do you choose?"

As the girl named Donna pondered her choice, a woman who had been in the Stew for her full seventy-two hours got up to leave, looking haggard but euphoric. She addressed the assemblage as if it were one person, which in a way it was.

"Goodbye, Stew," she called as she left, waving, "and thanks."

"You Were
Born Nude,
Weren't You?"

❡ The sky above Orange County that early autumn evening was mauve, smoggy and sullenly cold. It might have been on such a night eons ago that the first prehistoric human being took it into his head to drape himself in the fur of an animal. Smart fellow. I, on the other hand, the product of centuries of civilization leading up to *Women's Wear Daily,* was headed for a Nude Sensitivity Training Workshop. Instead of slipping a jacket on over my slacks and blouse, which on so raw a night would have been the sensible thing to do, I was about to take them and everything else off. I would do so in the presence of eleven equally naked strangers, partaking thereby in "a subcultural experiment to actively try new ways of relating."

I was going to examine for myself the conviction of Paul

86

"You Were Born Nude, Weren't You?"

Bindrim, who hopes history will remember him as an intrepid pioneer, that "clothing means we really don't trust each other. There's so much bullshit about an American's home being his castle, and such a *fetish* about privacy. After all, you were *born* nude, weren't you?" So far as I know I was, and visits to Esalen had removed my apprehensions about nakedness per se. Still, it seemed to me that a lot of people I knew could use more privacy, not less, and that a weekend with overdressed friends would have been far more alluring. But Bindrim's notions had to be reckoned with. Pictures of one of his previous workshops in my *Life* story had ignited furious controversy. Having heard so much argument pro and con, I felt obliged to experience his crusade for myself.

With an air of furtive mystery I was following mimeographed directions off the freeway in my rent-a-car. I and the other participants in the workshop, whoever they might prove to be, had agreed in writing not to "indulge in overt sexual expression" and to repose "in *individual* poolside sleeping bags." If we fraternized with each other in the week following our encounter, we had also agreed, it would be "at our own risk." Nor would we divulge to anybody the address of the house where we would be meeting. Public opinion is not sympathetic to Paul Bindrim, and locations for his nude encounters are not easy to find. When for some reason he cannot get the site he likes best—a secluded motel in the desert—he must make do with a suburban house that belongs to friends he pays to vacate it for the weekend.

That particular house suits him because it has a heatable pool, and his Nude Sensitivity Training depends a great deal on proximity to water. (Bindrim seems to take more literally than most Huxley's conviction that we are all "multiple amphibians.") But when we got to the house we were immediately told to go back out and repark our cars, scattering them around the vicinity so the neighbors wouldn't think anything funny was going on.

Please Touch

After this maneuver we sat, still clad, in the living room of the house, drumming our fingers on chair arms and coffee tables, silently whistling with fake nonchalance. To break the ice, Bindrim, who I thought resembled an exceptionally alert chimpanzee, explained the nasty-looking sore just below the right kneepant of his Bermuda shorts. It was the result of coral poisoning he had suffered on a recent holiday in Tahiti (the economy round-trip fare to which from Los Angeles is, or was then, $520).

Like a jolly camp director he divided us into committees to serve and clean up after the three meals we would share.

"All the food's been pre-prepared," Bindrim assured us. "Just help yourselves, whenever you like. Our *serious* meal will be Sunday lunch."

Feeling peckish, I was dismayed that Saturday dinner was far from "serious": store-bought cookies, apples, bananas, and instant tea or coffee. Thrift is a conspicuous virtue of Bindrim's. Anyone who admires the rustic luxury of his circular house in the Hollywood Hills is quickly assured he got it at a steal. For this twenty-four-hour marathon each of us had mailed in a $45 check—"a bargain price," said Bindrim, "especially considering you stand a good chance of having a Peak Experience."

I had been reading a lot about Peak Experiences, in the writings of Maslow, who coined the phrase, and elsewhere. I had been wondering how paid strangers could program something so private and elusive. I had a churlish notion that Peak Experiences were pretty much a matter of luck. Bindrim, however, believes he can induce "peaking" in 80 percent of the population. Dubious but hopeful, I had followed instructions and brought along my own "Peak Stimuli"—examples of "the things in this world you like the *very most* to see, to hear, to smell, to taste and to touch."

Assembling my Stimuli had been like getting outfitted for a mixed-media safari. Los Angeles, for all its fabled bounty,

"You Were Born Nude, Weren't You?"

was not my ideal shopping ground. I could imagine feeling pretty Peaky if I could somehow arrange simultaneously to see a New England maple forest in fall, hear an excellent brass quintet, smell newly washed clothes that had dried outdoors, hold the face of a man who had just come into a house in winter, and eat a cheeseburger of my own devising. Or I might Peak if I could snorkel over a coral reef while hearing crickets chirping while smelling the inside of a new car, drinking Clamato juice and dozing under a down comforter. But I had to make do with what was at hand. I brought along a rock I had picked up from the coast of Maine, a Sierra Club photograph of some fall leaves, a *Book of Common Prayer* from which I thought somebody with a resonant voice might read me the 139th Psalm, some good cheddar cheese and a brand new $2 leather luggage tag, from an intimidating Beverly Hills boutique, to smell. (Only later did Bindrim say how revealing this last selection was. "Leather," he informed me, "is the symbolic emotional expression of protecting a sensitive emotional state. Leather jackets, you know, are worn by people who don't know how to emotionally ice skate.")

Our hours together, Bindrim told us as we sat there with our clothes still very much on, would transport us all back to that wonderful, primordial time 10,000 years ago and more, when we were not vexed, harried, over-civilized human beings but free and happy animals. This mass regression would occur in what he called a "Womb Pool—a real Garden of Eden scene. Why *is* it," he lamented with no relevance that I could see, "that human beings hate animals so much? Intellect may be man's demise. Our intellects get us into trouble the same way a deer's antlers do. When the antlers get too big, the deer bumps into trees so that he can't retreat. It's the same with us. Our intellects prevent us from being ourselves."

To get acquainted, we were to introduce ourselves in speeches limited by a three-minute egg timer. When the sand ran out the timer was passed on to the person on the next speaker's right. Then each of us was to go around the circle and stare unswervingly into every other pair of eyes, an exercise which under the circumstances I found about as poignant as gazing at so many hard-boiled eggs. Next we were to express physically, not with words, whatever feelings this "eyeballing" had generated. Since in my case it had generated none to speak of, my repertoire of gestures was limited to gingerly pats on heads and shoulders. Other people, unencumbered by Eastern Seaboard reticence, were falling into each other's arms with emotion I could neither share nor comprehend. Finally, when we had done all these nonverbal tricks, we were to say what we thought of, or rather felt about, each other.

Maxine proved as forlorn as she looked; she said she had often considered suicide. A vast Mexican named Ramon, who had come north from a border town for the weekend, was also sad. "Sometimes," he said, "I think I am only the machine to make money. I am tired of people thinking I am strong just because I am big."

A swashbuckling "freelance counselor" with an auburn beard named Jay said attending this workshop was "the bravest thing I've ever done, and I was considered pretty brave in the infantry." A twenty-four-year-old named Roger, whose extreme and overall case of acne was never commented on by anyone during the entire weekend, felt an urge to challenge a young man of his own age named Dick. The two "fenced" with rolled-up magazines, looking like chorus boys from "West Side Story." When their "duel" was over they hugged. Bindrim beamed.

"Too often," he said, "you guys are afraid to let each other see your tender, feminine sides." Lloyd, also in his early twenties, said he had heard about nude therapy at a meeting of his chapter of Mensa, the organization for people with demonstrably high IQs. He also confided that he had finally found a girl he could tell he loved.

"I'm not sure it will end in marriage," he said. "We're just

"You Were Born Nude, Weren't You?"

winging it. But we've been to some pretty good places already." Lorna said she thought she was too thin. Mary didn't like being bowlegged. I said I had always felt that my body was clumsy.

Amenities done, we repaired to our absent hosts' bedrooms, labeled "MEN" and "WOMEN," to undress. We emerged shyly, hidden behind bath towels, and plunged as soon as we could into the 98.6-degree "Womb Pool." All any of us wore was our glasses. Esoteric Japanese flute music was playing on the stereo. Fences and shrubbery protected us, I hoped, from neighboring windows. In the pool we lined up in two facing rows. Each of us was to float twice, like a figure on a sarcophagus, up and down the rows of people, supported from below by the hands of all the others. This was supposed to induce a feeling of "infinite amniotic support," but I thought instead how infinitely stupid it had been of me to have my hair set, for $14 plus tip, that very afternoon. The only comforting thing was that the pool water, while hardly a liquid Eden, was at least a lot pleasanter than the chill night air.

Next we formed a circle and took turns going into the middle to be passed around from one to another in a "Trust Exercise" I had encountered before in terrestrial groups, here playfully called the "Rock and Roll." Jay, the "freelance counselor," particularly relished all this tactility. He did all he could to prolong his contacts with rocking, rolling women.

After a time, when Bindrim said we could disband and play alone, I pretended to be a polliwog or a paramecium. Then we all shivered out of the pool and into the house.

"We must remember," Bindrim said, "that we are *land*-based animals. We want to learn to be free in an air-and-ground atmosphere as well as in water." Inside, the lamps had all been turned out except for a psychedelic light show being projected onto a blank wall, and onto us too. Beatles' music replaced the Japanese flutes. The colored lights were pretty. We danced, mostly alone. Somebody mentioned erections.

91

"That subject always comes up," Bindrim said. "Some guys are afraid they will erect and some are afraid they won't. Don't worry about it." In fact, most guys didn't.

Later, when the lights went back on, we sat down with varying degrees of self-consciousness to "evaluate," as Bindrim said, "our interactions in the pool." Lloyd began the evaluations.

"*Some* people," he said, "passed other people around as if they were just sacks of potatoes."

"Anyone special in mind, Lloyd?" asked Bindrim.

"Well, yes," Lloyd said, looking my way, "I meant *you,* Jane. Did anyone else notice the way she passed people around, as if she couldn't wait until it was all over?" Several nodded.

"Well," I said in self-defense, "some of the men *were* quite heavy."

"In the *water?*" scoffed Lloyd. "Lorna's a lot shorter and lighter than you are, and I didn't see *her* minding. She was tender. She *cared.*"

"Well," I said, "maybe it's partly that I'm shy."

"THERE!" exclaimed Bindrim, wagging his finger at me from across the room, "did you see her face when she said that? She looked just like a shy little girl. I *believed* her. Jane, I'll bet you used to be a shy little girl. Were you?"

"*Was* I?" I said. "A lot of the time I still am."

Jay was chastised for having done a good bit of pinching and suggestive moaning during our "pool interactions." Maxine said, "He strikes me as just a big phony. You think you're pretty terrific, Jay, don't you?"

Jay paused for a minute. "Well yes," he said, "I do. In fact I'm superior to everyone in this room."

"Did you say you do *counseling* for a living?" someone asked.

"Oh, a little here and there, free lance," he said, as if he were talking of writing poems. He rolled his eyes at one of the girls.

At 4 a.m., having evaluated all our interactions in more detail than I might have thought possible, we crawled into our lone poolside sleeping bags. Bindrim bade us good night and ordered us not to utter a sound until he gave us a signal in the morning. The low cloud bank obscured the stars and moon. When we woke up the sky was still leaden, but Bindrim's choice of music was a majestic surprise: Berlioz' *Requiem,* a Brandenburg Concerto and some Vivaldi. ("Anywhere near the city," he had explained, "we have to have music to drown out the noise of the planes. If we had these sessions in the mountains somewhere we could just listen to the sounds of nature.")

Spared the usual nagging problem of deciding what to wear, or what to say for that matter, we ate quick stand-up breakfasts and slipped back into the Womb Pool. I still felt shy, but the music and the warm water were soothing, and not talking was ecstatic. I wished I had a body-temperature pool of my own, and thought how sweet was silence. I watched my fingernails grow more transparent the longer I was immersed, and busied myself looking at faces. Ramon resembled a giant Aztec Buddha, and like me had found a private place at the deep end of the pool. I felt strangely miffed that Ted, who had a profile like a head on a Roman coin, seemed drawn to Lorna.

He and she and most of the others paired off in the shallow end of the pool for more intense eyeballing, which led to touches and hugs. No words were needed to make it clear that many members regretted their promise not to indulge in "overt sexual contact." Many members, in fact, plainly regarded the whole experience as a frustrating tease. But Bindrim had his license as a clinical psychologist to think of.

He slipped into the pool and silently joined us, motioning us to assemble in threes and fours instead of twos. At 11 a.m.

93

he ended the silence, summoning us indoors to sit in a circle with our arms around each other. For me, that ended the spell. Silence, except for poolside music, had been golden indeed, but now Bindrim was reading Kahlil Gibran and playing a banal recorded poem called "The Junk Man." I longed to be thousands of miles away with other arms, or none at all, around me.

Lloyd, however, found "The Junk Man" touching. He burst into tears—not of sadness, he insisted, but of joy that at last he had found a girl to love. Bindrim doubted that was why he wept.

"Stay with the tears!" he ordered. "Feel them! Close your eyes! You're angry at someone, aren't you? Who is it?"

"It's—it's Miss Cavanaugh," Lloyd blurted. "My first-grade teacher. She was a dried-up, dead old bitch. She was a witch. I'll bet she died a virgin."

"What's Miss Cavanaugh doing to you now?" Bindrim asked Lloyd, whose eyes were squeezed tightly shut.

"She's kicking me out of the classroom," said Lloyd, "and I don't even know why. I haven't done anything wrong."

"Tell her!" urged Bindrim.

"You goddamn bitch!" said Lloyd. "You're punishing me for no reason! I'd like to tear your hair out by the roots!"

Bindrim leapt across he room and grabbed from a box a Sears, Roebuck catalogue, which he thrust at Lloyd.

"Here's her hair," he said. "Go ahead! Tear it out!"

Lloyd did so, ravaging the catalogue into a mass of ragged confetti. But still he looked frustrated.

"Your face looks as if you'd like to bite somebody," Bindrim said. "Would you?"

"Yes," said Lloyd. "My father." This time Bindrim gave him a raw potato. Lloyd gagged as he bit into it, but seemed to feel better. To every workshop Bindrim brings a kit of such supplies: potatoes to bite, catalogues and phone books to rip,

94

magazines to roll up and use as clubs, pieces of snappable wood to fracture, pillows to punch and nippled plastic baby bottles to bite, or sometimes to fill with warm milk.

"Different people," he said, "express anger differently. There are whippers, biters, slappers, stranglers and throwers. The idea is to regress, if possible, to the trauma that caused the distortion. That's the way to start toward a Peak Experience."

Next to regress was Maxine, who savagely hit a pillow she pretended was her unsympathetic mother.

"Fantasy," said Bindrim, "is terribly important. Our culture ignores it entirely. Another thing our culture ignores is the area of the crotch. Genitally speaking we're so *terribly* negatively conditioned. After all, where would your head end be without your butt end?"

Pondering this, we looked uncomfortably at each other. Bindrim scanned the room, trying to decide who among us should be first to demonstrate the next technique.

"Jane?" he said. "Didn't you say yesterday that *you* weren't comfortable with your body?"

"Oh," I answered with quick cowardice, "that was yesterday. I've gotten over it."

So Lorna was chosen for the exercise called "Crotch Eyeballing." First she was to stand up in front of a full-length mirror and tell us what she thought as she looked at her reflected body. It seemed she considered herself not only generally too thin but afflicted with thighs too far apart from each other ("see?" she pointed out, "you can see the air between them"), and flabby breasts.

"So what?" said Ted. "A woman your age is bound to sag a little. Besides, you have very pretty nipples."

"I *do?*" Lorna seemed pleased. But she was not for long allowed to keep standing. Bindrim arranged some sofa cushions in a row on the floor, and told her to lie down on top of them.

Please Touch

Her upper half rested on one, her lower half—with feet toward us—was elevated higher, on two cushions. No longer did she look pleased.

Bindrim bent down over her and grabbed her ankles, holding her legs way up in the air and far apart from each other, so that the effect was a huge "V." He directed somebody to prop up the full-length mirror in front of Lorna, so that she could have a complete view of her exposed nether side. He kept on holding her legs up and apart by the ankles.

"*This*," he told us all, "is where it's at. This is where we're so *damned* negatively conditioned." Thoughts ran through my head about the dignity of mankind in general and the lost dignity of Lorna in particular. She might as well have been a slain hog strung up in an *abattoir*. It occurred to me that private parts were private for a reason.

"Now, Lorna," Bindrim asked her, "please tell us who in this room you'd least like to have know about this area of yourself."

"For some reason," said Lorna in an understandably weak voice, "I'd pick Katy."

"Okay," said Bindrim, removing the full-length mirror so everybody could "eyeball" what Lorna had seen, "tell Katy. Tell her what things happen in your crotch. Say 'Katy, this is where I shit, fuck, piss and masturbate.' "

"I think," said Lorna as she eyeballed us all from that extraordinary vantage point, "that Katy already *knows* that." It was the only faintly funny thing anybody said all weekend.

Later Dick and Maxine submitted to having their crotches eyeballed. Bindrim said he was only sorry there wasn't time for all of us to have this experience, which Maxine claimed had "done more for me than three years of therapy."

Bindrim has ambitious plans. He hopes to conduct sessions in Advanced Nudity, lasting forty-eight hours instead of

"You Were Born Nude, Weren't You?"

twenty-four. "Maybe we'll avoid the clothed part in the beginning," he speculates. "Maybe that's just a waste of time. I'd like to try body painting. I'd like to see what I could do with videotape. I might like to try a marathon in the racial area, too. Nudity shouldn't be forced on anybody, of course, but it would be good for just about anyone."

He is careful to avoid breaking any ordinances, and although many human potential movement people cringe at the sound of his name, his reputation is growing nationally. His biggest following, not surprisingly, is in California, where some enthusiasts have tried to get him to lead marathons for teenagers—clothed, since naked ones for minors would not be legal. "I think it's a shame," one man wrote in a mimeographed letter to everyone on Bindrim's mailing list, "that my daughters have to wait until they're twenty-one to be straightened out by Paul Bindrim."

It was by accident that Bindrim took up his present line of work. Several years ago he and a woman friend, tired of their usual weekend routines, decided for a lark to visit a nudist colony near San Bernardino.

"I thought it might be pretty weird," he said, "but the people there turned out to be much easier to get acquainted with than those at the yacht club where I kept my boat. We went several times, and loved it. But after a while it got to be too much of a hassle to drive forty miles just to take my pants off."

Around that time Bindrim was earning a living leading clothed weekend therapy marathons. Toward the end of one of these everyone spontaneously stripped and jumped into a swimming pool. A fat woman in that group found to her delight that people were not horrified to see her naked.

"Some women who are overweight and ugly on land don't seem to be so in the water," said Bindrim. "Excess flab isn't burdensome in water. It's not an entrapment the way it is on land. You might find such a woman very attractive and inter-

97

esting in the water"—which would be fine, presumably, if you were a merman—"but even though she'd have to get out, eventually, the experience could change her self-image as nothing else could."

In that same historic group was a forty-year-old man who had never had a date with a woman in all his life. "He splashed around bareass and had a great time," said Bindrim, "and yelled, 'Look! It's me!' I didn't drive *that* man out of his mind; I restored him to it." And so began the present regime of nude weekend marathons followed by evening reunion groups, some clad and some not, at Bindrim's house in the Hollywood Hills.

We had sandwiches for our "serious" Sunday lunch. By turns, in an hour-long session, we summarized into a tape-recorder microphone our views of the marathon. I said I had liked the silence part a lot. Several men said they wished sex had not been proscribed. Bindrim said he could sympathize, but laws were laws. Then we were free to put our clothes on and take to the freeways. Some seemed reluctant to leave, but not me. Maybe on some sunny, balmy day, with people not so humorless, whom I loved and would like to look at, who had no programs or games or gimmicks up their metaphorical sleeves, I might find being undressed a Peak Experience, but . . .

"Hey!" I said to Bindrim. "What about our Peak Stimuli? Nobody had a Peak Experience! How come? What was the point of our bringing all this stuff?"

"Well," said Bindrim, "we don't always get around to that. If you'd like to learn to use your Stimuli by yourself, without the group, I have a paper here that will tell you how. You can buy a copy for $1.25."

I declined, dressed, found my rent-a-car and drove away,

"You Were Born Nude, Weren't You?"

reflecting with mounting melancholy that for me it had been not a Peak but a Pique—or maybe a Valley—Experience. My body had been naked, but never for a minute the rest of me.

"I Hope You Leave Your Brain to Harvard"

❡ The black man was really the color of brown sugar, like his turtleneck sweatshirt, and he was answering a question of mine.

"What can you do to have soul, to get yourself together? Well, you can snap your fingers a lot and buy some Aretha records instead of all that Bach and Beethoven. You can be more human. You can let the walls down. You can *listen* to people. Get to know more black people. Whatever made you come here, anyway?"

"I want to know how black people feel."

"Why do you want to know that?"

"Because I'm alive now."

"Do you *feel* alive, in that position?" It was five o'clock in the morning, as it so often seemed to be in the months I was joining encounter groups, and in fact I did not feel nearly as alive as I like to. Like some larva in mid-metamorphosis I was half in and half out of the sleeping bag I had borrowed for this interracial weekend marathon at a church in San Francisco. I stretched some and sat up more. We were split into two groups. There were ten people in the next room next door, and nine others in the room with me. I was afraid the other nine were misunderstanding me.

"But I really do know quite a few black people," I told them. "It's just that I can't honestly call any of them my good friends. Those I do know I haven't seen in a while, and they probably would think it was phony and patronizing for me to suddenly call them up, so soon after Martin Luther King, and ask them over for dinner. They might think I was some obnoxious do-gooder, trying too late to make amends. Oh, there are a couple of people in my office who probably wouldn't think that, and there's my cleaning woman . . ."

"*Cleaning* woman! *Cleaning* woman?" The shocked disbelief of the rest of my group, black and white both, was just about unanimous. Those who had been nearly dozing perked up.

"You don't mean to say *you* have a black cleaning woman?" a white woman asked. "Didn't you hear Larry say how it felt for him to have his mother work as a domestic for white people?"

"Yes, sure I heard him," I said, "and I could sympathize, but Mary isn't my maid in that sense. She isn't some loyal, hand-wringing family retainer who rolls her eyes and pulls in my waist cincher. She's a businesslike employee who comes twice a month and stays in my apartment for six hours at the most. I pay her $15 a time."

"Big deal," somebody said. "You call that a salary? I'll bet she calls you 'Miss Jane,' too."

"As a matter of fact I guess she does," I said, "but not be-

101

cause I ever told her to. It happens that she works for some other friends of mine, too, and she's always called them Miss Roma and Miss Virginia and Mr. Russell and so on. None of us ever asked her to, though."

"Maybe so, but she still cleans up your mess, right?"

"Right," I said. "She does. She does it better than I do, and I don't have time to do it, and she does, and she needs the money, and I pay her, and it seems to work out all right."

"Black women clean better than white women, right?" The white man who asked me this was named Emmett. He had professed earlier to "envy the blacks their pipeline from gut to mouth. I envy them their roundness, their fullness, their vibrance. I wish I could dance the way you do," he said to the blacks present. "I'd like to dance that way and *be* that way."

"Shit, man," said Larry.

"It's true, though," said Mike, who was the leader of this encounter. "I don't mind admitting it. We *do* dance better. We *do* have rhythm." Now Mike picked up Emmett's question: "Black women clean better than white women, right?"

"Look," I said with exasperation, *"any* woman cleans better than I do. I'm really not very good at it. I'm terrible at it. What else, by the way, is Mary supposed to do for a living? She isn't trained to be a microbiologist or a CPA, and I don't think she'd care to learn—she's fifty years old or so."

"Why don't you just give her the money," somebody suggested, "and hire a white cleaning woman?"

"For one thing," I answered, "I don't *have* all that much money. For another thing, I don't happen to know of any white cleaning women. God knows I have nothing against the idea, but it seems all my friends either have none at all or else black ones."

"Great, groovy, terrific, that makes it all all right, doesn't it, knowing you're not alone in your guilt? Don't you see that you're a white racist?"

"Me?"

"I Hope You Leave Your Brain to Harvard"

"Yeah, you, who'd you *think* was a white racist?"

"Lester Maddox?"

"Oh, come *on,* baby, where you been?"

"Richard Nixon?"

"That's a little more like it," said Larry, a gigantic man with skin the color of a piano, who had said how much, in childhood, he always hated having white men pat his "kinky woolly nigger head" for good luck. What white racism meant to him, he said, was a five-inch scar on his head, and tales of his grandfather's lynching in South Carolina, and the fact that he could not walk calmly along a beach without being questioned by the police. And there was his mother's job as a white family's maid.

"I don't hate *you,*" he told me, "but I do hate the idea that you don't see what's wrong with hiring a black."

"What would Mary think of this conversation?" somebody asked.

"She'd probably wonder what all the fuss was about," I said.

"Yeah, that's the sad part, she probably would."

"But she's not some dumb, stupid, conniving, grinning Butterfly McQueen," I protested, "she's more sort of—"

"Cut out that intellectual crap," a deep voice commanded, "and let's get to where it's at. Butterfield *who?*"

"Butterfly McQueen, who played Prissy in 'Gone with the Wind'—the little housemaid who comes mincing up to say 'Miss Scarlett, I don't know nothin' 'bout birthin' babies.' "

"Oh, baby, don't you see that that's the most racist movie ever made?"

"Don't *you* see?"

This argument transpired under the auspices of Esalen's Bay Area office. It could as easily have erupted in Cleveland or St. Louis or Atlanta or any number of other places where concerned social agencies have taken to holding interracial encounter groups. The usual pattern of these encounters is for

103

earnest, well-meaning and vulnerable white liberals like me to pay $50 or $70 to spend a weekend trading ideas and feelings with black people, some of whom are reluctant to come unless they're paid.

"I don't *need* a seminar in black-white problems," as one said during a New York encounter. "I live with being black all the time. My whole life is a continuous seminar in this problem. Why should I want to come down here and eat with you in your ridiculous restaurants? Why should I take a black trip on a white landscape?"

Or, as a black lecturer named Eric Lincoln told a largely white audience in Boston, "Ninety percent of our psychic energy is dissipated in being black. There isn't much agreement among us on 'we,' but there's total agreement on 'they.' We walk very close to the edge of the abyss. We play a balancing game, and we're victims of excruciating anxiety. Many blacks see training as irrelevant and dysfunctional. The key word isn't love, it's *change*. We have to change systems, not persons."

The man who didn't want a black trip on a white landscape was addressing a roomful of white housing-project managers. They had gathered to debate the advisability of renaming a project for Malcolm X instead of Stephen Collins Foster. In another New York confrontation I saw a group of foremen and other representatives of "lower management" wear black masks to see how their employees felt. Black men present wore white masks, for the reverse reason.

Another group I was in had only one black member, a witty and attractive woman who looked thirty-five but claimed to be "a lot older." She had a master's degree and had felt inclined at times to go on and get a doctorate, "but that would just remove me *too* far from my community," she said. "My having an M.A. makes it hard enough for them to understand me. Especially men. Sure I wish there were a man in my life, but it's tough nowadays to get along with black men.

"I Hope You Leave Your Brain to Harvard"

Black women have been women a long time, but black men have just *become* men in the last few years."

A group at Bethel, in an NTL program for the wives of intern trainers, had two black members. They made no reference to color until the final meeting. But just as everyone was about to say goodbye, with the usual round of hugs, one of the black women sprang at the other for attempting to "pass," and for "playing up to the white ladies." The accused one was reduced to startled, guilty tears. Not even the trainer knew what to do. That particular group ended, as groups will sometimes, on an unresolved note.

A remarkable interracial encounter took place in January 1969 in the Boston studio of radio station WBZ. Eight people spent twenty-two hours together, nonstop, in what became a celebrated program called "T-Group 15," so named because it was edited down to fifteen consecutive, commercial-free hours.

WBZ persuaded four white members of the city's School Committee, an organization not legendary for its attention to black neighborhoods, to meet with four black parents. The black parents represented an *ad hoc* committee to boycott the system and take over control of their children's schools. The issue was decentralization; the mood was acrimony. Even in Boston, where the ingredients in the ethnic melting pot never really have melted, a more polarized gathering could hardly have been arranged.

I heard a tape of that show. Its star—at first its villain—was Louise Day Hicks, chronic member and sometime chairman of the School Committee. I did a story on Mrs. Hicks when she ran for mayor of Boston in 1967. A large white woman who oftens wears kelly green, she lives in a large green house in a neighborhood scarcely less Irish than Dublin. She has long championed such conservative sentiments as "Boston

105

for Bostonians!" and "Neighborhood Schools for Neighborhood Children!,," which her plentiful adversaries take to mean white schools for white children and never mind the others. In Roxbury and in Boston's black neighborhoods, her name symbolizes racism.

"I hope you leave your brain to Harvard," said one of the black men to Mrs. Hicks in the course of the T-group broadcast, "so we can really get a look into that brain, because there's some curious things going on in your head."

It turned out in the course of those twenty-two hours that nobody had much idea what was going on in anyone else's head. At first the eight people sat far apart from each other. Only very gradually could their trainers, Irwin Rubin, an MIT professor, and Jack Jones, a graduate student at Boston University, persuade them to inch closer together. A third human relations expert, MIT professor Malcolm Knowles, was narrator. He introduced the program as "the most profound experiment ever attempted in broadcasting." He said that in its course the T-group members would "tear at the walls of race, education and personal communications, and in so doing lay bare many of the barriers built into each of us."

Rubin started the wall-tearing by playing some records, asking the group to listen carefully to the lyrics. One was the droning, haunting song of the Beatles, accompanied with Indian instruments, that laments the idea of lost love and the tragedy of people who hide themselves behind a "wall of illusion." The T-group members to whom this music seemed new paid dutiful attention. They did not find it easy to oblige, however, when they were asked by Rubin to tell what the song meant in their own words.

"That the blacks and whites are going to marry and conquer the world?"

"That there were two lovers who were in love?"

"No," said Rubin patiently, "but rather what's going to

106

happen to love that's grown cold. That maybe someday we'll realize that somebody's going to make us change, and that the power to change is within each one of us."

"But I question whether there ever really *was* any love between us," said one of the black women. "I agree that nobody's going to change us but ourselves, but I'm wondering whether we ever really *did* love each other. In fact, I have serious doubts about it."

"My concern," said Rubin after a time, "is that we're not going to solve any problems out there until we deal with the barriers that are in here."

And so, in a space seventeen by seventeen feet, over a period of nearly a full day, the barriers were assaulted. It turned out that the blacks and whites eventually could see each other as individuals, unconnected with their official roles. It turned out that Mrs. Hicks was sick and tired of being considered a scapegoat. It turned out that several of the whites really wanted to know (even as late as January 1969) the semantic difference between "Negro" and "black." They were as attentive as children at story hour when a black woman told them how "the generations born in slavery had no history. There was no one to say 'Boy, I knew your grandpa.' As far as that boy was concerned, he *had* no grandpa. He had nothing except what his mother gave him, which was an expurgated version of Christianity, taking out most of the love and militancy and leaving in just the humility."

It even dawned on the participants that regardless of their official roles, they all, more importantly, were parents concerned with the welfare of their children. In time they came to see that their opposite numbers "didn't come from Mars, aren't anarchists who'll go back planting bombs." As one among them said, "we *do* have these ridiculous illusions and myths about each other"—illusions which in a shorter time than twenty-two hours might never have been dislodged.

But the great rapprochement occurred between Mrs. Hicks and Mrs. Elizabeth Bristol, an imposing black woman. Rubin asked the group members if they would care to "give each other something." Mrs. Hicks volunteered, "I'll give to Elizabeth. I admire her honesty, her forthrightness, her down-to-earthness, and I would hope to give her some compassion and understanding of the problem."

Then Mrs. Bristol told at length how her own feelings had altered in those hours. "I still say she has a long way to go," she said of Mrs. Hicks, "but . . . I think she *has* changed her opinion of black people . . . and I'll tell you this, I'm glad now that I can talk with some degree of knowledge about Louise Day Hicks. Even if I don't agree with your opinions on certain issues, I can see you as an individual and not as someone to fight—as someone I can pick up the phone and call, and say 'Mrs. Hicks, this is Mrs. Bristol, can I have your ear?' "

When the seventeen by seventeen room was emptied, after the twenty-two hours, Louise Day Hicks offered to give anybody who might need one a ride home in her car. Before she left she asked Elizabeth Bristol: "Will you call me?"

"I sure will," said Mrs. Bristol.

Help See
Own Way
Behave

¶ Extremes entice me, perhaps because I represent so many middles. It was in the middle of the nineteen-thirties, in the middle of the sign of Taurus and in the middle of the Middle West that my middle-class parents named me Jane. I have never been sorry they did, yet it was with a sense of oddly mounting excitement one wet November noontime that I stood reading a sign on the door of a Roman Catholic retreat in northern Massachusetts. Scrawled with a Magic Marker and already runny from the rain, the sign read "ABANDON BACK-HOME NAMES, ALL YE WHO ENTER HERE."

Inside that house I need not—in fact *could* not—be Jane, the vagabond journalist from New York via Illinois and Michigan. My identity, my marital status, my "interesting" "career" with its all-expense trips to such places as Gangtok, Tangier and Garden City, Kansas, would all be irrelevant. The thirty-nine people I would meet in that house, most of them total strangers, would react not to my labels and biography and credentials but just to me, and I in the same spirit to them. The NTL had organized this $350 "Advanced Personal Growth Laboratory," for people who had missed, or who wanted more of, the two-week version held annually at Bethel, Maine. My own interest had first been kindled at Bethel a few months earlier. I visited there the last four days of the 1968 summer session, hoping thereby to sample the flavor of the place and of the whole organization. Four days wasn't enough time, though. When I dropped in on the Advanced Personal Growth Lab (which everybody I met told me I simply must do), I was greeted warily. The lab members, who had spent nearly a fortnight developing their own special jargon, names, and camaraderie, weren't happy to have a spectator. Only after a good deal of talk and voting and ceremony did they let me in.

"You can't possibly *begin* to understand what this is all about," several of them told me, "coming in this way at the last minute. Why weren't you here at the beginning?"

Because I had never heard of it before, that was why, but I wished I had. Later, traveling around the country, I gathered that to enthusiasts of sensitivity training that lab means what the Davis Cup means to tennis fans, or the *Ring* to lovers of Wagner. During the phone conversation that convinced me to sign up for the Massachusetts version, I scribbled a note quoting my informant. The note said: "DAMN GOOD EXAMPLE, COMPLETE RESURRECTION, HELP SEE OWN WAY BEHAVE, NOV. 9–17, HAMILTON, MASS."

Persuaded, and eager to plunge into the mystique of the lab, I flew east from California. A lawyer friend named Bob fetched me at the Boston airport. He was as delighted as I with the prospect of resurrection, but the task of rechristening perplexed us both. We went back to his car and sat there, pondering possible new names, for a full twenty minutes. We ruled out the classically simple names we both already had, and vowed to be imaginative.

Something from nature, perhaps? Maple? No, too much like Mabel. From Greek mythology? I felt shamefully ignorant about that. Scarlett? That might be pleasantly ambiguous, suggesting both the color and Scarlett O'Hara, who had such enviable attributes as the smallest waist in six counties and a flirtatious air. But, as Bob reminded me, she was also bitchy and overpowering: did I want to come across that way?

Of course I didn't. Good old Bob, he was so sensible. In fact, he said, that was the trouble: everyone thought of him as Good Old Reliable Bob—the one who always meets planes, draws up wills, fills in at parties, visits hospitals. Nobody thought of him as dashing, which was why he rejected Acorn as a new name. Acorns are promising, but they turn into good old reliable oaks. That gave me an idea: my new name must hint at something that had roots, which were what I most lacked and most longed for.

"Well," said Bob, "how about a willow tree?" Willows, he advised me, have roots so formidable they're always getting entangled in sewer pipes; besides which the trees are graceful and flexible, budding early in the spring and turning a pretty color in the fall. Moreover, it occurred to me that I had grown up in a house on Willow Road. That settled it: Willow I would be. Bob decided on Cumulus, after the cloud formation he thought could produce not only gentle, nourishing rains but also violent thunderstorms and blizzards.

Inside we made name tags, and began a little awkwardly to encounter the other thirty-eight people who for those eight days would be our world. They looked like (and later turned out to be) housewives, psychologists, professors, psychiatrists, dancers and businessmen. They spoke in many accents, and lit their cigarettes with matches from laundries and restaurants as

111

far away as Edmonton, Alberta. But we talked of why we had chosen our new names, not of professions and origins. Ginger had taken her name, she said, because she hoped to be less lethargic than usual. Stanley's honored a dead brother. Chico said his real name had a burdensome "IV" after it.

We were told we could change our names as often as we liked. Cumulus eventually had a metamorphosis and became Panther, and I soon abandoned Willow to put on a new name tag reading "Arizona."

"No," I kept assuring people, "*not* because it means 'Arid Zone,' and not because of the battleship—who'd want connotations like those?" The real reason was that Willow felt too pretentious and fragile. Arizona, a whole state where a lot went on, seemed safer. Unlikely things bloomed there, conifers and cottonwoods along with cactuses. Besides, Arizona to me meant convalescence, comfort, a big friendly kitchen and a giant double-hearthed fireplace.

Our Massachusetts quarters, converted from the estate of a rich family, were much more spartan. The fireplace no longer worked. Men were housed on the third floor, women on the second, everybody in one of several curtained cubicles in a room. My room, dominated by a graphic bleeding-heart crucifix, had five cubicles. Two of the others were taken, one by a short middle-aged widow with a kind face named Lucy, and the other by an olive-skinned girl with an enigmatic European accent named Tanya. I could easily imagine Lucy on real-life home ground: she would live nearby, and have a bird-feeding station in the yard. Not until I chanced to see Tanya's toothpaste, however, could I guess that she was Greek. It was labeled ΚΟΛΓΣΙΤ.

Our four trainers had new names, too. The chief among them was a wiry small man who looked to be in his forties and who always made me think of a Scottish bagpiper. He told us to call him Conchis, after the hero of Fowles' novel *The Magus*. In real life he was John Weir, just resigned from

112

the faculty of the University of Southern California in order to become a full-time itinerant group leader. His wife Joyce, here called Noel, would lead sessions in Body Movement. Ted Kroeber, who teaches psychology at San Francisco State College, would also assist Weir, and so would my old friend Michael Kahn, in this incarnation called Les Glass after J. D. Salinger's paterfamilias.

Weir decreed a silent lunch, and then a silent free period. Not really at ease, I went outside and did something that always gives me a comfortable feeling of abandon: I rolled down a hill. It was a wet hill, but it still felt good. In the retreat living room, where we next assembled, all the furniture had been removed except the phonograph. The Weirs don't think much of tables and chairs, but their labs rely greatly on music.

"There's a place somewhere in this room where you'll feel comfortable," Noel told us all as she put a record on. "Find that place." Gauchely, tentatively we moved about the room. I found my place near the hearth.

"Gradually," Noel told us, "ooze to the floor." We oozed. "You have no bones," she said. "You can't keep your knees up. You're just a blob. Your eyes are closed. If you touch other blobs, it doesn't matter. Now, let your ooze coagulate into a ball, so that your head touches your knees and your organism is a tight, round unit." Obediently we coagulated.

"Now, very gradually, stretch out and discover that you have a backbone! You can move! You can crawl!" With eyes still shut we did crawl, like the most primitive of vertebrates. "It's all right," she said, "if you bump into others." Bump we did. As the music played on we advanced to more sophisticated phyla. In time we were given permission to walk around on all fours, and to stand up on our hind legs.

"Now open your eyes," Noel said, "and feel how it is to see without focusing." We felt how it was. I reached to touch a metal sconce on the wall as if I had never beheld such a thing, or anything else, in all my life.

113

"Now notice," Noel said, "that there are other creatures around you." Indeed there were, and they began to cluster in friendly fours, fives and eights. My cluster was a small one, patently composed of leftovers. I ended up with one arm entwined in that of a very shy, very blond man in a polo shirt named Orpheus. His other arm was linked with that of a short fortyish brunette, with tears in her eyes, named Lili Marlene.

Evolving from a blob of ooze to an anthropoid did not affect me as it did most. I felt numb and anti-social, and somewhat afraid. The others in the lab, several of whom seemed already to know each other, gathered gaily before dinner on the second floor landing, stashing their liquor bottles by the naked toes of a statue of the Virgin Mary. Ordinarily that juxtaposition would amuse me, but now I felt out of phase and sorry for myself. I retreated to my cubicle and read a book. "Help See Own Way Behave" was a valid promise: my whole life I have escaped unpleasantness by reading.

I still felt clenched and wary after dinner, when we were shepherded to the basement. There we danced with our hands, sat on the floor for back-to-back conversations, and chose partners of our own sex for an exercise in Trust. We took turns lying on the floor and having our partners stretch our heads, legs and arms, moving each appendage about in the widest arc possible, to determine how willing we were to relax. I already liked Lucy, my roommate and partner, but when she cradled my head in her hands from behind, to lift it off the floor, I untrustingly did all the work. I expended much unnecessary energy, the way I do when I ride a horse.

Later, at our first "Community Meeting," came what Esalen experience should have taught me would be the inevitable controversy: should or shouldn't we subdivide into small groups? Naturally, after a lot of argument, we did. Our microcosm was split into three "family groups," each to divide its days into three periods: Improvisations, Graphics and Noel's sessions in Body Movement. Evenings the whole community would gather to sit on the living room floor and talk of whatever issues had not been covered in the "families." I was assigned to Conchis' group. So were my shy blond friend Orpheus, the melancholy Lili Marlene, a belligerent Green Hornet, a lanky suntanned blonde named Francie, a bratty young girl called Holly, Camilla, Yvonne, Isaiah, Captain Pinkerton and a Negro named Henry.

Our day began with Improvisations, the first session of which resembled the end of Antonioni's movie "Blow-Up." We had an imaginary tug-of-war with an imaginary rope, and then played imaginary volleyball. When the games were over we slumped into heaps on the floor, as exhausted as if we had used a real rope, ball and net. Childishness, we were discovering, was fun, but not merely fun. Regression would be the motif of the whole eight days. Maybe if we had had lollipops, or the nerve to suck our thumbs, we wouldn't have smoked as much as we did.

Another Improvisations period we went up in threes to the front of the room to occupy a trio of chairs. The person at either end tried to talk divertingly enough to get the full attention of the one in the middle. The middle man's job was to sustain both conversations. It vexed me, when I was in the middle, that Orpheus, who sat on my left side, wouldn't challenge me with questions. When I told him this later he said that taking initiative was the big problem of his whole life.

"I can keep something going if somebody else starts it," he said, "but I can't be the one to initiate." Another day he told us that he had been raised to prize modesty and decorum above all other virtues. All through childhood his mother had warned him never to raise his voice. She had succeeded so well that he now could scarcely speak audibly. That afternoon he and I went for a walk on the grounds of the former estate. We found an abandoned indoor handball court, which turned out to serve quite nicely as an echo chamber. We went inside and screamed as loud as we could. Orpheus' pale skin grew

115

scarlet as he roared and yelled. Making noise has never been my problem, but the yelling made me feel better, too. I think, in fact, that there ought to be soundproof chambers the size of phone booths in airports and bus stations, where frustrated bypassers could pay a quarter to go in and scream out their anxieties.

Another morning we were sent to the front of the room in pairs, and told to converse in gibberish. One of us was supposed to be trying to sell something—it didn't matter what—to the other. Francie, my partner, was trying to sell me a handbag, but I mistook it for a toaster, and said in my flawless gibberish that I already had two, so no sale. I thought this was good fun, but when our little skit was over Francie was furious. My gibberish sounded to her like German which she, being Jewish, took to mean that "Arizona must be anti-Semitic."

The accusation staggered me. I had meant my gibberish to resemble some impossble hybrid Afro-Slavic tongue, but on reflection I could understand Francie's train of thought. Jewishness had been the chief topic of the previous night's community meeting. Those of us who weren't Jewish—the majority, it surprisingly turned out—felt that those who were constituted an obvious in-group. Paranoia was rampant on both sides. The Jews assumed that we Goyim were against them, and vice versa. The implications were sobering. It was as if we were recapitulating the whole history of human relations since the Diaspora. There was much talk of the Torah, references to the Wandering Jew myth and bad jokes about Kaddish cheese.

In vain I longed for the *chutzpah* to wail that you didn't have to be Jewish to feel lost, and to proclaim myself as the original Wandering Shikse, not to say Dude, Honkie, WASP, Yankee, Gringo and Roundeyes. I did ask if anybody would care to join me in singing the Doxology, but the joke, such as it was, fell flat.

Help See Own Way Behave

Lucy, the widow, was the first to admit in a Community Meeting that she felt like a loner. Most of us rushed to agree that we did, too. A bearded European named Big Karl (as opposed to a merely mustached Little Karl) professed his loneliness with such vehemence that one would have thought he had a patent on it. I told him he seemed pompous and arrogant.

"Diagnoses I don't need," he replied. He charged that an in-group of Jews, trainers and Bostonians made those of us who fell into none of these categories, him in particular, feel left out.

"Who here feels part of Big Karl's in-group?" asked Conchis. Nearly everyone in the room got up to surround Big Karl. I didn't. I felt as self-conscious as I had in seventh grade, when I stood alone on one corner of an intersection waiting for the school bus because I lacked the nerve to cross the street and join the other kids. As such self-pitying memories rushed to mind I felt like crying. Later, when everyone else was dancing, I did cry, on—of all places—the shoulder of Big Karl.

Theories about conspiracies and in-groups continued to thrive. The next morning a middle-aged businessman in the lab, who apparently had spotted me as a fellow square and social isolate, asked over breakfast if I thought our leaders had doctorates.

"I'd feel a *little* better if I thought they had," he confided. He believed the group was up to no good at all, and wondered if I'd care to talk about it over dinner with him on Wednesday night. I turned him down, but with the approach of Wednesday —the only free, unstructured evening in the whole eight days —I felt more and more nervous. Aloofness still plagued me. I hadn't made any friends, really, and friends were what I needed Wednesday night. That night assumed for me the significance of New Year's Eve and the Junior Prom rolled into one ominous metaphor: freedom.

For me the most heavenly thing about the lab was knowing

that my day was all scheduled, that I need not choose between TWA and American, Los Angeles and Chicago. I was Arizona, not Jane, and all I had to decide was how to spend Wednesday evening. I didn't want to stay, as some were planning to do, in the retreat house—that would have been like not going home for Christmas from college. I wasn't invited to join certain expeditions being planned to restaurants in Ipswich and Boston. I didn't want to go off with the businessman. Luckily for me, Lili Marlene and Henry felt the same way. With excited pride we formed a scheme to leave our little society, for as long as it would take us to eat a steak dinner in the real world. The restaurant we would go to was just a few miles away, but the psychological distance was immense.

Our sortie was even more fraught with melodrama than I expected it to be. No nuance of the journey was too trivial, in plan or execution, for us to pounce on and magnify. The decision about who should drive Henry's car, for example, was monumental. Since the car was small, Henry volunteered to sit in the tiny back seat himself, "so you ladies can be more comfortable." This meant, however that one of us ladies would have to do the driving.

Lili Marlene said she was damned if she would, though she had a license and knew how, because driving a man around happened to be a special aversion of hers. It happens to be a special aversion of mine, too, but since Henry thought he was doing us a favor not to drive, I sighed like a martyr and took the wheel for a couple of miles. But then, as grandiosely as if I were being jailed for a principle, I announced that I wanted to trade places with Henry.

Emboldened by this display of moral courage, I later demanded that the waitress replace an ice-cold bottle of Beaujolais with another at room temperature. Henry and Lili Marlene discussed at some length my amazing reserves of bravado. Every time we passed the salt back and forth we would analyze what the gesture really meant. Not until dessert did we get to abstractions.

"You know," Henry said, "I love every single person in the lab—the same amount."

"That's impossible," Lili Marlene and I protested. "Some people there are much more lovable than others. You're not a dumb guy; you ought to be able to tell that."

But the next morning, in Graphics, we understood. Each of us was issued a twenty-inch by twelve-inch strip of shelf paper and told to sit there with closed eyes for a full ninety minutes, "experiencing" the paper.

"When you think you've learned all there is to learn," said Conchis, "stay with it." Having scarcely more attention span than a hummingbird, I was pleased to discover the properties of my paper: a rough side and a smooth, edges to cut with, ways it could be used to stroke, fondle, caress and hit. It became a club, a Hallowe'en mask, a *Playbill,* a piece of ancient papyrus, a bounceable ball, a mantilla, a bouquet of flowers, a glove. I punched holes in it. I pretended it was lace. Other people were making similar discoveries about their papers. Most were laughing.

Henry, however, was audibly so upset we all opened our eyes. "All that punching and throwing and ripping and poking," he said, "reminded me of when I was a little boy, and we had to live on a certain street in a certain house because we were niggers. The other boys would always gang up on me and beat me up and chase me. The only good thing was they chased me so much I got to run well enough to win a letter on the track team.

"But later it was the same thing all over. I was the first black patrolman the state-highway police ever hired, and most of them in the police barracks wouldn't eat with me. They'd point at me and say things to each other like 'Get a load of *him*—it looks like they'll let *anything* in nowadays.' It's just

119

lately that I've gotten over that sort of resentment. Now do you see what I mean when I say I love everybody here? I don't hate mankind; I hate what men *do* to each other. I hate violence. I want to protect my piece of paper, not rip it up."

My own favorite Graphics period, in which I crept boldly from the periphery of things to the melodramatic center, came to be known in the folklore of the group as The Great Finger-Paint Fight, featuring Holly vs. Arizona.

Holly seemed to me to be all the things I conspicuously wasn't: pert, popular, vivacious enough to be a cheerleader. To the extent that she had made any impression on me at all, which wasn't much, she annoyed me. She and I were at opposite ends of a long table covered with an unbroken stretch of paper on which we were all to do a mass mural in finger paint. My section of the mural was dazzling. It had an amber tree against a blue-green background, resplendent with fruits and flowers and the all-important roots. It was tastefully connected with the paintings of my neighbors on either side, and so touchingly symbolic that I paused to stand back and admire it. As I did so a handful of mud-colored glop came careening down the length of the room to land right in the middle of my beautiful tree. Holly had hurled it. I was so heartbroken I nearly wept. It was as if a hurricane had uprooted my tree. But not until the others in the group said: "What are you going to do, *let* her ruin it?" did it cross my mind to retaliate.

I threw a handful of my paint at Holly's picture, then she more at mine, and she some at me, and I at her. Pretty soon the two of us had squared off facing each other in an unrestrained free-for-all. Everybody else stood back as we plastered the walls and windows of the room, not to say each other, with multicolored finger paint. Somebody removed my bespattered glasses. The cheering spectators chose sides.

120

"I'll lay you two-to-one odds on Arizona," somebody said.

"You have everything I want," Holly yelled. *"I'd* like to have a pretty tree *too,* you know."

"You always ruin everything of mine!" I retorted. "Besides, you never have to help with the dishes!" Plainly we were regressing *à deux* and becoming each other's sister. Soon all the other women in the group joined in too, gleefully smearing us and each other with paint. In time the men got into the act. Everybody's faces and clothes turned hopelessly technicolor. The paint grew cold and flaky as it dried on our skin and even inside our clothes, but nobody cared.

"Hey, Arizona," Francie said, apparently convinced at last that I wasn't anti-Semitic, "let's have a tribal-cleaning ritual. I've got a car; let's you and me take everybody's dirty clothes to the laundromat after lunch. I've never even *been* to a laundromat."

That sounded fine. Our triumphantly dirty group was the envy of the others as we waited in line for lunch. In the line I stood next to a woman named Gretchen from another group, whom I had liked in our only previous talk. She had said "I'm not from Boston—I'm from another large, in fact, *very* large, Eastern Seaboard metropolis." I had been missing such signs of wit. Wit is tolerated in encounter groups, but not encouraged. It is regarded as an irrelevant defense, and an evasion of what in some circles is known as the nitty-gritty. Maybe so, but it is a defense I cling to myself and cherish in others.

I was therefore amazed when sympathetic Gretchen made an ugly face at me when I asked if she'd had a nice morning.

"May I ask," I said to her rather icily when lunch was done, "why you stuck your tongue out at me?"

"Not at *you,*" she replied. "Don't be silly. I was just so upset about the morning *I'd* had. They took me on a fantasy trip all the way back to when I was three years old, and it was really harrowing."

Oh God, I thought, how unperceptive of me. How many

other potential friends had I lost through such unreal, imagined slights? How inaccurate was my radar? The fun of the paint fight faded entirely as I brooded about such matters. As Francie and I drove off with a huge bag of dirty clothes I cried, brightening only long enough to explain the arcane symbolic mysteries of the Maytag Wash Cycle. When we returned for our Body Movement class I cried again, this time on the shoulder of Orpheus.

"I don't even know what I'm crying about," I sobbed to him. "I guess it's just because I don't know what I'm doing or where I'm going in this world."

"That seems a plenty good reason," he said, and his consoling tone made me weep all the more. I was still in tears when Noel directed us to lie down on the floor and listen to the music. She assigned us to imagine that each of us was a drop of water—any water anywhere—and to do whatever that drop of water would do. First I envisioned my own tears, then water leaping in a mountain brook. Then I saw a coral reef like one I had once snorkeled over in Puerto Rico, in which there swam a school of nearly transparent tropical fish.

Then I became a fish myself, only not tropical but a haddock like one I had caught the previous summer in Maine. I was big, sleek and silver, flashing with sturdy grace around the floor of the ocean. The music continued. Others in the group had risen to dance out their water fantasies, but I was still prone, vaguely mimicking the motions of swimming.

As that same fish, I spied a worm dangling from the end of a hook. I bit it and was caught. The funny part was I didn't care. I didn't mind even being hauled up out of the ocean, having the hook ripped from my mouth and being tossed into a wooden box on the bottom of the boat with other fish, there to thrash and finally expire. Nor did I later object when I was beheaded, degutted and served, with boiled potatoes and tiny fresh new peas. No longer sobbing, I slowly rose to a standing position.

Help See Own Way Behave

Noel, who had changed the record, now was saying: "Each of us has a personal myth inside him he wants to act out. Act out yours." I still didn't feel exactly sprightly, but at least I was on my feet. I trudged around examining the room's peripheries, methodically inspecting all four corners, stopping in none, always going on. (As I say, I've always felt attracted to extremes.) When I got to the corner with the phonograph where Noel was, I ignored her outstretched hand. I didn't even look at her, or for that matter, at anyone. I just went on, hardly noticing that others were acting out their myths, too.

Slowly my trudge became a sort of dance, in which I circled the other dancers warily, still not stopping, thinking "this one's interesting, yes, but what about *him,* over there? And who are *they?* Might I like them better? What's going on in the other room?" That's my myth, all right, I thought (and still do think): I'm far too seldom content with where I am, and often ruinously curious about where I'm not.

But finally I tired of motion. I stopped arbitrarily, figuring (with what for me was a revelation) that maybe if I just stayed in one place somebody would find me. Somebody did: Lili Marlene. I don't know how I fit into her myth, but she hovered and danced around me like a loving, protective mother. I thought, disloyally, that it might have been nice to have been found by a man. But having emerged so recently from fishhood—true to my scribbled promise "COMPLETE RESURRECTION"—I was scarcely what you could call nubile.

That phonograph was on and busy all the time, even before breakfast. People who had previously shied away from demure foxtrots were now devising abandoned and dramatic new steps to records by Feliciano, Leonard Cohen and the Doors. Even I, with a gimpy foot and a long history of athletic ineptitude, was taking part. Less and less did I retreat to my curtained cubicle, or brood about people in my "real life" outside. In fact, when one of those friends phoned long-dis-

123

tance, I rather snappishly said: "But I'm *not* Jane this week at all, don't you *see?* I'm Arizona!"

Mine was by no means the only resurrection. One night the widow Lucy, whose lifelong strengths had been logic and practicality, announced she was going to make a point of staying up later than anybody else. She did, too, leaving a note that said "Goodnight everyone—I'm the last one up and it's 4:17 a.m.!" She also stopped making her bed, which was as much a breakthrough as it would have been for me to start making mine. Congratulating her on this feat, we all felt more interconnected than ever.

"I feel as if I had thirty-nine other egos as well as my own," said the Green Hornet, "like the eye of a bee."

The primmest person in the whole lab was probably Amanda, whose coiffure was always perfect and voice always modulated. One lunch hour she asked Conchis to pass her the butter. Instead of doing so conventionally he rose from his chair, walked all the way down and around the long table to bring it to her personally. He smeared some of it, very gradually, all over her face. Amazed but then enchanted, she smeared some back on him. For a full fifteen minutes they stood there, amiably massaging butter into each other's faces. The kitchen staff, who had already witnessed the finger-paint fight, all stood by beaming. Amanda, as Jacques told her later, looked more beautiful than she had all week.

Jacques was changing, too. Never allowed to go barefoot as a boy, he now went around not only shoeless but shirtless, unshaven and adorned with hippie beads he picked up in Ipswich that fateful Wednesday night. (Eight months later I learned that his transformation had been more than superficial. He had grown a full beard and radically altered the hiring policies of his chain of retail stores.)

My lawyer friend Panther, *né* Cumulus, spent an hour or so being led around the house blindfolded, so that he could experience—as he never had since childhood—how it felt to

124

rely on others instead of on himself. The feeling so beguiled him that he asked the woman whose Liberty of London scarf had served as his blindfold if she would let him keep it—"a thing I'd never *dream* of doing," he said, "in my regular life." Naturally she let him keep it; naturally he was delighted.

Big Karl, who let it slip that in real life he was a metallurgist, made a dramatic pronouncement at a community meeting. "I used to think there were two things," he said. "Steel and shit. Now I've discovered that there's a third: flesh and blood."

"I haven't phoned my wife all week," Chico said, "so things are going to be a little tough when I get home. But later on it'll be fantastic. I've learned here what I never found out in eleven years of marriage: that you can make love with your *eyes* as well as with your body. I can't wait to show her."

Toward the end of the meeting Conchis rather abruptly turned out all the lights, leaving us leaning bewildered against the walls of a pitch-dark room. It was, as a behavioral science graduate student might say, quite a dynamic. The bolder people groped their way around the room, finding special friends and forming whispering, cuddling groups. Such groups developed on either side of me, but I was alone, still too forlorn to strike out myself in search of camaraderie. I was infinitely grateful when Jacques and Gretchen came over to me, uncannily aware of my aloneness. Jacques gave me a kiss, and Gretchen sat down to put her arm around me. It was positively Proustian. I felt as if I were a baby again (not a baby fish, but a human infant), whose parents had come to her nursery bedside to tuck her safely in. I felt loved.

That feeling multiplied, in me and in us all, the next day. In our final Body Movement session we stood in a circle. One by one, as music played, we went forward with closed eyes as all the others in the "family group" simultaneously touched us. This exercise, as melting as any experience of my life, was clearly a demonstration of *agape,* not *eros.* We called it a "love

125

bath" because our whole bodies, from earlobes to kneecaps to heels, were barraged with affection. Out of context it might have seemed part of a Maoist plot to arouse and destroy the whole free world, but in context it was exquisite. My old Midwestern reluctance to be demonstrative with other people dissolved. Afterward I felt as interdependent as one of a litter of newborn kittens, requiring at all times to be in physical contact with somebody else. Within us all burgeoned a love of mankind in general and our fellow lab members in particular. I have not elsewhere found the like of that love.

For a collective farewell rite on the final Sunday morning, all forty of us joined hands to form a huge circle. We swayed back and forth to music for a short while. Then Conchis broke the circle, leading us around the room in a snaking, uncoiling, spiraling "jelly roll" so that each of us was brought into contact with every one of the others. Now I could see the sense of eyeballing. When the eyes you look into have had a chance to become important to you, the exercise can touch the core of your soul.

"Hi," said Orpheus' eyes, "you and I have already said goodbye haven't we?"

"Sorry I never got to know you more," said Holly's.

"There's real affection between us, isn't there?" said Gretchen's.

"Funny, I never thought I'd even like you," said Isaiah, "but now, oddly enough, I love you."

Then the time came for us to part hands and eyes and resume our places among the real people—those who had not spent these past eight days amid such exposure, risk, regression, insights, trust and love. Conchis dismissed us with a poem by Blake:

> He who binds to himself a joy
> Does the wingèd life destroy;

> But he who kisses the bird as it flies
> Lives in eternity's sun rise.

Then, in his own language, he added some prose advice: "Don't talk about it, whatever it is," he said. "Get off your ass and *do* it. Stick with it. If it hurts, it's probably good."

As I packed my clothes—including a cardigan permanently stained with dried finger paint—I tried to summarize what I had learned. No lessons that other people, in and out of the movement, hadn't been trying to teach me for years: that I could love strangers and they me, that anger can be converted into strength and force, that tears can melt anguish, and that staying put can be more rewarding than keeping in motion. Banal truths, really, but this time they hit home, because these eight days I had trusted the people in charge and yielded to them. They were gentle and wise as well as messianic. Their style was not shrill; they did not push and shove. They admitted their own limits, gave of themselves incessantly, and perceived in me and in us all something more than we knew was there. Having felt inflated with helium, I thought how hard it would be to become Jane Howard again.

As I made my way from my cubicle down the stairs and out the door to the real world, I set my suitcase down at least a dozen times for effusive, last-minute hugs. I could not have been sadder to leave had I spent eight weeks in that house, instead of just eight days. But I was saved from maudlin tears by a farewell one new friend called out as I left the house: "Goodbye, Arizona, Bubbi."

Notes toward
a History

❡ The genealogy of the human potential movement is as hard to trace as a foundling baby's. Foundlings have no known ancestors, but the movement is alleged to have preposterously many. One of these came to my attention one afternoon when I emerged from a dip in the swimming pool of the Chateau Marmont Hotel in Hollywood 90046, to chat with an affable young astrologer. He wondered what had brought me to California. When I told him, he said he knew all about encounters, and offered an unsolicited piece for my mosaic.

"You know who *invented* all that group stuff, don't you?" he asked. "It was Ho Chi Minh, twenty years ago."

"Really?" I said. But I filed his tip away in a folder optimistically labeled "History." The folder was already chubby

128

with suggestions that the movement stemmed from Socrates, who after all had counseled people even as trainers do now to Know Thyself, and from ancient forms of Judaism. Another note mentioned Christ's early followers, who assembled furtively in each other's homes before the church was made legal for what somebody said had been "spiritual growth meetings."

I had also been advised that the movement was traceable to the early nineteenth-century German hypnotist Friedrich Anton Mesmer, to the Russian vagabond-mystic Georgiu Gurdjieff, to George Herbert Mead's idea of "social behaviorism," and to the psychiatrist Harry Stack Sullivan, like Mead a Chicagoan. Early in this century Sullivan conceived of psychiatry as an interpersonal rather than a strictly individual matter. The living American psychologist B. F. Skinner, whose theories of "operant conditioning" are applied in many groups, is considered influential, too. A scholarly friend had mentioned in a letter how "early Calvinist clergymen used to get together about once a month to criticize each other's manners, morals and deportment." He further wondered how relevant it might be that characters in Chekhov and Dostoevsky often seemed to upbraid each other with ruthlessly candid comments like: "Oh, Dmitri Andreyevitch, you're such a *bore!*"

I felt I might drown in confusion, if not in the Chateau Marmont pool, unless I could impose some sense on all this chaos. Help finally came in the form of a wise and knowledgeable letter from Dr. Kenneth Benne, a founder and still a prominent leader of the NTL. He suggested that I break the history of the movement down into three different frameworks.

"The use of groups for growth purposes, at the level of folk practice, is as old as human life on earth," he wrote. "It is as silly to say who invented groups in this sense as it is to say who 'invented' fire, or the wheel. The *family* is a small group designed to influence, guide and direct the growth of its younger members. The *classroom* is a group, designed to facilitate the learning of its members. The *religious sect* is a group designed to coach and influence the commitment of its members in certain beliefs and ways of behaving."

My notes abounded, in fact, with references to religions and sects. Someone had told me that Benedictine and Trappist monasteries had held weekly "Chapter of Faults" seminars to discuss the monks' shortcomings, and that eighteenth-century Methodists had held similar "class meetings." Martin Buber's much more recent "I-thou" idea informs nearly all manifestations of the present small group movement. So does Søren Kierkegaard's belief that "to will to be that self which one truly is is indeed the opposite of despair."

Benne's second framework was "the scientific study of small groups, how they work, how they influence their individual members, how they can be changed and altered. These relatively recent studies," he wrote, "have little focus on the use of groups in practice. Considering how important groups have been in folk practice for so long, these studies were rather late in coming." He referred me to Edward Shils' chapter on the scientific study of groups in a book edited by Lerner and Lasswell called *Policy Sciences: Recent Developments in Scope and Method* (Stanford University Press, 1951). He also mentioned a 1955 survey of scientific studies of small groups by A. Paul Hare and E. F. Bargatta. *The Encyclopedia of Social Sciences* had so many more references to scholarly treatises on groups that I decided it would be presumptuous, not to say impossible, to try to encompass them.

Suffice to say that the present movement really does stem in part from a German sociologist named Dr. Ferdinand Tönnies, who in the late 1880s first distinguished between *Gesselschaft* (an impersonal, bureaucratic hierarchy), and *Gemeinschaft* (a closer, more personal community). Toward the end of the century, gropings toward *Gemeinschaft* increased. In 1905 an American physician named Joseph Pratt helped cure tuberculosis victims by assembling them in an early version of the therapeutic encounter group. Trigant Burrow, another American doctor, contributed to the same cause at about the same time. He saw mental disorder as a disturbance in communication, created largely by a patient's "privately cherished and secretly guarded" image of himself. Burrow's aim was for people to express themselves as they really were "by exposing the socially-determined basis of [their] self-image."

In 1913, in Vienna, Dr. J. L. Moreno organized a coterie of prostitutes into a trade union. ("I didn't meet them socially," he is careful to say, "I was too much of a snob or a square.") Moreno learned how unconcerned Socialists, Communists and the Roman Catholic Church all were about the prostitutes' troubles. He enlisted the help of lawyers, doctors and hospitals, and organized the women into a therapeutic weekly *kaffeeklatsch*. It struck him that "they helped each other far more than any of us could help them." Soon afterward they were acting out their problems, as encounter group members now widely do, in psychodramas.

In the 1920s an American named Frank Buchman founded what was to become a worldwide religious organization variously known as the Buchmanites, the Oxford Group and the Moral Re-Armament movement. His followers soon multiplied by the thousands in England, the Netherlands, South Africa and the United States. Like early Christian penitents before them and Park Avenue psychoanalysands after them, they regarded confession as the first step toward conversion. Candor was rampant at their meetings, which were often called "house parties," and which must have resembled some of today's encounter groups.

Philip Toynbee reminisces about such gatherings in his book *Friends Apart: A Story of the Thirties*. In his student days at Oxford, Toynbee writes, there prevailed " . . . a fluency of communication which . . . at its facile worst is simply due to a common indifference and lack of respect. It was in this . . . lamentable spirit that I and several other communists used to sit in the lounge of an Oxford hotel, titillating our stuffed, impersonal minds with the blundering personalities of the Truth game. 'What do you think of me?' we would ask each other, or, at a later point, 'Whom do you like least among us and why?' The game is detestable because it must either give real pain and embarrassment or none at all, and if it gives none at all the players must be so indifferent to each other that no confidence should have been made between them."

By the 1930s small groups had become the serious focus of scientific attention. During World War II much of humanity was involuntarily exposed—in battalions and foxholes and air-raid shelters—to "intensive group experiences" with random assemblages of strangers. Such enforced rapport on so wide a scale doubtless helped create a receptive climate for the present widespread concern with groups. Meanwhile industries were at work toward the same end. In the late 1930s the Roethlisberger and Dickson experiments were carried on at the Western Electric Company in Chicago. These experiments with factory workers led to a phenomenon popularly called the "Hawthorne Effect," which means approximately that people's behavior changes when attention is paid to them.

Dr. Kurt Lewin came to the United States from Nazi Germany intent on testing theories whereby self-help groups might learn to avoid the totalitarianism he had barely escaped. The small group struck him as the obvious link between individual and social dynamics. His theories were concerned with the social restraints imposed on groups by technology, economics, law and politics.

Many of Lewin's ideas have become important to students of group dynamics, none more so than his concept of "Force-Field Analysis," which holds that events are determined by immediate forces rather than distant ones. Behavior could be changed, he thought, if people could identify which forces restrained them from desirable action and which ones drove them on toward it. He helped found the Research Center for Group Dynamics at the Massachusetts Institute of Technology, and the Commission on Community Interrelations of the American Jewish Congress. For a state interracial commission in Connecticut he organized what was called a Basic Skill Training Group, designed to seek out causes of and cures for prejudice. Experiments like this were later rechristened T-groups. They convinced Lewin, as one historian writes, that "no amount of *telling* people what to do could compare with having them 'discover' the same information for themselves."

Along came Leland P. Bradford, an Illinoisan who had worked with the WPA and other agencies involved with adult education. Bradford also believed that laboratories could teach far more effectively than lecturers. He and his colleagues Kenneth Benne (a philosopher) and Ronald Lippitt (a social psychologist) had been experimenting with laboratory groups, which they saw as a potent means of translating scientific theory into social change. Groups, they thought, could be used to re-educate people's attitudes, values and behavior. They admired what Lippitt writes of as Lewin's "deep sensitivity to social problems and commitment to use his resources as a social scientist to do something about them." Sharing this commitment, with Lewin's guidance they founded the NTL, at first a division of the National Education Association.

At about the same time UCLA and the University of California at Berkeley were developing a joint Industrial Relations Institute to design programs for labor-management relations and community service. East met West when some NTL men were attracted to UCLA and began the Western Training Laboratories. The term "sensitivity training" was coined there in 1954 to cover programs meant to make people more effective managers and executives. Eastern T-groups, meanwhile, were being influenced by Douglas McGregor's theories of humanistic (as opposed to authoritarian) management. A tension

133

began that still exists between groups designed for personal growth and those planned to bring about organizational change.

Several people chided me for not including a "Tavistock study group" in my itinerary. They were referring to the Group Relations Conferences, held mostly on New England college campuses in summertime. So far these Tavistock groups have affected about 1,000 mental-health professionals and others who are concerned more with groups as a whole than with interpersonal relations of group members. These groups were first transplanted to the United States (from the Tavistock Institute of Human Relations in London) in 1965, largely through the efforts of Dr. Margaret Rioch. Dr. Rioch is associated with the Washington (D.C.) School of Psychiatry and the National Institute of Mental Health.

"Tavistock groups are emotionally right wing," one of their alumni told me. "They're to the NTL what the NTL is to Esalen. But they can be terrifically powerful." They stem mostly from the wartime work of the English psychologist Dr. Wilfred Bion, who studied such concepts as mob rule and methods of selection of leaders for the British armed forces. Many consider Bion, who now lives in Los Angeles, as important an ancestor of the present group movement as Lewin.

Other ideas imported from Europe have also flourished. From Vienna Dr. Frederick S. Perls, one of the most conspicuous and controversial figures in all the movement, brought contagious enthusiasm for his Gestalt therapy. His methods, Perls believed, are best practiced in workshops "which make all individual therapy obsolete. "Trust in the group," Perls has declared, "seems to me greater than trust in the therapist. It is always a deeply moving experience for the group and for me to see the previously robotized corpses begin to return to life."

George Bach, arrived from Latvia, was meanwhile formu-

134

lating his theories about intensive group psychotherapy. Aldous Huxley was conceiving of man as a multiple amphibian with vast untapped resources. Carl Rogers, then working with groups of hospitalized veterans in Chicago, was beginning to think that "well people get better the same way sick people get well," and to develop his now-famous ideas of "client-centered therapy." Abraham Maslow was carving out his theories that science should study not only the sick but also the well. Maslow suggested that human beings should go beyond adjustment and attempt to transcend—to be "self-actualizing" and to aspire to more "peak experiences." He also conceived of a "hierarchy of needs," starting with physical and going on up from security to social to ego to self-fulfillment. "A need satisfied no longer motivates," Maslow pointed out. "Our perception of what people need colors our assumptions about human behavior.

"What Freud did," Maslow also said, "was to supply us with the sick half of psychology. Now we have to fill it out with the healthy half. Freud left out the aspirations, realizable hopes, and godlike qualities. Psychologists can't keep on ducking responsibility for these things."

"Even Freud," William Schutz agrees, "wouldn't be a Freudian today. His whole career was marked by development."

Concurrently, the organization called Alcoholics Anonymous was using techniques of public confession and group support to persuade drunks to forsake liquor. "My name is Karen and I'm an alcoholic," a ritual speech would start, and thus Karens in smoke-filled auditoriums all over the United States, and later all over the world, would relate how AA had made possible their return to sobriety. One of AA's success cases was Charles Dederich, who on Wednesday nights in 1959 took to holding "free-association" discussion groups at his small apartment in Santa Monica. These boisterous, rigorously honest meetings came to attract more drug addicts than alcoholics. Holding to the idea that acknowledging a character disorder was the first step toward curing it, they led to the founding of Synanon. Some two thousand such self-help groups, all relying on group discussion and group support as a means of erasing specific problems, have since arisen, among them the recently voguish and apparently effective Weight Watchers.

In the early 1960s the movement assumed more shape. In 1959 the Western Behavioral Sciences Institute was founded in La Jolla, attracting some of the most inventive and protean innovators in the various uses of small groups. The NTL was growing fast. Followers of Maslow and Rogers founded the American Institute of Humanistic Psychology. Meanwhile, Michael Murphy and his former Stanford classmate Richard Price hit on a grandiose scheme for using the sixty-two Big Sur acres Murphy had just inherited. They decided to establish there "a center to explore and expand and enhance the human potential," and call it Esalen. Described in a recent bulletin as "a forum and facility for discovery and recovery," Esalen has since grown from an occasional weekend retreat center to a year-round seminar and workshop facility, with branches and projects far removed from the Big Sur.

Because one of Murphy's most cherished hopes was to mix Eastern mysticism with Western pragmatism, Esalen became among other things a kind of *ashram*. Murphy had been a serious student of meditation for some ten years, including eighteen months spent in India. He was convinced that technological America could well use some of the benefits of Asian contemplation. Thus Esalen has become particularly hospitable to the doctrines of Zen, Hindu, Buddhist, and other Asian philosophies.*

* The former Harvard professor Dr. Richard Alpert, who with Dr. Timothy Leary made LSD famous, has been in residence at Esalen's Big Sur headquarters, known as Baba Ram Dass, the name he acquired during his Far-Eastern travel. So have Gia-Fu Feng, a specialist in the Chinese "meditation-in-motion" method called Tai-Chi-Chuan, and the Dalai Lama's former interpreter, Sonam Kazi.

Notes toward a History

The movement's infatuation with the East, which has spread far beyond Esalen, is much discussed and by no means universally applauded. Many doubt the relevance of Indian philosophy to contemporary American problems.

"The yoga system," says Stanley Keleman, "is based on an already depressed people who suffer from overwhelming heat and lack of food. Theirs is an inhalation, inspirational philosophy. It was by inhaling that they could hope to capture God and take him in. Western philosophy is more a matter of exhaling. Here the idea is to grow, to make contact with your world. Indians don't provide a fit atmosphere and environment for their children to live in, but the whole basis of Western civilization is a strong sense of self and of the individual. It's true that we've lost our old sense of community and tribal existence. The hippies over-value this loss, not realizing that our culture has already moved, in a tremendous achievement, from emphasis on communalism to individualism. This doesn't strike me in the slightest as anything we should worry about or regret."

"The doctrines and ideas of the Far East," another student of the movement points out, "can only thrive in societies where a great segment of the population is free to, or obliged to, concentrate on something other than production. The people who have time to question what we're all doing here on this earth are either terribly rich or else terribly poor—afflicted either with abject poverty or abject affluence."

(When one abjectly affluent woman wondered, during an Esalen meditation workshop, *"why* we should have to sit cross-legged for yoga when we've been trained all our lives to sit on chairs, unlike the Indians who haven't?" Murphy said he thought she might have a point there.)

Esalen was such a fast and legendary success that other "Growth Centers," similar in motive though unblessed with hot steam baths or magnificent real estate, have sprung up at the rate of one a month. The most established of the others is

Kairos, outside San Diego. Dr. Benne, like many of his colleagues, is somewhat dubious about these institutions, which fall into the third framework he suggested in his letter to me: "The professional use of small groups to release and facilitate the growth of persons who participate in them ... to make use of groups in practice more conscious, more knowledgeable, more skilled, and more professional." Such places, he wrote, "don't draw sharp lines between education and therapy, and have released all sorts of non-professional use of small groups by people with small knowledge or professional skill."

Be that as it may, the growth centers continue to grow, and so do all the other species of groups in the movement. Some followers of such matters foresee that encounter groups will eventually wane, but nobody seems to think that will happen very soon.

I much preferred discussing the movement with James and Elizabeth Heber Bugental to talking with the poolside astrologer. Bugental is one of the original humanistic psychologists, and his wife is one of a growing category of improbably radiant former nuns. I had heard enough about them to go out of my way to meet them. Having failed to track them down in California, my only chance was to catch them after a workshop outside New York and drive them in a rent-a-car to their plane at Kennedy Airport. The trip was inconvenient, but their literate good sense made it worthwhile.

"It would really be great," Elizabeth Bugental said, "if people could learn to *genuinely* encounter each other without even needing groups—if they could learn to switch gears and peel off facades when necessary, as a matter of course. It wouldn't put us out of business if that happened, either; we could then use encounter groups to heighten and deepen the growth expe-

138

rience, and make it really mystical. Right now, encounter groups are a kind of vestibule experience. What they do so far is help people get their feet in the door and give them a taste of how things *can* be."

"Blamers Assume the Spaghetti Position"

¶ "You think I came here because I *wanted* to? With *them?* You must be out of your mind." Barbara was sixteen, and she seemed to be adolescing before our very eyes, like a flower growing in a fast-motion movie. Every one of her teeth was imprisoned in metal braces. Her hair would have hung to her waist had it not been caught up in a classic, pretty chignon. Maybe the rest of Barbara could look classic and pretty, too, someday, but right now all she looked was venomous and sullen. She was referring, with more hatred than I have ever seen any child show any parents, to her father Aaron and her stepmother Lydia, who sat to her right.

The several other children in that circle of fifty-one people were scarcely more vivacious when their turns came to say why they had come to this Weekend Seminar in Family Life.

"I was dragged," said a boy of fifteen named Peter, whose voice could crack even in a three-syllable speech.

"They *made* me come," mumbled thirteen-year-old Joann.

"I wanted to stay home and work on my terrarium," said Teddy, who was ten, "but they forced me to come here."

"I didn't have anything else to do," admitted a seven-year-old named Nancy.

The parents who had coerced these and other children to the weekend were somewhat more articulate.

"We feel we've been losing touch with Peter," said a woman named Ethel whose fingernails were so bitten that a quarter-inch of flesh covered their top ends. "I used to live only for Peter, but lately I've been thinking maybe I ought to pay more attention to my own life. And Ralph seems more distant from me, too."

"We've all been tending to go off in our separate directions, and the directions never seem to intersect," said Ralph, a gray-looking man in his forties. "I think perhaps it has to do with the alienation that pervades . . ."

"Shut up," cut in Peter. "You're always lecturing."

"Yeah," said Peter's younger sister Adrienne. "Dad's always off trying to save the world, and he can't even unify his own family."

Next in the circle to introduce herself was Charlotte. "I came because Dean asked me to," she said. "He hardly ever asks me anywhere. I was so excited I hired a sitter to take care of our kids. I never get to be with him alone."

"We all came," said a kind-looking paterfamilias named Howard, "because I'm a psychologist myself, and I wanted to see you at work, and have my wife and kids see you, too."

By "you" he meant Virginia Satir, the leader of this weekend and probably the most peripatetic of all circuit riders. She has no fixed abode or address, preferring to swoop from one airport to another with seven suitcases filled with flowing gowns which sustain her image as a Wagnerian heroine. When people marvel at her gypsy life she assures them "there are about twenty-five places in the world I call my 'Virginia Corners'—places where I keep a few clothes and maybe some *objets d'art* I've picked up here and there." In her case "here and there" might mean the Yukon, Milwaukee, Australia, Seattle, Kenya, Boston, Idaho, Japan, Chicago or New Zealand.

Now she had lighted outside New York City, for a weekend sponsored by the growth center called Aureon. The crowd she had drawn looked alert and prosperous and more interesting than many I had seen, but I was skeptical. Spring had come. New chartreuse outgrowths had just appeared at the end of darker green branches of pine trees. I hoped that whatever happened in the windowless auditorium where we sat could compete with what was happening outdoors. Also, having come as a family of one, I felt defensively alone.

Virginia, whose last name is pronounced Sa-TEER, is nobody's natural mother.

"I've never birthed any," she said, "but I've raised four: two step and two foster." The staccato-style book *Conjoint Family Therapy,* however, is all hers. Its thesis is that the family member whom most therapists would label the "patient" is in fact a victim of a "disturbed communications network." Her methods for getting all members of families back into touch with each other are much emulated.

"Sometimes," as she said to this group, "a family feels like a can of moving worms. Sometimes kids do what is called fighting, which is actually love-making in reverse." She prefers folksy metaphors to psychological jargon, which she considers "sterile and very hideous."

"Families," she said, "often remind me of the woman who always served roast beef cut in two, and cooked in two different pans. She did this because her mother had taught her to, and her mother's mother had taught *her* to. And *her* mother, when somebody asked, said she cooked *her* roasts that way

142

because when she was a young bride she didn't have a big enough pan, and had to use two little ones. That's the way a lot of pointless family traditions get started. Our biggest problem as human beings is not knowing that we don't know."

We would spend the weekend, Virginia said, making "journeys into our own inner space," in order to get in touch with our feelings. When any emotion was mentioned she would ask: "Where in your body do you *feel* that?," and oblige the person to locate an anxiety in his chest, butterflies in his stomach, tightness in the shoulders or whatever other symptoms wherever.

"Stay with whatever feeling you're experiencing," she said, "because another one will replace it immediately if you do. Let yourself be in touch with yourself. Trade diplomacy for integrity. If you're straight with yourself, you'll have more of yourself there to deal with the problem." (I never met a circuit rider who sooner or later, somehow, did not express this idea. If the human potential movement had a coat of arms, the motto emblazoned on it would surely be "STAY WITH THE FEELING." As another trainer put it, "a feeling is energy. It has to be stored somewhere. Where did you put it? Where did it go?")

"I love to make up old sayings," Virginia said. "One of them is this: children divide the world into two classes, parents and people; and parents do the same thing, only their two classes are *children* and people. I hope we'll see before we leave that we're all people.

"You came into this world like a mule, with no pride of ancestry and no hope of posterity. You were programmed to grow, but you had no information as to how to go about it: you just did it. Think of all the things you learned when you were two years old! There are some very accomplished and distinguished people in this room, but I don't think anybody here has learned more as an adult than all of us learned when we were two. You may think it's too late now to change, but

143

it never is. You may not remember, but if you take on faith that there was a time when you couldn't talk, and wore diapers, you'll see what I mean. A baby can think and feel as soon as he's two hours old. He starts learning then, and he never stops."

At several points in the human potential circuit I had run across the thesis that the family is a "system," as amenable as any larger system to programmed change. NTL summer programs include labs for entire families. Robert Blake applies his "Grid System" to families as well as to companies. Many social scientists regret popular misconceptions of the American family, a lot of which come from television.

"I've got a great formula for a successful TV family show," Richard Farson said once. "All you have to do is be sure the woman is smarter than the man, the children smarter than the woman, and the animals smarter than the children." Farson also lamented that "there is very little intimacy in family life now—little of the intimacy of shared feelings, of 'This is what it's like to be me,' or of asking 'What's it like to be you right now?' Somehow we dare not risk becoming vulnerable to each other. But we're going to have to find new ways of applying our new social technologies. We need to devise ways for people to reach the goals they have set for family life.

"It's too bad we have such terrible resistance to applying science to the things that matter most to us. In families, as in civil rights, the great paradox in improvement is that it simply brings increased discontent and the need for more improvement. There ought to be networks of families who can be responsive to each other in crisis, and who can monitor each other's family lives so that they can have the feedback they need to achieve their goals."

Most families I have known would shrink with horror from the prospect of such monitors and networks and barrages of

"Blamers Assume the Spaghetti Position"

feedback, but there are those who feel otherwise. I first learned of this at a family microlab during a convention of humanistic psychologists. In that encounter, a roomful of adults had been instructed to cluster into family-sized groups. Everyone in each group was to choose a family role. I became the "mother" of the group I joined. Somebody else was the "father," and three other grownups were our "children"—a bellicose teen-age son, a sprightly, pretty twelve-year-old girl, and a mousy girl of seven. Each of us was issued a crayon. We would express ourselves with colored lines on a big sheet of paper. Talk was forbidden, because children aren't as verbally adroit as adults, whereas everyone can handle a crayon with equal facility.

That exercise taught me something about myself. I covered the whole big sheet of paper with ever-widening concentric green circles. Engaging in a playful skirmish at one corner of the paper with my "son" and his black crayon, I never noticed all the while that my younger "daughter's" yellow crayon had not ventured from the place where she started. I ignored her entirely, the way I have ignored unobtrusive people in real life.

Virginia Satir now led us in a similar exercise. "People are different in their families from the way they are outside," she said. She told all fifty-one of us to mingle in the middle of the room and reorganize into "second families" in which we would see ourselves as people, not as players of preassigned, nearly inflexible roles. As if it were dancing school I was pleased to be chosen quickly by the psychologist named Howard. He had prematurely white hair and an amiable manner.

"Let's get *her* for our 'daughter,' " he whispered conspiratorially, pointing to the sullen Barbara. Fine, I thought. We asked Barbara if she'd care to join our "family." She shrugged with surpassing nonchalance. We found three folding chairs and sat down together, as Virginia told us to do, to talk of our impressions of each other.

145

Please Touch

Barbara said she felt as miserable as we thought she looked, because her real parents had made her come here instead of letting her go to a reunion of CIT's she had worked with the past summer. Never again, so far as she knew, would they all be reassembled.

"CIT's?" inquired Howard.

"Counselors-in-Training," Barbara replied witheringly, as if he had asked her what "USA" meant. She fidgeted, writhed and avoided our eyes. That he was a psychologist and I a writer interested her not at all. Only when I mentioned that an article of mine on ice cream had drawn more reader mail than any other, ever, did she look at me directly.

"I'm a real ice-cream freak," I said. At this Barbara actually smiled. "I like ice cream, too," she said. I asked if there were any adults anywhere in the world whom she liked for themselves. She thought a while and said she guessed not.

It turned out there was a good deal more to know about her. She had recently lost thirty-five pounds on a crash diet. Her older brother used drugs and was presently in a special treatment center. She had seriously thought of killing herself. I wished I could go right out then and get her some butter crunch or chocolate chip.

All around us other newly formed "second families" were conversing animatedly. Then Virginia interrupted and said we should return to our real family units, first introducing our new families to our real ones. Barbara did not choose to present Howard or me to her father and stepmother. "Family members usually get stuck in a hole," Virginia told the whole group. "Why don't you talk now about how you classify each other in *your* families?"

Another unattached woman named Winifred and I talked of how we struck each other: she seemed to me "competent" and I seemed to her a "student"—impressions which depressed us both. I noticed that things weren't going well with Barbara and her real family. She and her father were staring at opposite walls, and her stepmother's efforts to make gay chatter were in vain.

Virginia wandered around the room and paused for a while with Ralph, Ethel, Adrienne and Peter—the pedant, the nail-biter, the rude girl and the boy who still looked as if he wished he were elsewhere.

"He's angry," Ethel said of her son. "He's angry all the time, but he never lets me know why. It wasn't always that way. We used to be so close. Once a friend and I rode the subway all the way into town from where we live, in Kew Gardens. When we got to Bloomingdale's she turned to me and said: 'Do you realize you've talked *all this way* about Peter?' But why shouldn't I? All his life his teachers and everyone else told me Peter was special, Peter was gifted, Peter was bright. It seemed he gave me the fun and the contact I didn't get from his father. Peter really *did* mean too much to me, I guess. I guess I hounded him too much about quitting piano lessons, and maybe about a lot of other things."

"Yeah, 'maybe' you did," said Peter.

"I feel so cut off," said Ethel, with a quaver in her voice.

Virginia asked Ethel and Peter to stand up and stage a typical argument.

"Practice the piano!" said Ethel.

"I don't want to, you bitch," said Peter. Virginia asked Ethel to stand shaking her finger at Peter, and Peter to respond with a gesture of pushing away. That, said Virginia, was the way things were between these two people—on the surface. Then she restaged the tableau to illustrate what the real emotions were between them: Ethel hanging her head in shame, and Peter shielding himself—rather than pushing his mother away—with his hands. Then she asked them to sit down facing each other.

"I don't know when you two last saw each other," said Virginia, "but this is Ethel and this is Peter. She also wears a Mother's hat, and he wears the hat of a Son. He's a young man who happened, a long time ago, to come out of her. I wonder how you look to each other now, at this moment in time."

"Well," said Ethel, "you don't look as bad in long hair as you *might.*"

"So you see him as having long hair," observed Virginia. "What else?"

"I think I like him," said Ethel, "but then I always did."

"Not 'always,' " prodded Virginia, "but *right now.*"

"I *like* him right now," said Ethel, "he's got a nice face, even when he scowls."

"I used to have a book called *The Glossary of My Interpretation of What You Really Are,*" said Virginia, "but I threw it away, because I saw how inaccurate it was. Peter, how do you see Ethel?"

"I see she has . . ."

"Can you tell *her?*"

"I see you have short hair," Peter said, "and I see you look hurt, but kind, sort of . . ."

"I can see you aren't looking at each other as you are and thinking descriptively," said Virginia. "Until we reach our feelings of intimacy and tenderness, we have to waste a lot of time being angry . . ."

". . . and other cruddy stuff," said Peter.

"Yes, and other cruddy stuff," said Virginia. "Ralph, how do *you* feel about this scene?"

"Like pushing the two of them closer together," said Ralph. At Virginia's direction he got up and did so, so that his wife and their son were obliged to embrace. Ralph and his daughter Adrienne looked on. Adrienne giggled. Virginia asked why.

"Because I heard Mom tell Pete he smelled like cigarettes," she said.

"Why are there tears in your eyes?" Virginia asked Ralph.

"Because I feel good to see Peter and Ethel together," he

148

said. "I feel glad that they are able to undertake a position of such rapport, because I had assumed that that sort of empathy no longer was a possible course of action . . ."

"Oh, Daddy," said Adrienne, "stop lecturing."

"Where would *you* like to be in relation to the rest of your family, Adrienne?" asked Virginia. Ralph was standing over Peter and Ethel, who still sat with their arms around each other on facing folding chairs.

"Maybe next to Dad," said Adrienne. "I feel sort of sorry for him." She did go and join her father, and after a time the son and mother stood up, and the whole family stood in a circle, unembarrassed by the presence of forty-seven other people in the room, with their arms all around each other.

Virginia remembered a quote from Bob Hope: " 'So-and-so wasn't cuddled, so he curdled.' We should all remember that skin contact doesn't have to mean rape. We usually think of physical contact as expressing only two things: romance and utility. We seldom touch each other just for the sake of touching. One of the terrible things in family life, as soon as babies grow up, is that people quit using what can be one of the most helpful kinds of contact there is—just using hands. Adults can use hands in so many other ways than slapping, dragging, pinching, pushing, pulling or patting to mean 'there-there.'

"By the way, a grown woman should never pat a grown man that way. A beau I had a long time ago, when I knew from borscht, told me so. I still know from borscht in a lot of ways, but I do know that. And I know that mothers and sons are often afraid to touch each other, because touching means romance, and romance means rape. Touching is one of the ways we can learn about each other's worlds."

After supper we reassembled in our second families to learn more about communicating. "Most of us are so busy being what someone else wants us to be," said Virginia, "that we don't know how to listen. There are four wrong ways people communicate. You can blame, you can placate, you can be ir-

149

relevant or you can be 'reasonable.' There's something incomplete about each way. The blamer leaves out what he feels about the other person, the placater leaves out what he feels about himself, the reasonable one leaves out what he *feels* about the subject being discussed and the irrelevant one leaves out everything. Let's practice finding out how these styles feel. Okay? First, let all the mothers be placaters, and all the fathers be blamers, and the first children irrelevant and the second children placaters. Go ahead, have a discussion about some plan your family is making."

"Where would you like to go for vacation this year, dear?" I placatingly asked my "husband."

"Anyplace as long as it doesn't turn out to be as mosquito-infested as that cabin you picked last summer," said Howard blamingly. "I tried to get some work done, but with no screens and in such small quarters, and with *her* making so much noise"—he was indicating Barbara—"it sure wasn't much of a bargain."

"I've got a history test tomorrow," said Barbara irrelevantly, twirling a lock of her hair.

"Oh, darling," I said to Howard, "you're right, it *was* wrong of me, we'll find someplace really *nice* this year, it's *so* important that you have your peace and quiet . . ."

"Okay," interrupted Virginia, "now switch. Mothers blame, fathers placate, first children blame, second children be irrelevant."

"Where we gonna go on vacation?" demanded Barbara.

"Wherever you want to go, sweetheart," said Howard. "Your mother and I want you to have every advantage we never had ourselves."

"You mean those advantages we can afford on *your* salary," I snarled. "That doesn't leave much, does it? And besides, how come you still haven't built those bookshelves for the den?"

"Yeah, how come?" broke in Barbara. "Judy's father builds

stuff for the house all the time, and their house looks great—
it's not a dump like ours."

"You're probably right, dear," said Howard, nearly gag-
ging, "I really ought to be more industrious, I *have* neglected
you both. . . ."

"Now I'd like you to assume postures that illustrate the
roles you're playing," said Virginia. "I'll show you what I
mean. This is the Spaghetti Position: it shows how Placaters
are." She got down on the floor and arranged herself in a limp
pile, and then stood up. "This is the Blamer's Position," she
said, standing angrily with one finger pointing out shaking at
an unseen adversary. "Now, take the positions you just had in
your families." Barbara and I stood with our fingers shaking
at Howard, who lay cringing on the floor. "Now," said Virginia, "let's have the fathers be blamers, the mothers be reasonable and the children be irrelevant."

"Why the hell don't you decide where we *are* going for vacation?" Howard asked me.

"I'm going to do that right now," I said sweetly, "just as
soon as I finish sewing name tags in Barbara's camp things.
Barbara dear, do you like this new sweater?"

"The curtains in this room are really stupid," said Barbara.
And so the exercise went.

For me there was some jarring unsolicited feedback. "Boy,"
said Howard, "when you were being a blamer back there, I
really was scared for a while. I had the feeling that being
bitchy came easy to you."

The next morning Virginia led us in communications exercises. They were designed to show the utility of getting any
message across without direct eye contact, and without being
close enough to touch. She had children stand up and parents
sit at their feet, so adults could know how it felt to be small.
Many teenagers missed this session, because they had slept

151

outside all night, on shower curtains and under bedspreads. I wished I had gone with them, but realized they would have considered me a geriatric case. I was discovering in myself some of the fawning attitude toward youth that characterizes much of our society. I gave to kids under twenty the deference due great and wise old age.

Then, with closed eyes, we held hands and experimented with different degrees of pressure.

"All of me was in my hand," said Peter of the contact he had had with his father. "It was a good feeling, sort of secure."

"It made me feel so good I wanted to laugh," said a mother.

"When you said just to 'contact' she squeezed too much," one boy said of his mother. "But when you said 'pressure,' she didn't squeeze hard enough."

"We can have eyes and ears in our hands," said Virginia. "We die in our relationships if we don't have contact. But just because you want to make advances to me doesn't mean I have to accept them. There are ways of saying 'at this point in time I'd like to be by myself,' without being placating, blaming or irrelevant. If you say 'look, I feel like being alone right now,' *congruently,* without adding 'because' this or 'because' that, it's hard to take that as a rejection."

During the coffee break I asked Aaron, Barbara's father, if he had learned much from the communications exercises. I had noticed that he and his daughter had only touched or talked to each other when Virginia ordered them to.

"Oh yes," Aaron said. "This is very useful. It will help me in business. I happen to be a manufacturer's representative—a salesman—and it's quite true that if you believe in your product, you have to communicate with your voice and the way you look and your handshake and everything else."

"Did you think it helped much with Barbara?"

"That one?" Aaron shook his head. "I'm not sure I can

ever get through to her. Her or her stepmother either. Must be something wrong with the way I reach out to them." He went off for a short walk by himself.

In the next session Virginia asked Aaron and Lydia and Barbara to show how things were within their family. "I feel great loneliness in our family," said Lydia. "There are whole days of complete silence—not literally silence, but when nothing of any importance gets said."

"I don't like to feel that I have to be nice just because Lydia wants me to," said Barbara. "If I'm nice I want it to be because I *feel* like being nice myself."

"But when does she ever feel like it?" Lydia asked rhetorically. "I'd like Barbara to just let me put my arm around her once in a while, but she never does. I'd like her and Aaron to make me know I counted for something with them."

"Have you ever *told* Aaron that?" asked Virginia.

"I'll tell him now," said Lydia. "Aaron, I'd like to count in your life. I'd like to know I mattered to you."

"But you do," said Aaron with pure surprise. "I feel that you and I are—are inseparable."

"How come we never even talk, then?" asked Lydia.

"We do, now don't exaggerate," said Aaron. "It's true, though, that I can't carry on a conversation much after eleven o'clock at night, and it's true that early morning is when I have to make all my business telephone calls, or else I won't reach my customers. And it's true, unfortunately, that we don't spend much of the rest of the day together."

"What about dinner time?" asked Virginia. "I'd like to try something. I'd like for the three of you to pretend that this room is your apartment, and that it's the hour when Lydia is cooking dinner and Barbara is home from school and Aaron is home from the office. Go around this room the way you'd go around your own house." They did so, each barely noticing the others.

"Is that the way things are with the three of you?" asked

153

Virginia. They nodded. "How does it strike *you*, Aaron, this pattern?"

"Well," said Aaron, "it violates the basic principle of modern technology. It's time-and-effort-consuming to wander around this way."

"Do you mean that if we travel this way in relation to each other we'll never really meet?" Aaron nodded. Virginia asked them to wander around again, this time joining hands when they encountered each other, for a count of no less than ten. They did so. "How did that feel?" Virginia asked.

"Well," said Aaron, "like an improvement over the other way. It seemed more purposeful."

"I think what you're all really trying to avoid," said Virginia, "is the idea of clutch. You all think that if the others really catch you they'll never let you go. Aaron feels that if Lydia ever gets him into the kitchen to chat while she cooks he'll never get out. Barbara feels the same way."

"That's right," said Lydia. "They're both eluding me. I touch Barbara, but there's nothing in the muscles that touches me back."

"I've got an idea," said Virginia. "Aaron, can you give Lydia a piggy-back ride?" Aaron was a tall and burly man.

"Sure," he said, and he did. "Lydia," said Virginia, "you tell him where you want to go. Let him know what you want."

"Let's go over that way," said Lydia. "Now let's turn. Go back to the center, now. Okay?"

"How're you doing?" asked Virginia.

"It's nice to get a free ride," said Lydia, "but I feel as if I'm very heavy for him to carry."

"Is she too heavy?" asked Virginia.

"No, she's light," said Aaron, "but it's beginning to be a little rough on the knees."

"Okay, you can let her down," said Virginia, "but remember one thing: *tell* her when you're going to drop her." Aaron did, and then they stood facing each other, looking a little shy.

"How do you feel now?" asked Virginia.

"Like hugging her," said Aaron, "but I feel a little diffident with all these people around."

"How do *you* feel?" Virginia asked Lydia.

"Great," she said, "but I wish Aaron would smile." Aaron did, and he did embrace her. Barbara remained in a corner of the room. But her scowl, at least, had vanished.

"God Forbid
You Should
Change Anything"

⟨ "Why would anybody want to use those encounterish T-group things in *schools?*" asked a woman I know whose distress with her town's board of education was such that she almost single-handedly founded a radical and much-praised private school. She would be surprised to discover soulmates among the leaders of the human potential movement. They find the same fault with existing educational hierarchies that she and I do. If I had a child I would not want him to be taught by most of the teachers I had myself. Certainly I would shield him from most of those I saw breezing their derisive way through "Ed School" when I was in college. But there are people in the movement to whom I would entrust him gladly. Their aim would jibe with mine: to make him turn out funny,

156

solemn, kind, interesting to others and himself, decisive, open both to ideas and emotions, and reverently curious about combinations of words and colors and shapes and sounds and numbers. They would seek to obsess him not with popularity and politeness and getting his picture in the yearbook a lot, but with the supreme lifelong habit of asking and learning.

In the year I spent observing small groups, I thought a lot about my hypothetical child and his hypothetical schooling. The movement has grand ambitions for using such small groups, and various other versions of sensitivity training, in schools. Administrators and faculty can profit (and in some adventurous instances have) by going away for T-groups and workshops. Students can benefit (and sometimes have) by exposure to "affective education," a human potential term favored by teachers who think there has been too much emphasis on "cognitive" or strictly cerebral learning, and not enough on feeling and imagination.

Such experiments, even when they triumph, are controversial. Their goals are flexibility and openness and candor. No institutions need these goals more than schools do, but none are more hesitant about working toward them. Administrators are conservative, parents skeptical, and school boards notoriously suspicious about innovations. "Reforming a school system," to paraphrase Abraham Maslow, "is like melting a glacier." To strive to melt glaciers is to ask for trouble.

"No school system can change," said James A. Kimple of the South Brunswick Township system in New Jersey, "unless the administrator gets down off his pedestal." Kimple, the superintendent, got down off his and went with his principals to an NTL summer laboratory at Bethel. Doing so, he says, "saved us about five years of trying to sort out relationships and achieve mutual confidence, trust and sensitivity to one another." Kimple was enthusiastic enough to solicit federal funds for hiring the best professional trainers he could find, to lead T-groups that eventually touched his whole system.

157

Please Touch

Kimple would find a kindred spirit in Charles Dederich of Synanon, who shares his belief that "learning is an attitude. We're trying," Dederich said, "to design a way in which learning is sucked into people from inside, rather than jammed in from outside. We consider the regular American system of education a total failure."

"Yes," I said, "it's pretty bad."

"I said it's a *total failure,*" repeated Dederich.

In 1969 I followed two much-headlined brouhahas about sensitivity training in affluent suburban high schools. One was spread by the wire services after alarmed coverage in the *Chicago Tribune*. It dealt with some unofficial extracurricular exercises run by an English teacher at the Boltwood Division of the Evanston Township High School. The eager 27-year-old in charge of those sessions was Thomas Klein. Klein believes that "personal growth" is a more important objective of English classes than literature. I can't agree with that, but I think it unfortunate that his efforts to involve and excite his students should have been so controversial. Many of his students and their parents were enthusiastic about the nonverbal exercises he conducted, and found them quite valuable. A couple of anonymous complaints to the *Tribune,* however, made him seem more a pariah than a minor folk hero. He doesn't teach at that school any more.

A few months later the *New York Times* picked up some coverage from the extremely conservative *Darien Review* of a weekend sensitivity training laboratory. A typing teacher who had attended that lab disagreed vociferously with most others present, who had found it helpful. Her outraged report polarized Darien. Three hundred citizens assembled at an open school-board meeting which somebody said resembled "a dirty version of the Salem witch hunt."

The lab in question had been led by Peter Caffentzis. It was part of a ten-session program designed to prepare teachers to handle forthcoming courses in "Family Life and Sex Educa-

158

tion." Caffentzis is employed by a federally supported Connecticut organization called SPRED, which is an acronym for "school progress reaches each district." He had previously led 24 other labs for some 650 Connecticut school people. He was hurt by the Darien controversy, but not surprised.

"We have to anticipate negative responses," he said, "because we're not exposing people to a neutral event but to something very powerful." Many teachers, he thinks, "don't know how to listen. They're a defensive, over-answering group of people who use opinion as fact and have forgotten whatever learning theory they were taught, if any.

"They've never, never had to design a learning environment. All they can do is transfer notes from lectures to tests. If *they're* not willing to experiment, how can their kids benefit? They often lack an adequate theoretical framework from which to operate. They get so they don't value the best thing they have, their intuitions. They look to others for approbation."

Caffentzis went to Food Trades Vocational High School in Manhattan. For years, until his wife persuaded him to quit, he worked as a bartender in his Greek father's restaurant. At 27 he went to college to study psychology. He was hired to teach disturbed children and accidentally hit on a classroom technique that resembled encounter groups. Somebody who admired him in action suggested he go to a summer lab at Bethel. He went there for a total of three summers, and was so impressed he thought of shaving all his hair off to imitate his mentor William Schutz (then Bill and now Will, then merely bald and now bearded). Now Caffentzis is completing a doctoral dissertation at Yeshiva University on "Use of T-Groups to Increase Flexible Behavior in Schools."

"Educational institutions," Caffentzis says, "are the only ones I know of where one mistake can kill you. Failed experiments usually result in firing. The way systems respond to mistakes is to cast out the individual, rather than to research the

159

error. I'm trying to get people to see that our society's way of life is artificial. People say T-groups are artificial, but hey, look, like how about 30 kids in one room facing the same way for 35 minutes? What's natural about that?

"The main idea is 'God forbid you should change anything,' " says Caffentzis, "but I won't buy that. I'll probably be in trouble for the rest of my life."

Gloria Siemons in 1968 taught first grade at the Foothill Elementary School in the Goleta Heights section of Santa Barbara, California. Sociologists would describe her six-year-olds as products of upward-mobile, middle-class America. In one class two of the boys were, or had been, on tranquilizers. Mrs. Siemons tries to "instill in the kids preparation for uncertainty, to help them to cope, absorb, not overreact, not be overdefensive and get them to acknowledge their feelings instead of repressing them.

"The child," she says, "is alive and wiggly, but his environment is usually deadening."

The environment was far from deadening the day I visited her classroom. It was a few weeks after I met Mrs. Siemons and eight other teachers then working as part of the Ford Foundation–Esalen project for "affective education." First thing in the morning she assembled her charges in a circle in the front of the room.

"I'd like each of you to feel what's happening inside of you right now," she said. "What's your heart doing? How are you breathing? See if you can get to talk with *yourself,* without being aware of other things. Think about what you feel in your stomach. When you're ready, try to put it into words. Take all your feelings and worries, butterflies, excitement and happiness, and put them in the middle of the circle."

"I've got monsters in my stomach," one boy said.

"Put the monsters on the rug," said Mrs. Siemons. "There,

that feels *much* better. Nicky," she said to one of a pair of noisily scuffling children, "I'm feeling very angry with you right now, and with you, too, Eric."

The first-graders' mothers were visiting that day. They made joint finger paintings with their children and took turns leading them and being led by them on "blind walks" on a hillside in the schoolyard. Later, in the gymnasium, they played games using sheets. First the children were told to curl up and hide under the sheets, pretending to be bean seeds.

"When I see that you really *are* a bean seed, and not a first-grade child under a sheet, I will come and water you and make you grow slowly, s-l-o-w-l-y, the way a plant really grows," said Mrs. Siemons. Later she had the mothers get under the sheets, too, to show that they also could grow. When they reached their full height the teacher asked them to *"look* at your child. Take him in your arms and experience the full shape of him. If you're able to, lift him up to your own height. Then go back down on the floor with him, and touch him any way you like." For surprisingly many mothers it seemed a radical novelty to hold their children. For nearly all, it seemed moving.

"A lot of people in the community object," Mrs. Siemons later said. "They say 'those kids aren't learning, they're having *fun.'* But I tell them I can't really teach a child unless and until he is having fun. Kids can blame and resent and hold grudges as much as anybody else. Like anybody else they've got to feel involved in what they're doing, and in touch with themselves."

I wouldn't want my child to be a cultist, but I would be delighted to expose him to the uproarious zeal I witnessed one day at the Synanon school in Santa Monica. Then a year-old institution, the school was already getting applications from as far away as England.

Please Touch

"These kids," as one of their teachers told me, "are taking a real trip on Greek culture. They decided to saturate themselves in it, and believe me they're getting *saturated*. It's terrific the way they're learning to relate their own lives to some far-off culture. Some of them, if you can imagine, used to be lonely, monosyllabic mumblers."

Not much mumbling went on in this imaginary Mount Olympus. Thirty children, ranging in age from seven to twenty, were engaged in what academic textbooks might call "sociodramatic role-playing." Each had assumed the identity of a Greek god, or a privileged moral, and they were playing a Hellenic version of the Synanon Game. When I went in the game was "on" Zeus, a big fat black kid.

"You know, Zeus," said another child, "you have the whole world at your fingertips, and you just sit there and play with us. Who do you think you are? What's that you have in your mouth, a thunderbolt?"

"Yeah," said Leda. "You come sidling up to me like a beautiful swan, but when are you gonna give me some child support for those eggs I laid?"

"Jesus Christ," another kid whispered *sotto voce,* "was that girl *hatched?*"

"What kind of woman are *you?"* someone asked Leda, "that you go around letting swans make love to you?"

"Look," someone else told Zeus, "if you're gonna go around making people have babies, you could at least be yourself, instead of some animal. A bull! A cuckoo bird! A black cloud! Really, Zeus, how can we trust you?"

"What about Dionysus?" asked Zeus. *"He's* the idiot, he's the dumb one. Why do you always get drunk, Dionysus?"

"I dig grapes," said Dionysus.

"Well, you dig them a little too much, if you ask me," said Vulcan. "You're a *rotten* role model. You lie around all day while a whole lot of Greek people work their asses off like slaves."

"God Forbid You Should Change Anything"

"I happen to be very tight with the common people," said Dionysus. "Me and Prometheus, we got friends there, we identify."

Athena was asked, "Why don't you get a new tunic and fix yourself up? Why does intelligence have to be so masculine and warlike? *Be* the goddess of wisdom—be wise enough to throw that helmet away and identify with being a girl."

Talk turned to Persephone's protracted visits to hell. "It isn't so bad there," she said. "You get luxuries. Of course you have to put up with all those deadheads."

"Hades, you must feel insecure about your appearance," someone guessed, "otherwise how come you make yourself invisible all the time?"

"Oh shut up, Apollo, you talk too much. You're so ugly and horny."

"*I'm* not ugly, *Pan's* the one who's ugly. He can't get any women to look at him, probably because of his hairy goat's legs. He forces girls to turn themselves into bushes and reeds, and then he uses them as flutes. That must be what they mean by 'playboy.' "

"He needs a good chiropodist."

"How do *you* feel, Hercules, being able to do all those fantastic feats of strength but with nothing between your ears? Just because somebody told you to do twelve impossible things, does that mean you had to *do* it?"

"What about Iris? She's so busy making rainbows the mail never gets delivered."

Later I talked to the Synanon schoolmaster, Dede Harvey. "These kids," he said, "are learning that being honest is the only comfortable way to live. They have a freedom to *be* that you don't see much in the world outside. On their own they sense a need for both discipline and tender care, and they figure out very quickly that they don't get any status by being a dropout. They've taught me far more than I ever learned getting a university degree."

Please Touch

For some years Carl Rogers had wanted to test an idea that "the basic encounter group can be an instrument for self-directed change in school systems." He chose the Immaculate Heart College in Los Angeles, which certifies seventy teachers a year and staffs and supervises eight high and fifty elementary schools. Using a private foundation grant, Rogers has worked with the college through the Western Behavioral Sciences Institute and later through the Center for the Study of the Person. Cardinal McIntyre forbade the use of the program in the elementary and high schools, but it still thrives in the college.

At the college I talked with an ex-nun faculty member named Veronica Flynn, a veteran of many encounter groups and one of the most contagiously happy people I have ever met anywhere. "Administrators feel threatened," she said, "by tumultuous emotional change, even when all around them those who have done the changing say it's the best thing that ever happened to them. Many prefer withdrawing into administrative safety to growing. They don't recognize that whatever is basically human about us is good, and should be shared."

Dr. Flynn sometimes leads encounter groups at the college. "But we never know much in advance when they're going to be," she said. "You can't program 'thou shalt encounter.' It's the kind of thing that has to evolve, not be imposed. When a group of faculty or students or anybody else wants an encounter, as part of a one-hour class or for a weekend retreat, then we have it. But only then."

"The encounter group," says Dr. William Coulson, who has helped lead the Immaculate Heart project, "simply fortifies the staff's willingness to run risks. Sometimes to be creative you have to run the risk of looking foolish. The individual is strengthened in encounter groups. He learns to trust his experience."

Coulson, quoted in *San Diego* magazine, sees "the encounter group as a medium of harnessing the energy of the student

164

"God Forbid You Should Change Anything"

revolutionary, who seems to be seeking the outright destruction of education as it is structured today because he considers it irrelevant. He can *talk* about it in encounter groups, and this can lead to changes without throwing rocks. The encounter group can be an angry, tearful, verbally violent student revolt packed into a room. That's better than roaming around the campus tearing things apart. Some say that getting people to talk frankly to each other is dangerous. But we say the alternative—absolute anarchy—is more dangerous."

"Remember, It's Only a Pillow!"

❡ When I was a child my forte was spelling bees. When all else failed, as all else often seemed to, I could always console myself by getting an A, or an A minus anyway, in English. Words, then and ever since, have been my strength, my refuge, and what some would call my defense mechanism. I like Roscoe's WNEW Metro-Media rock station, but there's little danger of my forsaking the Gutenberg, pre-McLuhan heritage. Words have served and enchanted me so reliably that I regard any attack on them with narrow-eyed suspicion. Just such an attack is very much a part of the human potential movement. The attack is known irreverently as Bod Biz, and more ponderously by such verbose names as New Multi-Modal Methods of Nonverbal Communication. The idea is that talking and writing aren't the only ways to get messages across.

The Bod Biz people contend that we can learn a lot more than we might suppose about each other without ever exchanging a single sentence, and that many sentences that do get uttered are wasteful, dishonest and evasive. The Bod Biz people think that gestures unaccompanied by any speech can be at least as eloquent as a conversation, sometimes more so. If I want to get to know you, the Bod Biz people suggest, I don't necessarily have to talk to you. I can smell you, massage you, merely touch you, feel your face, read your posture or guide you blindfolded from this room onto that lawn. Our culture, the nonverbal people believe, is too much attuned to sight and not enough to touch. They propose to correct this imbalance.

"The most spiritual person," one leader says, "is the one who's in touch with his body. The soul and the emotions flower through the body." Even the most timid and conservative T-groups are assailing cultural taboos against touching. It is rare to find a group whose members do not at some point take turns being lifted up in the air from below by the hands of the others, so that everybody has a chance to get rocked in a hammock of human fingers. (The sensation, which I experienced several times, is delightful.)

In the hagiography of Bod Biz there are many saints—Ida Rolf, Charlotte Selver, Ann Halprin, Bernard Gunther, Mary Whitehouse and Albert Pesso, among numerous others. Each has an evangelistic clientele, convinced that its idol is possessed of some mystic entree to true and total awareness. They all go around having weekend groups and otherwise spreading the gospel that our bodies are trying to tell us something: the truth.

The first ones I met were Ann Halprin and Bernie Gunther. Mrs. Halprin led a spontaneous dance session to drumbeats at a convention in 1968. I dropped in, started dancing, and felt considerably more in touch with myself (not to say sweaty) as a result. Gunther, a former weight-lifter, more or less invented the famous Esalen massage, which is accurately described as not only a physical but a mystical experience. He is also the author of numerous nonverbal exercises. Ida Rolf is a formidable woman who looks like Santa Claus and points out that "people don't move 'normally,' they move *averagely*." Although her technique of "structural realignment" is supposed to hurt a lot while it lasts, she has many devotees.

The Bod Biz person I chanced to spend most time with was Mary Whitehouse, who looks patrician in an Eastern way (and is in fact a graduate of Wellesley), and lithe in a patrician way (and was in fact a dancer). "But straight, ordinary dance struck me as being terribly sterile," she says. "It had lost the thing Isadora Duncan gave it that made it a vital art form." Having heard particularly rhapsodic accounts of weekend workshops she holds called "Movement in Depth," I signed up for one. I spent a Friday evening, most of a Saturday and half of a Sunday in her studio on Santa Monica Boulevard, with fourteen other leotarded people who were trying to get in touch with themselves.

We were not, as Mary kept telling us, dancing. "Finding out how the body moves is generic to dance, belongs to dance," she said, "but it is much broader than dance. The phrase 'dance therapy' has so much in it that I don't like and don't mean. My work is functional rather than expressive.

"Movement can help change tension," Mary said, "as much as relaxing can. Movement is a river you go swimming in, it's the flow of energy that carries you along. What you find, as you work with the movement [she meant physical, not human potential] is a dramatic physical corroboration of the pattern you know is essentially true of you. You get aware of what's inward." At one point in the weekend the music stopped, and we were told to stand frozen where and as we were. I froze with my hands held protectively in front of myself, almost like

168

a boxer's, as if I were afraid somebody might hit me. Clearly nobody had reason to or was about to, and this unplanned stance told me something undeniable if not pleasant about myself: that I am needlessly guarded.

Questions arise as a Whitehouse weekend continues. Are you open or closed? Are you running from or toward? Are your eyes closed because it's more comfortable that way, or because you don't want to look? Sometimes Mary played phonograph records, including a lengthy sequence of Indian raga music. Once in a while she would pound a drum or beat a gong as we swam in the "river of movement" around the room. Sometimes we were alone, sometimes not. I wasn't much interested in my partners. As they say in groups, I wasn't really into it. It occurred to me to go up and join one couple but I didn't presume to interrupt them.

"If you're not involved," Mary asked me, "is the feeling of being out of it directed against yourself? The risk would come if you knew you would be destroying something for Ann and Davis, and nevertheless went up near enough to see whether they would block you out, reject you, or whether your just *being* there would start something different for them. But if you just say, 'Oh, they're busy,' and stay here instead of exploring, then you'll never know where that impulse might have led you.

"As your movement brings you into orbit with somebody else—if you inadvertently touch somebody, or somebody goes by you—put your feelers out to see if that changes things. I set no premium on being angry or nasty, or proving that you can be violent as such, but I am interested in avoiding the business of *always* being kind, generous and loving. There are ways of learning to stand the fact that the time is not *right* to be with somebody else, and to be strong enough to show that fact to others."

Half a dozen or so of Mary's followers, whom it is tempting to call disciples, have their own studios. They are much more inclined than she is nowadays to go on the workshop-lecture circuit. She is content, for the time being, to hold weekend workshops in her studio. She is, as they say, going through some changes, in a state (as who in the human potential circles is not?) of analysis and inquiry. She even doubts the worth of groups. "I've found out over and over," she said, "that groups stopped the individuals from doing the things they needed. I think there's a lot more to be said for private work than some people think. I keep trying to avoid a method attitude. It's the inner, psychic movement that's continuous. You have to qualify where it's at for you, here and now. It's a semantic problem, of communicating not information but attitudes. I've been doing this for fifteen years, and the words are just now, slowly, beginning to come. I haven't got yet to the place where I can go directly to the source of what movement is. It's descriptive, poetic, intuitional and feeling. About all reading can tell you is that you've missed something."

But some practitioners of Bod Biz are fluent in discussing the merits of nonverbal communication. "Training isn't behavior," says John Weir. "I can say 'I hate you' or 'I love you,' but if all I do is *say* it, you're not likely to be convinced. Talking is a very pale, poor subtitle for behavior. I guess maybe this started toward the end of one of my early labs, ten or twelve years ago, when Guy A said, 'I really don't know you,' and Guy B said, 'I don't know you, either,' and I got the idea of telling them both: 'Why don't you walk to the center of the room and *do* something?' They did—they went and hugged each other, as it happened—and that taught them far more than they had known before, or could have learned otherwise.

"Joyce, meanwhile, observed that people in talking T-groups weren't really getting to know each other at all." Joyce Weir, like Mary Whitehouse, is a former professional dancer. Like Mary she co-leads laboratories with her husband, and sometimes with others. Joyce is as forthright and gentle and free of cumbersome neuroses as anybody on the group circuit. She is, as the blacks say, together. (So is her husband.)

"In Joyce's dance experience," John explained, "she had seen people communicate without talking, and she saw that in groups the process could be the same. She tried her own invention—having people express themselves with gestures rather than words. We tried it in T-groups and it was an immediate, tremendous success. In no time at all people were asking for it. We introduced it to the NTL in 1962, and right away the people who'd been exposed to it picked it up and took it off."

At the Weirs' lab I went to, people who swore they had never danced before in all their lives now did so, pliantly. I was moving with much more fluidity and grace than usual, and so were many others. The phonograph was on nearly all the time in the eight days that lab lasted—in between and after sessions until late at night, and even before breakfast, we danced as routinely as at home we read the paper. It was Joyce's encouragement, in our sessions in Body Movement, that loosened us up and metamorphosed us into dancing fools.

In one of these sessions she directed us all to collide with each other. Cheerful, slightly martial music was played as we lined up in parallel rows. The heads of both lines were told to cross to the bottom of the line opposite, which meant bumping into each other en route. The way people bumped was most revealing. Some did so with vigor and zest, but I went to elaborately playful lengths to avoid any confrontation at all, contriving frivolous do-si-dos, the same way in real, daily "back-home" life I go to unpleasant lengths to avoid unpleasantness.

In another Body Movement session, a few days later, we stood in a circle and were told to make the angriest gestures we could think of with (in turn) our arms, shoulders, feet, hands, heads and so on, working gradually up to a pitch of

171

anger no longer feigned. Then each of us was to step to the center of the room and act out whatever was the most angry thing we'd ever thought of doing in all our lives. However awful it was, we were supposed to act it out completely, in a kind of dance. Pillows from sofas were used as props, to be beaten, struck, pounded, thrashed and abused by people who imagined them to "be" whoever it was had made them mad.

Most of the angry gestures amounted to ritual murders. Many people had to be reminded: "Remember, it's only a pillow!" When I went to the center of the circle I didn't feel nearly as violent as some of the earlier people had seemed to. I thought I might do an amusing little vignette of the ire I remembered having felt in childhood for my sister. Today I like her almost more than anybody, but when I was nine and she was seven thoughts of sororicide seethed in both our heads. I pantomimed grabbing the tongs from the fireplace of our old living room. I took the tongs to the center of the room where I imagined our old walnut dining table to be, with her on the other side of the table. I feinted, now this way and now that, as if to chase her, round and round the imaginary table, chasing her and meaning to hit her. I got more and more into the spirit of things, and finally I did catch her, and beat her. Then she became the pillow, or rather the pillow became her, and I beat it with the imaginary tongs, yelling: "You little brat!"

"Remember," Joyce urged me, "it's only a pillow—it's all right, GET HER!" Since I hadn't said who my victim was I was amazed that Joyce could guess the gender. I kept on beating and stomping until Joyce asked, "Is she gone?" I said yes. But retired back in the circle, watching a couple of men "kill" their fathers, I knew I hadn't really finished her off. Newly released rage bubbled within me, and I knew I would have to go back and annihilate her. I did, yelling more, and beating on the hapless pillow till I was out of breath. This time it worked. An exhilarating and utterly novel flood of energy coursed through me. I wondered how much strength I had been deploying over the years to keep all that rage under tasteful wraps, and whether all the sequences of syllables in the world could have taught me the lesson this nearly wordless act had taught. But poor Ann—for that was, and I rejoice still is, my sister's name.

"Now I Leave
My Heart
at Home"

¶ Big Jim didn't need any of this sensitivity stuff. Big Jim loved his wife and he loved his family and he loved his work. He loved getting up in the morning and driving off to the plant almost as much as he loved returning home (outside Philadelphia) at night. Especially he loved coming home after a business trip. "I'd rather eat hamburger at home," Big Jim liked to say, "than sirloin on the road." He told us he saw his life as a range of mountains, one peak after another, just waiting to be ascended, "like a sort of challenge."

We called him Big Jim partly because our group also included a shorter, younger Jim, but also because he was so imposing. He was not at all loath to share his beliefs with us. The New Deal, for him a live issue even in late 1968, had defi-

174

nitely been a mistake. Anybody who wore a beard was *ipso facto* emotionally unstable. If the shiftless people in Appalachia and Harlem would just show a little initiative, self-made men like him would not have to be so heavily taxed to provide "doles" and "handouts." Nothing but their own sloth deprived those people of what he had: a wife who annually dyed Easter eggs, a quartet of children who insisted that he, not one of them, say the blessing at Thanksgiving and who still, grown though they were, hung up their stockings Christmas Eve. He also had a garden full of azaleas and peonies and zinnias. There was one thing he wanted to make clear to us about that garden, though: he could do without fussing over the lawn. "If there's one thing I hate," he made clear, "it's grass."

At this several in the room snickered, especially Phil. Phil had told us he'd just seen the movie, "I Love You, Alice B. Toklas," and therein learned a whole new connotation for the word "grass." Jeff and Stan knew it without having seen the movie. Jeff and Stan both wore long sideburns, and shocked the older, more settled men in that five-day lab by admitting there were things they cared more about than their jobs. Stan talked of a summer he had spent working on a kibbutz in Israel.

"But why would *you* want to do that?" asked Dom with profound bewilderment. "You're not even Jewish."

"For the experience," said Stan. Dom shrugged. His idea of fun, he said, would be to take the fastest possible supersonic plane to the south of France, where he had already been on several business trips, and "spend a week or two just laying on the Riviera."

Jeff had a particularly startling ambition. He hoped to save enough money to quit and take his wife to live in a fishing village in Portugal, where he would paint seascapes. Sylvia said she had been to Portugal on a round-the-world trip, and had met there a very nice American girl married to a "native" young man who was "terribly handsome, but do you know

175

what he *did?* He sold *postcards!"* Sylvia, whose plucked eyebrows made her resemble a seagull in flight, was in charge of all the sales personnel for a large chain of department stores. She looked awfully competent and, beneath a brittle veneer, awfully unhappy.

These people were among thirty whose souls I saw bared and before whom I bared part of my own at an intercompany laboratory for executives held in late November at a motel on Cape Cod. As that five-day lab began I despaired of ever caring about any of them. My usual reaction to business and businessmen is something between a yawn and a frown. I automatically throw out the business section of the Sunday *Times.* I pay ungratefully little heed to the world of commerce and the people who, by oiling its wheels, certainly benefit me as much as the next American consumer. Yet industry is one of the most receptive and adventurous patrons of sensitivity techniques, and I was clearly obliged to look into the effect these techniques were having on business.

This Cape Cod lab, led by the estimable trainers Herbert Shepard and Al Fitz, who teach psychology at the Yale Medical School, was my longest but by no means my first encounter with encountering businessmen. The first time I ever went to Esalen I saw how the movement was changing an executive named Osborne Apthorpe. Oz, as he urged us all to call him, didn't look like my sort. He seemed like a character out of Jacqueline Susann by Chester Gould, with Ayn Rand for godmother. With that close-cropped crewcut, automatic smile and ridiculously firm handshake, how could he possibly have more than one dimension? I had heard that he controlled a vast amount of real estate in Oklahoma, but that seemed the only interesting thing about him. But then he said, "I had the Protestant ethic tattooed on my ass, the Foxchapel Country Club creed on my belly, and they anointed me with Old Spice and sent me out into the world to make good." I thought then that Oz couldn't be all bad.

"Now I Leave My Heart at Home"

As "they," whoever "they" were, had expected, Oz had made good in the world. But even with his name in *Who's Who,* and money enough to have bought up a lot of the Big Sur coastline himself, he still wasn't happy. His marriage had failed. He was desperately out of touch with his children. The girl he had been seeing was exasperated with his stuffiness. He wasn't pleased, either, with the way things were going between him and the hundreds of people in his employ. This was Oz's second encounter group. From the first he had emerged with enough ebullience to last him all the way back to Tulsa, where he rushed with delight to visit his neglected kids, scooping them into his arms and regarding them as if for the first time ever.

"What's the matter, Daddy?" his twelve-year-old daughter had demanded. "Are you on *drugs* or something?" Oz was stunned. "I guess she'd never seen me enthusiastic before. I guess the men who work for me hadn't, either." And so he had returned to Esalen, with the hope of learning more about conveying the feelings he had so long and so very nearly successfully concealed.

Oz was atypical of most businessmen in encounters, who don't go to groups on their own but because their companies send them. The Cape Cod lab I went to was sponsored by several corporations with headquarters up and down the Atlantic Seaboard. Committed to the idea that their middle-management executives could benefit by five days of sensitivity training, the corporations pooled funds to hire trainers to work periodically with selected staff members.

Later I heard that one of these corporations had quit the program, disillusioned with the way the groups affected its men. Other firms elsewhere have also had second thoughts about the merits of sensitivity, "maybe," as one social scientist reflected, "because the danger is not that the group will fail but that it will *work*." A *Wall Street Journal* survey of sensitivity training verified this danger. It cited the cases of several businessmen who went into T-groups autocratic, tough and competitive, and came back so radically changed that they lost their jobs. Aware of such a possibility, the article said, many corporations have "turned away from the free-swinging, traditional T-groups to carefully planned sessions dealing not with personalities but with specific company problems." Sensitivity training, a General Electric spokesman was quoted, "is designed to change an individual, not necessarily to change the environment he works in." For this reason many businesses have come to rely more on continuing internal programs than on off-site T-groups.

Not to say that the off-site T-group isn't a thriving institution. The NTL's calendar is filled with such labs all over the country, geared to the special needs of key executives, middle-management workers and, in a few cases each year, corporation presidents. Although a cliché of the movement has it that lieutenants of industry are more kindly disposed toward sensitivity training than captains, Leland Bradford says the NTL presidents' labs are invariably poignant.

"The more money and security people have," he says, "the less likely they are to want to let down their defenses. They've got more to risk and more to lose. But guys who run corporations of over $500 million often say that those seven or eight days are the most important days of their lives.

"These men are very lonely. They've been taught that any sign of weakness is despicable. For them, even a small revelation is cathartic. They're men who have nobody to talk to, no peers—even their wives usually just function as hostesses. Our labs let them talk about their anxieties and fears and strengths to other people, on their own level."

NTL prefers to work with companies which will commit five years of their time. As a sideline fact, Bradford says, "It's true that in almost every case the stock of the company has gone up. They become more financially healthy. The same forces that help individuals to learn help industries too."

"Now I Leave My Heart at Home"

This is so because to suppress feelings for the sake of ritual and politeness is also to suppress creativity and innovation. Such an atmosphere leads to what Chris Argyris of Yale University calls a "closed-circuit system." One such system was the dry-cleaning chain whose executives I had met during a workshop the previous June at a motel in the middle of Long Island. The firm had been a closed-circuit system, at least before new management had taken it over and hired Robert Allen to shake things up. Allen runs Scientific Resources, Inc.

"You guys," said Allen, "probably spend more time together than you do with your wives, but you don't really know each other. You aren't really friends, are you?"

"It's no good to get *too* close to people," said the dry-cleaning firm's new president. "I used to lead with my heart, but I found out that wasn't such a good idea. The first time I ever fired a guy it turned out he had five kids and a wife dying of cancer. I *listened* to him, and it wrecked me. Since then, I don't listen. I don't socialize. I don't want to meet the wives of guys I might have to fire. I don't feel comfortable being what I'm not, and I know I'm not a people person. Now I leave my heart at home."

"The best thing you could do for *me,*" said another, "would be to make it a seven-day work week. I sort of unwind over the weekend, and it takes me until Tuesday morning to get back in action. I know me Mondays, and so does my secretary. Somebody wants to see me on a Monday, I try to get her to put them off."

Allen told each of those men to show the others something on his person that would tell them something they wouldn't have known about him otherwise. One man took from his wallet the torn half of a dollar bill he and his brother had argued over thirty-five years earlier. "My mother got so sick of hearing us fight," he said, "that she tore the bill in two to show us how useless it was. The lesson stuck with us both."

Another man confessed immoderate pride in the cashmere

179

Please Touch

sweater he was wearing. "I don't know if it's a warped sense of pleasure or not," he said, "but I come from a poor family, and in certain things I like to go first class. Like I'd rather have one drink of Scotch than two of blended."

The company's president, a proud and self-made man, pointed to his wristwatch. "See this?" he said. "When I was a soldier in Germany all the guys wanted to go home with either watches or cameras. They were a lot cheaper there, but even so I couldn't afford the Swiss watch I had my heart set on. I promised myself I'd get one someday if it was the last thing I ever did. I had a phobia about it, the way my wife had a phobia for a baby grand piano. Now she has the piano and I have the watch and so what? Like how many beds can you sleep in at once? I have a different prospectus from life now. What do you do for an encore?"

That president had probably never heard of Abraham Maslow's concept of "higher-order needs," or of the difference between "D-motivation" (D for deficiency) and "B-motivation" (B for being). But that's what he was talking about all the same: values, and how once one's survival needs are met other, vaguer dissatisfactions still remain. The watch and the piano are not enough.

Such concerns are about to confront a great many people on a colossally expanded scale. Before long only one in five adults will be obliged to "work" to produce what the rest of the population requires. Automation continues to rob people of jobs, and many remaining jobs of their dignity. Students of such matters wonder what will replace work as the controller of people's behavior. And they wonder how people can be expected to have any regard for each other, or even themselves, if they can't take pride in what they do.

Men in high echelons, of course, only laugh wryly at the prospect of a work-free world. It won't happen in their lifetimes, at least not to them. It is they who must shepherd automation through its present growing pains, and they in particu-

180

lar who must get accustomed to and comfortable with change.

"It used to be that one guy would own a company," Leland Bradford says. "That guy would be strong, dominant and autocratic, and he would have arrived there by his own brilliance, hard work and other solid American virtues. But it isn't like that anymore. Now we have professional management, not ownership." In some quarters this is known as "entrepreneurial," as opposed to "dynamic," leadership. "A guy just doesn't have the same stake," Bradford says, "if he's only responsible to a board of directors, instead of to himself. In company after company, the poor president doesn't know as much as the scientists do. The scientists are usually way ahead of the bosses, because management now is so much more complex."

The state of technology has made such a situation inevitable, Argyris thinks. "Computer technology now makes it possible to generate and organize information far beyond the capacity of any one man to understand, much less evaluate," he says. "You've got to have a top management team to deal with the amount and complexity of information there is today."

Corporations aware of these baffling and accelerating changes spend millions of dollars a year to have their people opened and made more flexible. More and more companies deal in services (as opposed to goods and food). There is little to distinguish one tankful of gasoline or one jetliner voyage to Los Angeles from another, except for the width and sincerity of the staff's smiles. Technical expertise isn't the problem. Jollity and empathy are what the customers want. If you weren't born jolly and empathetic, you can learn these traits in a weekend or five-day workshop, or so claim the several firms that deal in sensitivity training. One man whom they changed, a perhaps apocryphal IBM employee, is said to have changed the plaque in his office from "THINK" to "THINK AND FEEL."

181

Please Touch

A lot of these programs are called O.D., meaning Organizational Development. One of the leading vendors of O.D., rumored to be the first behavioral scientist ever to become a millionaire, is Robert Blake, who with his partner, Jane Mouton, runs a firm called Scientific Methods, Inc. Blake's design is called the "Grid Lab." Grid Labs fall toward the cerebral, right-wing end of the human potential spectrum. They are based on charts that measure the degree to which managers are "people-oriented" or "production-oriented." Each trait to be measured is rated on a scale of one to nine. A 9.1 person cares more about production and less about firing an unproductive employee. A 1.9 is more worried about running a happy shop than competing. A 5.5 strives for balance and in so doing doesn't much impress anybody.

"The person who knows least about a company," Blake says, "is the one who's been in it longest. He's culturally entrapped. He can't change. It's in his muscles, his bones and under his fingernails." Blake's Grid Labs have spread to twenty-three countries, 700 companies and affected 150,000 people. The headquarters for all this activity are in Austin, Texas, which has a thriving "growth center" called Laos House. Austin also has sheltered my ubiquitous trainer friend Michael Kahn, along with my former president. I don't suppose Kahn's path and Johnson's have crossed, but the human potential business is full of surprises.

At the Cape Cod lab everybody's attention focused late the first night on Marilyn. Widowed five years earlier, she was aggressively defensive about the job she held with a large manufacturing company. "I wish I were a dingaling," she said. "Dingalings may be dumdums, but they're happier. My girlfriend's a dingaling, and she's perfectly happy because she's toilet-trained her three-year-old daughter. I wish that little could make *me* happy." Marilyn was accused of, and scolded for, phoniness. Why should she be content with small accomplishments, when obviously she was capable of larger ones? Why didn't she take more pride in supporting her own three children as well as holding down an important job? This went on for some time, until Marilyn asked: "Isn't it someone *else's* turn to be the dartboard?"

"I'm not sure I like that term 'dartboard,' " Herb Shepard said. "I don't see this as a dart-throwing session, unless you mean the kind of darts that have rubber suction cups instead of points."

"Oh, Herb," said Sylvia, the sales manager, "how can you *take* it? You've been so patient, putting up with all of us."

"Oh, Sylvia," Jeff mimicked, "how can you stand to be so damn *motherly?* Maybe that's why you never found a man, because you mothered the hell out of all of them." (Jeff had told us he had six children. "It was easy," he said.)

"That's not true," Sylvia protested, "I *have* found some, I *have* had chances. But the one I really wanted to marry—the only one I ever really cared for—he turned out to be as mean as a snake." Sylvia's false cheer melted. She cried. Stan comforted her. "I take back what I said about your looking like a used-car salesman," she said. He patted her on the back.

Many facades changed in the course of our five days on Cape Cod. Much of the unmasking took place in the course of extended and unstructured T-groups, during which people talked much more revealingly than seemed usual for any of them. Some of the changes were probably generated by the planned exercises Shepard gave us. In one the two groups into which we were divided competed at building paper towers. At an "auction" we made bids for colored cardboard, construction paper, Scotch tape, scissors, stapler, glue and staples, at prices starting at $25,000. Each team was supposed to design and construct a tower taller, stronger and more esthetically pleasing than the other's, using only the materials available. In figuring out such problems as the division of labor, we were

183

supposed to learn something about how each one of us functioned in a group, as well as about how groups interact and compete. I protested that this wasn't my kind of thing, that I had no knack whatever for engineering or building, and that I'd better just watch. But I was pressed into service as a color consultant, to advise where to put the yellow cardboard in relation to the red and the black. When Dom drew a design for the tower he envisioned on our blackboard, I feigned interest —not very cleverly, it seemed—and asked, "How many sides does that tower have?"

"Did you ever wonder how many sides *we* have?" Little Jim asked. When our team ran out of staples and had nothing else with which to stick parts of the tower together, somebody suggested we could cheat and use chewing gum. I ran helpfully to the motel desk to buy some. The finished tower didn't look like much, and the judges challenged our use of "strange and unauthorized organic fixatives." The other team won. We didn't care: By that time all of us were interested in learning more about each other.

Then, as part of a nonverbal afternoon, came the incident of the lemons. We split into groups of six and sat on the floor. In the middle of each group a sack of six lemons was opened. Each of us was to select a lemon and "get to know it" by inspecting, feeling, looking at, smelling and memorizing our individual lemons. Then all the lemons were reshuffled in the sack and set down again. We each had to find our own. It was quite easy; no lemon could have had quite the same ridge just below its navel that mine had, or its purple brand name stamped on it in quite the same blurred way. I would literally have known it anywhere. The others were retrieved with equal haste by their owners. We all were permitted to keep our lemons, as reminders that if pieces of fruit were so distinctive one from another, so must humans be.

We were getting that message anyway. We were so interested in talking to each other that nobody slept much, and most of us smoked a lot. "My mouth feels as if I've been licking ashtrays," said Marilyn. Fred, a blatantly unobtrusive man who had earlier said that most people here and elsewhere were "just zeroes" to him, mellowed and softened. He told us how in the yard outside his house he had watched a robin fluttering to feed her babies, keeping very still so as not to attract rapacious bluejays to the scene. Stan, who aspired to go to Portugal, told how he watched birds, too, and how he had seen a "psychotic and bigamous" wren in his yard build two houses for two wives.

This group would have struck the Big Sur set as hopelessly straight and square. The subject of sex scarcely came up. "I've only danced with one woman in my life," Art said, "and that's my wife. The first time we ever danced together, at a Sea Scout Hallowe'en party, my older brother came up and said 'If I ever catch you dancing that close with another woman, I'll knock your block off.' " I did hear Dom ask Hank, "Do you close your eyes when you kiss an individual? I don't." When we had a spontaneous evening of blowing soap bubbles and doing pictures with finger paint, some of them playfully painted each other's faces while they were at it. But not all. Big Jim cringed at the very idea. Some of the soap bubbles had cigar smoke in them, which made me feel a little sick.

After the bubble-blowing—which apparently was the only spontaneous and silly thing at least half of the people in the lab had done in their entire adulthood—we went back to our group room to talk. Hank, who had been our purchasing agent in the auction, said he didn't care much for hippies with long hair.

"I don't see that it costs that much to be clean," he said reasonably, in a Boston accent as thick as Louise Day Hicks's. "I have nothing against them, but once when I tried to talk to one of them in a far-out coffee house, I had to get out when the ventilation blew my way." Hank was a prime exponent of the virtues of holy matrimony. "I'm proud to be married," he

185

said, "and proud to wear my wedding ring. I love anniversaries and rituals. I hope we'll have three or four kids: I'd like to have a great big dinner table on Sundays with a big family there, like my father had."

Jeff, alluding to Big Jim's metaphor of life as a series of challenging mountain ranges, asked what my mountains were. "To finish this book," I said, "and to keep on writing and working, and to get married and have a baby."

"Whoa, there," said Art, "do you really want to get married? Why bother?"

"Because," I said, "I'm secretly square. I think a kid should have a daddy." This enormously pleased the men, who said, practically in unison, "Well, then? What's keeping you? Why don't you settle down? There must be men in your life."

"There *are*," I said, "and I like a lot of them. But I can't decide. I'm selfish and shallow . . ."

"Wait a minute," said Herb, "is that you talking or your puritan grandmother?"

"I guess it's partly her," I said, "because there's part of her and part of a lot of other people in me. But not just her. I really am shallow and selfish, along with a lot of nicer things."

Art hadn't said much, and I tried to deflect attention from myself by trying to draw him out. "How about you?" I asked him. "Do you miss your wife when you're not with her?"

"No."

"Does she miss you when you're away?"

"Yes."

"Why don't you . . . "

"Just a minute, Jane," said Herb, "you've gone too far. You shouldn't just keep grilling Art that way without giving something of yourself while you're at it. Reveal something of *you,* like 'that's the kind of trap *I* don't want to get into,' or maybe 'that's why *I've* avoided marriage . . . "

Dom wanted to talk about his company. "Kill or bill," he said, "that's all anybody there ever cares about. There are

186

"Now I Leave My Heart at Home"

white crosses all over the place. Destroy somebody else is the only way to get ahead there." As he spoke he poured himself a second highball. "We don't drink much at home," he explained. "My wife always says things like, 'What, a cocktail for the *second* time in a week? Aren't you afraid you'll turn into a drunk?' She cares about me, though. She wishes I wouldn't always wear the same blue suit with the same black tie. I don't mean I only have one suit and one tie, I mean . . ."

"Sure, baby," said Stan, "we know." He meant it; we did know. Dom needn't be nervous and frenetic with us. We all could be a little more relaxed with each other than we might ever have thought possible.

Later that night we sat around in our room, found a candle, and turned the light out. Herb felt moved to lead us in a "collective fantasy trip." He asked us to close our eyes, sit back and suppose that all of us, together, were entering a haunted, vacant house in the country, which we had reached by bus. The house, he said, had not been occupied for some while. Somewhere in that house was a treasure.

The ensuing fantasy, to which we all contributed, was rich with allusion to things all of us had revealed about ourselves. We decided to enter the house via the rusty, mouldy cellar door.

"It's scary in this house, and it smells," said Sylvia.

"Oh, it isn't *that* bad," I said. "What's in that trunk over there?"

"I think that's the trunk Jake was born in," said Herb. Jake actually was born to a theatrical family.

"There are yellow baby clothes in the trunk," said Marilyn, "and a rolled-up paper. Is it a map?"

It turned out to be a poem written ten years ago by Little Jim, which he had brought with him to this session, and now read. Nobody had thought of Little Jim as any kind of poet. Everybody was touched, some to the point of tears.

"There's a second cellar below this one," said Herb. "See,

187

the door is over there. Would anyone like to try to get down there?" Nobody wanted to; the prospect was too scary.

"There's a player piano," said Phil, "with the score of 'Moonlight and Roses' "—a song he had vigorously objected to having to hear, almost nonstop, on the motel's Muzak system. Then, in fantasy, we all trooped upstairs to a bedroom with a huge round bed on which fourteen bodies were decomposing. This thought was not quite as depressing as it sounded.

"The bodies are entirely decomposed now," said Stan, "and the bed is turning into a roulette wheel. There's only one bowlegged old lady left there, with crossed eyes. Let's just leave her, okay?"

"Sure," everyone agreed. "Hey, look," Hank said. "This chimney has loose bricks. Why, here's a dumb-waiter. This kitchen must have been built a long time ago, because everything's built to a scale so much smaller than people our size would need."

"Look at that big copper pot over there."

"Did you say 'pot'?"

"What does that calendar on the wall say," I asked, "1960 or 1690?" Nobody could quite tell. We went back to the room where the bowlegged lady waited. Somebody said there was a hairbrush on the dresser with faded gray hairs in it, and a silver handle. "Sure," I said, "and there are initials on the brush, and the initials are D.L.B." (a monogram which meant nothing to me or anyone I know).

"*What* initials did you say?" asked Herb. I told him. "Why, that's the name of my barge!" he said. "I call it DLB-407 after my three children: David, Eloise and Brian."

"What shall we do with that hairbrush?" asked Sylvia.

"Shake the pot at it!"

"Did someone say 'pot'?"

"Hey, look, there's a roll of rolled-up grass wallpaper."

"Did somebody say 'grass'?"

"Now I Leave My Heart at Home"

"Over there," said Herb, "is a 200-year-old soap bubble. Why, it's turned into a crystal ball! Maybe that's the treasure we've all come here to look for?"

That was just what it was. I was the only one to see myself in the ball, burping a baby, who somehow was blowing smoke bubbles, as a man looked on. Dom said he saw me being watched by 40 million people, which was how many he thought read *Life,* my lapsed connection with which impressed him immoderately. Hank was presiding over just the kind of Sunday dinner table he said he remembered from his own childhood and longed to have for himself. And there was Jeff with 23 children, and there was Art coming down in a parachute! I was the one who saw that.

"How did you know," Art asked, "that parachuting was one of my ambitions?" I hadn't known, but somehow this was my big night for E.S.P.

"Whoops," somebody said, "be careful! Art's parachute isn't opening!"

"Yes it is," Marilyn said, "he's landing in a pretty coral reef —and right next to it is a beautiful wooden house he built entirely by himself."

There too was Dom, taking an SST to the Suez Canal to work in a spaghetti field on a *kibosh,* which was how he pronounced *kibbutz.* There came Stan with a used car on his back. There came Fred and Jake, both talking a lot. There was Sylvia with a nice-looking man and a couple of what looked very much like stepchildren.

"I'd like to leave the house," said Big Jim. "There's a cemetery outside. Let's go look at it." But nobody wanted to join him.

The next and final morning we met to talk over all that had happened. Big Jim, who knew a lot about chemistry, told us about the soap bubbles we had blown. "A bubble," he said, "is composed of surfactant molecules (that's a contraction of surface-active molecules). Those molecules are like soldiers

189

which have united to form the bubble. When the bubble hits the ground, they will disappear. There's always the hope that the bubble will last, but it never does. Bubbles always burst. And it's the same way with soldiers who have got together here to form this bubble we've had."

Big Jim hurried back to Philadelphia to hamburgers and blissful domesticity. He left unchanged. Nobody else did, though. Reports I heard many months later intimated that other bubbles were still aloft.

"Have You Been in Good Contact with Your Legs This Week?"

¶ "The way *you* vibrate," I was told, "you're like a Ford that's been in the garage for a year. See that guy over there, the one who sort of hums like a Cadillac? He's got the right idea. Still, what you're doing is better than nothing. It's a start, anyway. Feel it?"

As a New York cab driver might have put it: what did they think, I was crazy? Sure I felt it. It wasn't exactly my standard posture, arms akimbo on hips, head back, pelvis forward, legs bent and involuntarily atremble. I had graduated to this exercise after mastering what felt like an even odder one: standing with the small of my back leaning against a tautly rolled Army blanket strapped to the top of a kitchen stepladder,

191

arms high aloft as I alternately sighed and gasped and heard others around me uttering stranger noises still:

"You bitch!"

"Leave me alone!"

"No! No! No!"

"I can't!"

"I won't!"

Some yelled like caged lions, some like whimpering babies, some like trapped moose. The room we were in, which happened to be at Esalen, sounded like a torture chamber and looked like a four-ring circus. There were three other stepladders besides mine. Against each one leaned another member of our five-day workshop in a new discipline called Bioenergetic Analysis. Each of the four of us was surrounded by a quizzical crowd of people awaiting their turns. And each was hovered over by a specialist whose mission in life is to rid clients of the "scar tissue" which hides evidence of early traumas, psychic and otherwise. The specialists were uncannily perceptive. "I can just look at your feet," one of them said, "and tell all I need to know about you." A couple of the men present agreed that they really did, as the doctors guessed, play "brother roles"—treating their wives like little sisters. One woman conceded she was a "virgin flirt"—the kind who holds back, expects men to go after her, but doesn't ever really yield. "Such a woman," said Stanley Keleman (whom I found the most imposing of the Bioenergetic therapists) "is always seventeen years old, even when she's fifty-eight and married. These roles were much more common under the double standard. So was that of the old authoritarian father figure, but don't worry, he's still alive and kicking somewhere."

A lot of us were alive and kicking right there in that room. In addition to the stepladders there were also four different piles of mattresses. The mattresses had a vexing tendency to slither apart when vibrating novices lay on them, kicking their legs at ninety-degree angles and pumping their arms up and

192

down like the chugging pistons of the oil derricks of El Segundo. (*Their* arms? Who am I kidding? *Our* arms.) It was a strange scene, but it had its folksy notes. One woman, obviously a veteran Bioenergetics devotee, offered a suggestion. "You know what I do to keep the mattresses from slithering apart?" she said. "I Velcro them together. Works real good."

One man, who complained of indecision, was told to "get in touch with your uncertainty. Stay with it. It will talk to you sooner or later, one way or the other." Some people submitted to having their jaws and foreheads and chests pressed by the formidably determined hands of the Bioenergists. They wanted us to mobilize all the energy we wasted suppressing feelings of anger and sex. Such feelings, they maintained, weren't nearly as lurid and shameful as we probably feared. If we'd breathe deeply enough and yell and kick properly, we might get them out of the way.

"You don't *have* a body," said Keleman, "you *are* your body. Your body is your past and your past is your body. Every muscular contraction in your body represents an unspoken *no*. Our aim is to get your body to speak out that *no,* so you can feel alive. The moment you start to flow you'll really feel all the anger in you. The problem isn't more aliveness, but bearing the aliveness we already have, freeing blocked energy from tight muscles to produce movement and feeling and life—the awe and mystery of breathing and being alive."

Keleman, who lives and works in Berkeley and wears a size XXXL cardigan, exudes an aura at once masculine and maternal. John and Joyce Weir, among others, swear by him. His following on the West Coast probably outnumbers the New York enthusiasts of his mentor Alexander Lowen. Lowen, the founder of Bioenergetic Analysis, is a chronic pipe-smoker who looks like an eager Jewish Spencer Tracy. He and Keleman were being assisted for this workshop, as they are in some others, by John Pierrakos of New York City and Jack McIntyre of Detroit. All but Keleman are medical doctors.

Please Touch

Twenty of us were there for five days to do their bidding. One workshop member, put off by the unearthly screams, cut out the first day, but the others stayed on. Most of them apparently planned to apply what they learned in their own encounter groups. Although Bioenergetics is essentially an individual, intrapersonal matter, many think it is best learned in a group setting. "A lot more dramatic things happen with groups around," said one enthusiast. "I guess it's because you build up toward a sort of collective energy level. People watch this stuff and get all involved. Each successive session gets more explosive."

With all that energy being liberated all over the place, we didn't need many clothes. We'd been told to bring bathing suits, but the several of us who had forgotten now stood around vibrating in just our underwear. I thought of how certain mothers, among them my own, used to caution their young to be sure and wear clean lingerie in case they got run over. Never would they have understood this scene, or believed that the prevailing mood was not erotic or prurient. The prevailing determination, so help me, was to set the energy aflow from the core of our beings to our skin. "When the energy or the feeling flows," Lowen said, "the skin has a better color, the breathing is deeper and fuller, circulation improves, and throat tensions diminish."

Sex was talked about, but without leering or mustache twirling. Maybe it was Keleman's influence. What he said about sex—some of it, anyway—might have reassured those mothers with the advice about underwear. "The amount of sexual licentiousness and experimentation that go on amid all this 'freedom' we have now," he said, "is a tremendous copout. Without the heart's commitment you have no human sexuality. The illusion prevalent in this culture is that we must deny either our heads or our bodies. That's untrue. You can't really hide your sexual feelings. They have to go somewhere. A woman who is fully identified with her sexual feelings attracts you as a total personality, not as a sexual object. Sexuality is an attitude toward life, a state of being. To be alive sexually is to regulate your own sexuality for deepest pleasure."

"Sometimes," Lowen contributed, "it would be better for people to get at a punching bag than to have sex. Sex is of course one of the strongest involuntary aspects of human functioning, but people misuse it. The mind fears sex because the conscious mind is obscured in the thought of orgasm. Orgasm signifies the discharge of all your excess energy. The self is submerged when it unites with another. The more you commit yourself to any activity, the more pleasure it will give you. To commit yourself to life is to commit yourself to your body. We should let the body take over, and not be so egotistically arrogant. The body will heal itself. It's a creation of nature. If nature can't sustain life, then nothing can.

"We must learn to let go and accept and express the body's feelings. Sex is primarily a function of the lower end of the body, and valid sexual movements develop when the feet are firmly rooted in the ground, which is to say the earth. Feeling moves up from below, not down from above. Only when the energy is able to flow all the way to the feet and come back from there can you be open. If a person is rooted in the earth he'll be okay, because he'll press down on the earth, and it will press back and send him energy."

Lowen, as his beliefs might suggest, is considered a neo-Reichian, which is to say a follower of the controversial psychoanalyst Wilhelm Reich. Lowen was in fact analyzed by Reich, an analysand of Freud himself. The difference between classical Reichian work and his own, Lowen said, is that "Reich tried to unfreeze the body from the eyes down, whereas I work more from the feet up. Reich thought that if a person could give in to sexual feelings everything else would be okay. I think anger and other repressed feelings often come before sex.

"The involuntary pelvic movements of sexuality do not

195

start from the head, but from the tail. Most people's sex is head-directed, and that's called fucking. True sex, as opposed to fucking, is spontaneous and concentrated in the lower end of the body. It's not the average pushing, ass-tightening shoving it in; it's a rocking of the whole body, starting from the lower end. The point of it isn't orgasm, but a free flow of energy, to make a person function better and enjoy life more.

"I wish it were true that if you could get a person to have an orgasm then all his problems would be over," Lowen said. "It is true, though, that as you get more integrated and more in touch with your feelings, then your sex will be better, too. If people don't come to terms with their bodies, they're lost. The way a person moves on a couch in this room is the product of 2,000 or 5,000 years of civilization."

Evenings we either had such discussions as these or saw movies of Lowen at work with his regular private patients. (One such film commenced with the memorable line: "Hello! Have you been in good contact with your legs this week?") Daytimes we would take turns "working." I drew big crowds when my turn came, probably because I was the most clinically challenging case around.

"Look at her eyes," somebody said. "Look at all that sadness and anger and fright. She pushes people away with her eyes."

They looked. "The look in your eyes is less afraid *right now*," someone else said. "No—you've lost it again—*there,* that's more like it was before, *there! That's it!*" Then somebody said to glare, to stick my jaw out, to be mad.

"But," I said to my bioenergist, "I'm *not* mad at *you.*" He sighed. Would I never get the point?

"Stand the way you are," he said, "and you're literally a pushover. You don't stand as if you were on your own two feet. You're like a good little girl who says 'yes' to everything. There are some things you *shouldn't* say 'yes' to. You'll say 'no' better if you stand with your knees bent. Keep them bent

196

all the time, in movie lines, at the supermarket, everywhere."

"I'll try to," I promised. Then somebody noticed my jaw.

"She's got what we call a glass jaw," said a dentist in the crowd. "It's a typical English jaw—you know, chin up, stiff upper lip, don't cry, that sort of thing."

"But I *do* cry sometimes," I said.

"Sometimes," Lowen said tantalizingly, "isn't enough for the hurt you've suffered in your life."

"Well," I said, "I *was* in this car accident last winter ..."

"That accounts for a lot of it, probably," he said, "but not all by any means. Come on over here and try the kicking." I lay down and kicked. "Not like *that*," he scolded, "not like a child in a tantrum, but assertively! Come *on!* Get *with* it! One! Two! Three! Four! It's fun, isn't it? See, the bottom half of your body doesn't *have* to be separated from the top half. You really have a great deal of anxiety." Suddenly he pressed his fingers down hard on my jaw. For some reason that did seem to send a rush of presumably unlocked energy through all of me. But when I sat up he asked, "See how tight the back of her neck is?"

The only thing I was any good at was banging on three piled mattresses and yelling *"No! No! No! No!"* I had this surprising flair because the requisite energy comes from above the waist, where in my case it was accessible. (My classic "pelvic block" wasn't so disgraceful; some people were blocked all the way up to the chest.) But I didn't know how to make a fist. Dove of peace that I'd falsely imagined myself to be, free of vexing aggressions, I didn't know you were supposed to wrap your thumb around your first two fingers. I learned, though, and progressed from hitting with my hands to using a tennis racket, thwacking down with a violent surge, and trying to release all the No!s of three decades of docility—of making Daddy and Mommy proud, of getting promoted, of having bylines, of being popular, of reflecting credit on the troop, the adviser room, the sorority, and doing whatever X, Y or Z

197

might want me to, lest X, Y or Z be depressed. If complying made *me* depressed, I'd pretend it didn't. Be polite. Have you written your thank-you notes yet? Smile. Hello-Grandmother-it's-wonderful-to-be-here. Hi-Jenny-how's-school? No-Edmund-I-can't-go-to-the-movies-tonight-but-do-call-next-week. No, damn it, *don't* call next week. Don't call ever! *No! No! No!*

Somebody else held his rib cage up too far. Others were too concerned about letting their stomachs stick out. Nearly everybody was afraid to reach out for love. "We all have that fear," Lowen said. "It's a question of how deep the fear goes." A minister broke down in tears when he realized that "most of my life has been spent holding people, at funerals and in hospitals, but whenever anyone tried to hold *me,* even when I desperately wanted them to, I somehow still couldn't let them." But now he was letting them; at least he was being held by a woman who suddenly marveled that the two lines she'd worn for years on her forehead, "like a macadam road," seemed to have disappeared.

An alumnus of a German boarding school, where it had been a matter of considerable pride never to cry, now also wept. Another young man I had met before and considered gently erudite was analyzed as having "a quality of ominous, menacing stillness. He's silent and rigid, as if he were saying 'Watch out for me, or I might have to kill you.' " That young man worked himself up to a laudable frenzy on his pile of mattresses.

"Don't leave me!" he yelled. *"Please don't leave me!"* I couldn't figure out whether his parents, thirty-some years earlier, had or hadn't left him. There was much talk of his and everybody's parents, whose specters were resurrected all over the place. Keleman traces many problems back to unresolved Oedipal conflicts. When one girl stood up before the group, he said, "You can tell by the tension in her chest how *she* is in the world. What she's saying to all men is 'I dare you to make

198

me love you, because if you don't, you're not a man, and I'm not a woman. I really want to be loved like a little girl, not a woman.' A girl shouldn't mobilize her father's genitality. She won't, as long as her father has a good relationship with her mother or at least with *some* woman. But if his sex life isn't right, then his unsatisfied condition will be projected onto the child, and she'll feel that her femininity is rejected. It's the same with sons and mothers. When things aren't right, a child senses it and generates fantasies about being Daddy's girl or Mommy's boy. He'll grow up resenting the parent of his own sex and unable ever to surrender or give in."

In some Bioenergetics workshops, though not in ours, people are taught how to vomit. "It's the right reaction to something unpalatable you've swallowed, physically or emotionally," said Lowen. "You don't have to accept what you don't like. You can get rid of it symbolically. Doing so puts you more in touch with the animal kind of thing. You know the way a dog's stomach retches, pumps in and out and discharges what it doesn't need? You can do the same thing. Drink two or three glasses of water, put your thumb down your throat, and release the energy you were using to suppress whatever it was you couldn't accept. In the same way, unrelaxed ass muscles lead to hemorrhoids and constipation, and a cold often means blocked-up tears."

After five days such funkiness scarcely fazed us. Even the raucous decibel level seemed less shattering. There was one frightening moment toward the end of the workshop, though. A pretty woman who had been lying on a mattress, kicking and shrieking in unspecified rage, suddenly went into what looked to my medically ignorant eyes like an epileptic convulsion. I thought she might die, right there. Her back arched and her irises rolled out of sight and she writhed off her pile of unvelcroed mattresses and onto the floor. Two bioenergists grabbed her, manipulated her, cajoled her, and with consummate gentle finesse brought her to. She sobbed for a while and then seemed to feel just fine, aside from having cut her finger on the edge of the window.

Her nine-year-old boy had come along from San Rafael to play with the several resident children at Esalen while she attended the Bioenergetics sessions. That night at supper he noticed the bandage on her hand. If I had not been sitting at their table to overhear their dialogue myself, I would have thought it too cloying to be true.

"How did you hurt your finger, Mommy?" the boy asked.

"I was working out some angry feelings I had about Grandma," his mother said.

"Why?" the boy wondered. "What did she do to make you mad? We haven't even *seen* her since last summer."

"It was things Grandma did a long time ago," said the mommy. "Things she did that made me mad when I was little like you are now. But when I was little I didn't show my feelings the way you do now. Getting mad, the way you do, is better, don't you think?"

"I guess it is, Mommy," said her son. "If people didn't know how to be angry they wouldn't be human, would they?"

Of There
and Then

❡ I lay down on a mattress as the group converged around me. Somebody took my glasses and I shut my eyes. I was told to picture myself as being very tiny and going into my body by any orifice I chose. Rather unimaginatively I entered by the mouth. In my mind's eye was a vivid picture of the minuscule me, dressed in the same white nylon turtleneck and red slacks I really was wearing that day. I clambered over giant white teeth which, despite their gold inlays, resembled the rocks where the ocean assaults the California coast. I slid down my slippery throat, feeling a little claustrophobic because it was so narrow, and on into the torso.

The journey, called a "guided daydream" or "body trip" and led by William Schutz, lasted an hour or so. From a sunny beach on Cape Cod, I went into a room lined with paisleyish red and yellow watered silk that looked like the endpapers of old books, and on to a zoo whose cage bars were in fact my ribs. Next I found a secret sliding rock panel behind my lungs. It led down to the intestines, which contained a roller coaster. A ride on that roller coaster led out of my body, which I entered a second time, more originally, through the eyes. The insides of my eyes were like tiny rooms with railings on all the walls, and tricky sliding floors like those in amusement parks. ("Could mean mental imbalance," Schutz later reflected.)

I went back to the beach where this time there was a congenial group of strangers. Their faces didn't register but their names, it was quite clear, were Robin, George, Sally and Kitty. Kitty was a baby. They offered me some of their picnic lunch and invited me to join them for a walk along the shore. I did so with pleasure. The walk led to a room with sticky red walls. As I described this room, aware even with shut eyes that the group was gathered close around to hear me, Schutz gently said: "There's a calendar on that wall. Can you tell me the date on the calendar?" Sure I could: I even threw in gratuitously that it was a Pan-American calendar, turned to April 1948, which was when I was finishing eighth grade and when my self-esteem had reached an all-time nadir.

Next came a loathsome game called German Dodgeball in the girls' gymnasium of Skokie Junior High School, the entire floor plan of which I was suddenly able to recall in precise Nabokovian detail. I wished aloud that I had contrived to get an excuse from the school nurse from this gym period. I had to wear an ugly, cumbersome leather-and-wire mask as a glasses guard, and I was self-conscious enough without it. Then, for some reason, came a side trip down to my feet, which I always (especially in eighth grade) had considered much too big, but which now seemed just the right size. And there was another detour to the hands and fingers, from which remote territory, I reported with delight, it was possible to return not by a laborious climb, but via a handy elevator that zoomed me non-stop right back up to the shoulder.

The upshot of all this, Schutz later theorized, was that I was in effect reborn, exorcised of my unflattering self-image as an awkward and ungainly thirteen-year-old. I had thought this ghost had been laid some time back, but apparently not. Exposing it thus in public fantasy acquainted me as nothing had before with the meaning of such words as *satori* and *nirvana*. For the first time since I had been at Esalen, I was told I didn't look uptight at all. Maybe it was even a Peak Experience.

This "body trip" was one of several departures I experienced from the encounter groups' customary reverence for the Here-and-Now. The theory is that in real life we often avoid the Here-and-Now, colluding to divert each other from its harshness. We chatter, instead, about how many miles we get to the gallon or what a pretty dress you're wearing or what sort of a president Humphrey would have made. To talk of *How you feel right this minute sitting in this room in that chair talking to me* is difficult and unsettling, but worthwhile: it makes us know what we really feel, which surprisingly many people don't.

Judiciously handled excursions into the There-and-Then, like my body trip, can be another route to the same goal. In other groups I became a dragonfly skimming over a pond, a turtle sunning on a raft, a lump of bread dough being kneaded, a Mediterranean peasant woman walking regally toward a well and (speaking of regal) Queen Elizabeth II herself, waving graciously to her subjects while being borne by courtiers around a room, on a kitchen table that served nicely for a royal coach. And once I was me, watching vanishing species of wild animals gambol as the sun went down over the highlands of Kenya (where in fact I never have been) and then retiring to a steep-roofed cottage with exposed beams and the right person inside.

Please Touch

The Kenya fantasy happened during an all-day meeting of an encounter-oriented New York City organization called the Riverside Community. One hundred or so of us were gathered in a large room in (of all the intrinsically uninspiring places) the Thirty-fourth Street YMCA. We split into subgroups of five, and were given five minutes in which to think where in the world and with whom we would go the next day if money were no object. When time was up, I was the first in my quintet to tell my fantasy. When the others followed with theirs I felt chagrined. Theirs weren't self-indulgent sprees. In their fantasies they had founded various agencies to help the undernourished, the downtrodden and the overlooked. (Or would mine have been nobler and more humanitarian, too, if I hadn't gone first?)

A good many There-and-Then excursions derive from the theories of two august and surpassingly self-confident living ancestors of the Human Potential Movement, Drs. Jacob L. Moreno and Frederick S. Perls.* Both are Viennese, and both feel fervently that groups provide the right *gemeinschaft* for the *angsts* of our *zeitgeist*. Both also speak a little condescendingly of their common late acquaintance Sigmund Freud. "I told Freud he put people on a couch and isolated them, which was entirely wrong," says Moreno. "We don't live on a couch; we live in groups from birth to death. Freud took people into the past, I take them into the present and future. Psychodrama deals with the Here-and-Now." Psychodrama, which Moreno rates second only to Sociometry among his own contributions to science, is a technique many encounter group theorists favor. A group member who wants to act out some critical scene from his past, or perhaps from his imagined future, is chosen to plan the drama. He will select other group members who remind him of his parents or his spouse or his

* Dr. Perls died in March, 1970, while this book was in proof.

children or whomever, to play those roles. Other people may be cast as his "alter egos," to voice thoughts he may forget to, or be unable to, articulate. The resulting proceedings can go on for hours, very affectingly.

Moreno's house overlooks the Hudson River. Perls has moved from Esalen to Lake Cowichan outside Vancouver, B.C., to found what he has referred to as a "kibbutz," a whole therapeutic community that will probably become an extension of the sessions he held in his circular stone living room at Esalen. At these sessions people were invited to come up one by one and occupy the "hot seat" next to his and opposite a vacant chair. The patient (a name which Perls, who is frankly a therapist, doesn't mind applying to subjects) relates and re-experiences a dream he has lately had. "Any dream you dream is real," Perls says, "and can be experienced in the present. Any dream has a top dog and an underdog" (corresponding roughly to the super-ego and the id). "Every part of the dream is a part of yourself. There are plenty of parts of our dreams we aren't willing to accept. You might not accept right now that you are a sterile, sadistic punisher," he said to one young woman who had just finished relating a dream, "but I'd like you at least to play that role." She did, badly. "This is all garbage!" Perls told her. "It's not even literature; it's anemic garbage production with no power. Until you uncover the cruelty in yourself, you won't come close to the power you have." (A point made also by George R. Bach.)

A dream, Perls believes, is an "existential message" which once a patient re-enacts its parts, can suggest "how to get past the impasse that makes your existence a nightmare and help you take your historical place in life." Fragmented, seemingly unrelated aspects of personalities are thus realigned into a new whole, or *gestalt*. The elements of the dream are personified and imagined to "sit" in the vacant chair across from the "hot seat." The dreamer then talks to his dream. The group watches with mounting empathy and often with great emotion. One young man about my age told of a dream in which he had seen his Aunt Evelyn die in a luncheonette. He realized after "being" his aunt, "being" her lunch, "being" the restaurant and being himself, that he did after all love his parents, from whom he had lately been estranged. He cried. So did many who watched, among them me. Another young man with a pasty face and a pasty, apologetic manner came forth to the "hot seat" to tell of a dream about a troll with crippled legs who was trapped in a dungeon where the sun never shone. He had in turn to "be" the troll, "be" his crippled legs, "be" the dungeon and "be" the door that barred him from the sun. In the course of enacting all these things he lay sobbing and writhing in the fetal position on the floor. Obviously his most central dilemmas—his impasse—had been reached. But he said to Perls, almost as if it were a question, "I'm not crippled; I'm not dead."

"Louder!" Perls demanded. "If you mean it, say it as if you did." The man said it louder and louder, but was still told his tone was unconvincing. Perls instructed him to go around the circle repeating the statement to each one of us. One by one he came up to us and said, in increasingly less hesitant tones, "I'm not crippled! I'm not dead!"

"Of course not," most of us said a little patronizingly.

"Like hell you're not!" said a fierce encounter veteran named Ben. "Tell me so I'll believe you, or I won't!"

"I'm really not crippled! I'm really not dead!" said the man in tones that suddenly were really confident and believable. Several people got up and formed a ring-around-the-rosy circle around him, chanting, "He's not crippled; he's not dead." It was like the finale of an operetta.

I had a Gestalt experience myself, led not by Perls, whom I found rather too formidable, but by Bill McGaw. It happened at Kairos. All of us in that weekend's workshop lay down on the floor with our eyes shut, silent for many minutes. Suddenly

Of There and Then

McGaw dinged on a gong, and the noise scrambled my
brains, tumbling usual associations haywire. Suddenly there
took shape inside my skull a picture of a rural mailbox on a
woodland country road, supported by a post stuck into the
earth and surrounded by a circle of multicolored tulips in full
bloom. They were pretty, but planted a trifle more symmetri-
cally than I would have liked. I was delighted with this fantasy, which clearly depicted one of my fondest wishes: to have
a rural house of my own. McGaw invited me to interpret it
the Gestalt therapy way, to *be* each element in the fantasy.

"Okay," I said, "I'm the mailbox. I give messages and get
them. I'm hoping for a lot of good long letters. I am the place
where reports are received and transmitted. If nothing's in me
I feel bleak and lonely, but still always hopeful. I am pressed
into the earth, which is warm and rich and loamy, with
worms. I am the earth; I am fertile and black and rooty and
rich. I am—or rather, we are—the tulips, beautiful and multicolored and longing to be wild. We are pretty; we enhance,
befriend and surround the mailbox. I am the road on which
the mailbox stands, a pretty unpretentious road where the
snow falls and piles and drifts in winter and grows gray and
melts and turns to slush and mud and then blooms and is lush
until the leaves turn red in autumn and fall to a mulch on the
ground. The road I am leads deeper into the country and
back out to the city. I am a road that connects with all the
other roads of the world." This was a surprisingly affirmative
and cheerful view of myself, for all its ribald and obviously
Freudian implications. Articulating it this way made me feel
better than I had in several harried weeks.

Vicarious There-and-Then experiences can be as affecting
as firsthand ones. In one group I belonged to, a young woman
said that even though she had a fond husband and three children, she had always been troubled by the fear that her father,
a proud European patriarch, had wished she was a boy. A
psychodrama was set up that began a hemisphere and two

207

generations away. She nominated two in the group who re-minded her of her parents, who had first met in Russia in the early part of this century when they both were plotting to es-cape from pogroms. Two others played her mother's parents, who schemed for the couple to marry. The brave young Rus-sian Jews made it to Ellis Island and all the way to Cleveland, where in time the Irish woman who played the mother an-nounced to the Italian man who played the father: "Isaac! We're going to have a baby!" "Isaac," who looked about as Russian Jewish as Elvis Presley, was nevertheless very con-vincing.

"Is good," he said. It was he who announced the sex of the child to the mother when she woke up from the anesthetic. "We have a daughter," he told her.

"Isaac!" the mother said, in some apprehension, "do you mind?"

"No," the father said. "Is good." And then the woman seemed to believe, as she never had before, that her parents accepted her for what she was, and so did the rest of the world.

One There-and-Then episode, at a marathon outside Chi-cago, was so theatrical that if I had not witnessed it I would have thought that—like the little boy's talk with his mother at the Bioenergetics session—it had come from the wastebasket of a mediocre playwright. This marathon group included a hippie named Leon, with steel-rimmed glasses and flowing hair, and a bald, stolid policeman named Nick.

"Look, man," Leon said to Nick. "I saw the pigs club a lot of my brothers and sisters at the Democratic convention. It puts me uptight just to sit here in the same room with you. You give me vibes of law and order, and I don't *need* that."

"I haven't said a thing about law and order," said Nick, "and I'm from Wisconsin, not Chicago. I think you're a nar-row-minded little jerk."

Of There and Then

"How do you feel about *yourself,* Nick?" asked Virginia Satir.

"Like a lion trapped in a net," answered Nick.

"What happens to lions trapped in nets?"

"They get put in cages for people to look at."

"What would you say to people looking at you in your cage?"

"I'd say, 'I don't like it in here; I'd like to be free.' "

"Give each part of you a voice," suggested Virginia. "The strong lion voice and the trapped, weak cage voice."

Nick's voice started out weak. "The Bible says the meek shall inherit the earth," he said, "but that's not what it's all about." Then the other voice took over. *"The strong have the power. You come up from down there. You've been meek too long. You and me are going to have a fight."*

"Just a minute, just a minute, wait, don't make a fuss, it'll be all right, don't get excited, wait till the next time . . ."

"The next time is now!"

"The other part of me," Nick volunteered, "is pallid, pale, gray, made of skins sewn together. It looks like a mouse or a rat. That's funny, I don't like mice and rats; I don't want part of me to be like that. But I guess part of me is. Or maybe it doesn't have to be like mice. Maybe the other part of me is more like a cloud. That's funny, the lion and the cloud: Why *shouldn't* they come together? Maybe they *can.*"

The gentle cloud part of Nick did tangle with the strong lion part. He sprang from his folding chair, sat down on the rug, took off one of his black loafers and stamped with savage fury on a speck that clearly was the cloud part of him. *"Go away, you fucking weak thing,"* he roared. *"I want to get rid of you."* His pen, glasses and watch flew all over the floor.

"Boy, you really gave it to me," said the cloud part of him, "but you know something? I don't mind; I feel better. I think maybe you can really use me. I think maybe we *can* work together."

Please Touch

Nick brought his two hands together, obeying Virginia's instructions to call his left hand Gentleness and his right hand Strength. First his hands were three octaves apart, then two, and then very slowly, inch by inch, they edged closer and closer toward each other in the middle, until they were near enough to touch but couldn't quite manage to. His face erupted from a mask of pain into tears. Then finally the two hands did meet, did touch, first just the tips of the fingers and then everything. The fingers slowly interlocked.

"Strength and Gentleness!" said Nick. "Maybe it can work. Might be a damn good match, baby." The hands revolved around each other, and he made a lattice of his fingers so that the strength and the gentleness showed through each other.

One trip Schutz led, the same week I had my guided daydream, took a Boston divorcee all the way back to her mother's womb, from which she emerged squalling like a newborn infant. As she wept for a puppy (whose death in her childhood she had never mourned) grew up, got married, and bore her own children, her voice dropped gradually to its present alto pitch. In another session that week a man of twenty-six, the same age at which his father had died, complained of an omnipresent fear of death. He was thereupon made to "die" in fantasy and to be "buried" and "reborn" while his group, by the spooky light of one candle, covered him with a sheet, picked him up and carried him around, and kept on humming the panacea Sanskrit mystery syllable "OM." He lay on a mattress writhing and moaning from the imaginary pain of terminal cancer, very nearly screaming, while his group leader told him: "You want to scream your unremitting terror but you really can't; you're in too much pain. All around you are doctors and nurses who are going to wake up tomorrow and go on living, but you won't, because *you are going to die.* This is *death!* This is what all fear is about. And now it is

210

coming to *you* . . ." Suddenly the young man quit writhing and lay quiet. Somebody covered his body and face with a sheet.

At a signal from the leader, the group lifted the mattress with the body on it, a little like the "Poor Jud is Dead" scene from *Oklahoma,* only not funny. They moved the body in procession in a big circle around the darkened room. It was deposited again on the floor, this time with the head facing in the opposite direction. Thus was the young man symbolically "buried," and told that when he felt like it he could choose to be reborn. Everybody waited expectantly. After a time he did get up, embracing in turn each one of his group members. He appeared vastly and genuinely relieved, and complained only that he felt hyperventilated. And then, since it was Esalen, he and all the members of his group walked by moonlight down the crooked dirt path to the bathhouse, to soak and reflect.

Pews Keep
People Apart

"If I ever really looked at the horrible darkness and despair I feel in my gut, I'd die. I can't stand it. Yet I do stand it, and whatever it is that holds me together is what I think of as God."
                                           —a member of an Episcopalian
                                              encounter group.

❡ After the automobile accident somebody came by my hospital room with a form for me to fill out. It asked, among other things, my religious affiliation. Rather flippantly I wrote "Pantheist," hoping thereby to dissuade any hand-wringers with turned-around collars from showering me with platitudes. But my answer wasn't entirely irreverent or untrue. The view of trees and butterflies from my hospital window really did give me the sort of solace I imagine other patients might get from clergymen. Ministers seldom waken in me any feelings of reverence and awe, but nature always does. So do most little children, and a number of grownups, and language and wine and music, even religious music. I love Masses and chorales and am immoderately fond of hymns. I like not only the genteel Protestant ones sung in the churches into whose collection baskets I dropped quarters (long before quarters stopped being silver), but the raunchy, maudlin, fundamentalist kind, too.

To paraphrase a classic hymn, beloved by all sects, "Change and decay in all around I see," all right, but I am by no means convinced that there is any "Thou, who changest not"—certainly not the trinitarian sort of Thou they told us about at Sunday School and Young People's. Billy Graham may crusade against th'encircling gloom, and Norman Vincent Peale may preside at private White House services, but they lose me and much of my generation. I would rather be preached to by Swami Satchidananda of the Integral Yoga Center in New York City (whose huge following includes at least one ex-Catholic, middle-aged, extremely straight grocer).

The human potential movement, however, has made me think that if the churches really wanted to they could lure us back, at least for a second look. A massive mutual transfusion is now in progress between organized religion and sensitivity training. In groups I have felt salvation, and in church congregations I have felt connection. This is as the human potential people mean it to be.

"We're taking religion back from the priests," says Abraham Maslow, "or rather turning them into social scientists."

"If psychology pushed to its deepest truths," says Rollo May, "it could not stop short of arriving at spiritual questions. We need a new mythology and a new set of symbols to express

213

modern man's inchoate yearning for meanings which can unite his experiences on all levels."

"Sensitivity training," says James V. Clark, "can teach people to see God and Christ in places where they might never have thought possible. They have seen Him where Martin Buber told us all to look, between man and man, and where Paul Tillich told us all to look, in our own depths. Sensitivity is not only a religious enterprise, but *the* most religious enterprise I know, because it lets people connect with their own capacities for love and power. Sensitivity training offers both a technology for the creation of meaningful religious development and an unparalleled laboratory for the study of the elements of religious experience itself."

Esalen, in a program Michael Murphy wishes would attract a fraction of the attention its hot baths and massages do, is conducting an interdisciplinary series on religion called "Theological Reflection on the Human Potential." The series is co-sponsored by a division of the National Council of Churches. Theologians and philosophers involved take part in encounter groups and other human potential disciplines. Then they try to relate these experiences to "such issues as the nature of God and man, liberation, redemption, God's will, creation and the good life. The revelation and growth-promoting experiences which such workshops facilitate," the Esalen catalogue goes on, "are significant for their theological-philosophical inquiry. Conversely, the increasing experiment with human potential may benefit greatly from theological reflection upon crucial experiences of change and growth."

Suppose a lady named Mrs. Minler. That's what other people call her, and that's how she thinks of herself. She is in her early seventies. Not long ago she went back to a city called Springfield, where she used to live right kitty-corner across the street from the Third Presbyterian Church. She had lived for

214

twelve years in Florida, ever since the death of her husband, and had not been back to Springfield except for this one time. Naturally she wanted to go once more to the Third Presbyterian Church, which in the old days had been as much a part of her as the taste of her own lips and gums.

Imagine Mrs. Minler's surprise when she stepped inside the church on that particular Sunday. Things weren't as they had been at all. Quite obviously something had happened to nice old Reverend Owens—he had gone away, to Heaven or elsewhere. There weren't even any pews in the church, just folding chairs arranged in circles of six, most of them occupied by people Mrs. Minler didn't recognize. On the altar were two large bottles of wine and several long loaves of French bread. Nowhere was there a robed, restively shuffling choir, waiting for the organist to sound the first notes of the Processional. Nowhere, in fact, was there any organist, only a guitarist dressed all in black and not wearing a tie, standing near the altar and singing as he played "Where Have All the Flowers Gone?"

Mrs. Minler wondered sadly what all this had to do with religion. She decided she would leave and just walk around the neighborhood until her relatives came to fetch her. But the new minister, who was waiting by the front door for the service to start, saw her dismay. He came up to talk to her. He was dressed in robes, but there was a sign Mrs. Minler didn't understand hung around his neck. It read "40,000." He did not explain the sign, but he told her he had replaced Reverend Owens three years earlier, and that they were about to have a special experimental service.

"It's called an Encounter Microlab Communion," he said, "and I'd like very much to have you stay for it."

"Where are the pews?" Mrs. Minler asked.

"Pews," said the reverend, "keep people apart from each other. The way people sit in any room—a church or a schoolroom—has a lot to do with what goes on between the people. We think church should be a place where people face each other, and face themselves. I see church as the place where my life is reflected the way it really is, the place where I can recognize tension and face it without going to pieces. Church is a place to celebrate as well as worship. Sometimes we have dances right in this room."

"Dances?" said Mrs. Minler.

The reverend smiled. "This must seem strange to you," he said, "but I think you might like our service. I hope you'll stay to have coffee, and we can talk about it more." He handed her a slip of paper that said "eleven," and pointed to a circle of six chairs with a big sign by it that also said "eleven." There were twenty such circles.

Mrs. Minler did not like the sound of "encounter micro-lab." A neighbor in Florida had told her about that sort of thing. That sort of thing involved a lot of compulsory touching and fondling of strangers. Mrs. Minler didn't even much like touching people she already knew. When her twin sons had been boys she had rarely embraced them, for fear it might spoil them. The only physical contact she'd ever had in this church, or in any other for that matter, was the accidental brushing of upper arms—followed by polite murmurs of apology—during the sharing of hymnals.

Only one of the chairs in Group Eleven was free. Mrs. Minler sat in it, between a colored man with long frizzy hair who looked about thirty and a white man who looked unusually delicate. When the guitarist in the black turtleneck had finished his song, the delicate man addressed the circle.

"For those of you who weren't at our last experimental service," he said, "let me explain that this, obviously, won't be like a regular communion service. We'll cover the same ground, but in an informal and more personal way. We'll read some Scripture and have an offering and share some bread and wine together, and talk about ourselves. But first let's introduce ourselves. We've tried to arrange it so that nobody's in the same circle with his husband or wife or whoever he came in with, so let's each tell our name—first name only—and then say whether we've been here before, and then share some feeling—not a thought, not a fact, but a *feeling* that we wouldn't mind having the others know. I'll start. My name is Anthony, and I've been coming here two years, and I'm feeling sad today because my roommate has just moved to Cleveland where he *thinks* he can start his *own* hairdressing salon. I'm not sure he can, and I'll miss him."

"Well," said the woman on Anthony's right, after a brief pause, "I'm Laura." Laura looked about nineteen. "I've never been here before at all, but a couple of my girlfriends from school have been coming a lot, and they told me I ought to come along with them, especially if I want to get to know Terry better. Terry's the guy playing the guitar. I like him."

The man next to Laura was tall and solid, with clear-rimmed glasses and an emblem in his lapel. "I'm Duane," he said. "My wife and children and I have been coming here ever since we moved to town eight months ago. I'm a landscape architect and I feel pretty good because I got three new contracts this week."

"My name is Sally," said the nervous, slender woman next to Duane. "My husband and I haven't decided yet whether to join this church or the Community Congregational. I like it here, but he's a little more conservative. He works at the Springfield National Bank. Maybe some of you know him. We have two children, a boy of twelve and a girl seven. We had another daughter in between, but last summer she drowned. It was a terrible thing, and . . ."

"I'm sure it *was* terrible, Sally," said Anthony. "Maybe we can talk about it some more later in the service. For now, maybe *you'd* like to tell us something?" This invitation was to the black man between Sally and Mrs. Minler.

217

Please Touch

"My name is Bob," said the man, "and I've been coming here four or five years, and I feel terrific today because my sister just had a baby boy and named him after me."

Then it was Mrs. Minler's turn. "I'm Evelyn Minler," she said, "and I used to come to this church when I lived right kitty-corner across the street, but I've been living in Sarasota, Florida for twelve years now, ever since my husband died. I must say I feel a little confused and upset by what's going on here."

"Tell us something else about *yourself,* Evelyn," said Laura.

"About myself? Well, I like to raise camellias."

"Beautiful," said Anthony. "Now, the service might begin with what we call the Evocation that starts 'Almighty God, to Whom all hearts are open . . .' but let's talk today, instead, about how open we really feel—how open we're willing to be to each other when we come to church."

And so they talked.

Such changes in liturgy are affecting many denominations. In the summer of 1968 I walked into a huge hotel ballroom in Washington, D.C. Of the 500 people there, the man on the stage and I seemed to be the only ones who weren't wearing what he called the "basic black" of Roman Catholic religious orders. All the others were nuns, fathers and brothers gathered to learn new ways to modify their liturgy and make it more appealing. The man on the stage (who was later to lead the Marriage Workshop I went to in San Diego) was Bill McGaw. He had just come back from the World Council of Churches meeting at Uppsala, Sweden, where he had demonstrated the same innovations he was about to show.

McGaw said that the tallest person in each circle of six should start by going around the circle and telling each of the others what his first impressions of them had been, and so on

218

until we had all exchanged impressions. He gave us several other instructions, in what amounted to a very gentle version of the Microlab. One of the exercises was for each of us to "write" a problem we had on an imaginary three-by-five index card. The cards were imaginarily shuffled, so that each of us was dealt one we hadn't written. We told what was written on our cards. The one I "wrote" said "fear of having chosen the wrong path." McGaw told us to choose any two of the problems and talk for a while about how it would feel to have those problems. Our group chose to talk about "not accepting people for what they are" and "inadequate understanding."

Then McGaw read the passage from John I:14 about Christ and the paralytic. He asked us all to image that scene: What might the weather have been that day? How did Christ look? How would it feel to be paralyzed? Before our circles disbanded, we were all to touch one another in some fashion. Amid the shoulder pats and hand squeezes came one surprise. A nun kissed a priest on the cheek.

"You needed that, Father," she said.

One could make a life work of visiting all the churches that have been affected by sensitivity training. I kept hearing of such experiments wherever I went. Some priests at the Ossining, New York, headquarters of the Maryknoll Seminary held an all-night marathon. A monastery outside Atlanta hired the Human Development Institute to expose it to sensitivity training. Several convents were having similar workshops. Four thousand Episcopal priests had been to encounter groups, and 2,000 were qualified to lead them. Unitarians and Presbyterians were actively involved, too. Had I checked into the Swedenborgians of Seattle? Did I know that the Reform Jews had officially sanctioned sensitivity training three or four years ago? Wouldn't I like to visit St. Paul's church of Englewood, New Jersey, which had an active program called "Groups for

Living"? Had I heard about what was going on in Chambersburg, Pennsylvania, in Appleton, Wisconsin, in Birmingham, Alabama? Following one such lead, I telephoned an Episcopalian minister in Wyoming. There too? There too.

"We fool a lot of people out here," said the reverend. Nor is he the only clergyman in his state who leads encounter groups, both for teenagers and for the public at large.

The Latter Day Saints, enjoined long ago by the Prophet Joseph Smith to "so organize the brethren that they might be freed from every encumbrance beneath the Celestial Kingdom by mutual bonds and mutual covenants of love and friendship one towards another," also were sponsoring group programs. An interdenominational Protestant organization called Yokefellows, based on the use of small confessional groups, had many chapters, some thousands of miles from its California headquarters.

Roman Catholic laymen often gather for three-day retreats called "Cursillos"—little courses in Christianity. An acquaintance of mine who had been to a Cursillo and also on a Synanon weekend "Trip" said "I got the same kind of terrific high from both of them. You come out much more aware than you were of textures, of life, of each other. You come out of the Cursillo singing a song called 'De Colores'—of the colors. You're more aware of colors, too. I talked to people both there and at Synanon that I'd never have met otherwise. It's really a mixed bag. And it really made me feel more *Christian* than anything else ever has."

A Los Angeles *Times* article quoted Dr. Melvin Wheatley of the Westwood Community Methodist Church as having told his congregation that "there is a basic truth in the psychedelic contention that most people go through life turned off. There are dimensions of memory and degrees of awareness available far beyond what most of us ever claim. Too many people are like the Pennsylvania Indians, who laboriously warmed themselves for generations by fires of twigs, while camping adjacent to fathomless beds of anthracite.

"The New Testament," Dr. Wheatley went on, "is not just concerned with life and death, but with degrees of awareness. All the days of our lives God seeks to stab our spirits more widely awake."

"Psychedelic is right!" said Laura, after the Scripture reading in Group Eleven at the Third Presbyterian Church. The reading had been from Chapter Four of Revelation, talking of "one on a throne" who looked like "a jasper and a sardine stone, and there was a rainbow round about the throne, and in sight like unto an emerald. And round about the throne were four and twenty seats; and upon the seats I saw four and twenty elders, sitting, clothed in white raiment; and they had on their heads crowns of gold. And out of the throne proceeded lightnings and thunderings and voices; and there were seven lamps of fire burning before the throne, which are the seven Spirits of God . . ."

"Fantastic," Anthony had agreed. Mrs. Minler, who didn't like to touch people, patted his hand. The young man with the guitar sang another song, about a dead young man. Its refrain went:

> And the only clue as to how he died
> Was a bayonet stuck in his side.

Mrs. Minler winced. She winced again when she realized what the "40,000" sign that the minister wore meant. That was how many American servicemen had been killed so far in Vietnam. Mrs. Minler had always assumed that the government must know best about such matters as the war, but she began to reconsider. She had never cared much for colored people, but the man next to her must be nice if he was so

221

pleased about his new nephew. And the hairdresser on the other side of her seemed to be what her husband would have called a "pansy," but he seemed kind, too.

When the service had finished, and each of them had had a chunk of French bread dipped in red wine, the hairdresser said that they would "pass the peace" among them. He gave the woman on the other side of him a gentle hug, and said "May the peace of the Lord be with you."

"And with you," said the woman, who in turn hugged the man on her other side. So it went around the circle, until it came time for the Negro man to pass the peace to Mrs. Minler. He hesitated, and took both her hands in his instead of giving her an embrace. She looked up and put her arms around him.

"Peace be with you, too," she said.

The Reverend James Adams of St. Mark's Episcopal Church on Capitol Hill in Washington, D.C., told me that his parish's January retreat would not be strictly sensitivity training. It sounded like part of the human potential movement, though—thirty-five people going off by themselves for a weekend, to divide into small groups and examine their feelings not only about the church and the Bible but about each other.

Adams' flock, whom he had described as "mostly young, over-bright and over-educated," looked conventional enough, and the setting was super-conventional: the National Headquarters of the 4-H Club. It was filled with Grant Wood prints oddly reminiscent of Soviet realism, and fringed satin banners adorned with the 4-H motto, which is:

I PLEDGE
    my HEAD to clearer thinking,
    my HEART to greater loyalty,
    my HANDS to larger service, and
    my HEALTH to better living for my club,
        my community and my country.

Pews Keep People Apart

The strawberry chiffon pie served in the cafeteria looked delicious, but it tasted as I imagine detergent must. All this was an incongruous background for the things the Episcopalians said, which could as easily have been overheard among what Californians call "Big Sur Heavies."

"What environment *would* you be comfortable in, Sue? Warm jello?"

"I don't know," said Sue. "I feel I've been losing touch with myself. Somewhere, someplace in me, I don't feel right."

"I feel pretty good," said a distinguished looking man named Dana, who reminded me for some reason of a retired admiral. "I feel that through all the months we've been together, I've related to everyone in this group, and that I like all of you and all of you like me."

"I've got news for you, Dana," said a girl in her early twenties.

"Really?" asked Dana.

"Yes. I feel I should tell you this: I've never liked you."

"Really?"

"It would be wrong for me to let you think you got along great with everybody in this group, because in my case, I've been polite and nice all along and let you think so, the way I'm polite and nice to my father, but what I really sort of feel is sorry for you, because you're not anywhere *near* as groovy as you think you are."

"I'll have to go along with that," said a young man named Bruce. "You really are a conceited, pompous bastard."

Dana looked stunned. "Well," he said, "I guess I should thank you for telling me that . . ."

A black woman came across the room to put her arm around Dana. "I admire Linda for telling you that," she said to Dana, "and I even think there's some truth in what she said, but I think you're a hell of a guy, too."

"Thanks, Nancy," said Dana. "I guess part of closeness is discovering the depth to which you're *not* understood, and finding out where you really stand. It's tough, but it's better than kidding yourself."

"I'm kind of the same way," said a bespectacled older man named Harry. "I live a very safe life. I don't reach out, because if I did I might get rejected, and I'm not happy about that idea. Not expecting anything is a way of staying where you are. There's no chance of getting involved if you say 'I know when I reach out I'll be rejected.'"

"Harry, do you ever act like what you really are? Or do you temper what you say and how you come across because of what you think the group expects of you? Older people, a lot of the time, have learned the rules for the group they're in, and they just find it easier to accept the rules, and not sweat it."

"I guess maybe I *do* do what's expected of me," said Harry, "rather than what I really want to do."

"What's wrong with us all," Adams told members of the group, "is that we aren't in touch with ourselves. Sin is separation. Separation is loneliness. Sin is where there's a vacuum, an abyss, between parts of yourself, or between you and other people. To me the tragedy of separation is that I'm separated from *me*. That's the part that really hurts.

"I've got a lot of things going on in me all the time, and there are some of them that I don't want to pay any attention to, like failure, ignorance, greed, dishonesty, temper, cowardice. And hate. And fear. I don't want to be with some essence of myself that it's difficult to come to grips with. But in blocking off those things, I also block off the things that are good.

"You can't turn yourself off a little bit. If I blot out that in me which I don't like, that part of me that I *do* like dies down, too. Paul said the wages of sin was death, and he was right. If you're out of touch with yourself, man, then you're really dead."

Pews Keep People Apart

"How would our society look," James V. Clark once asked a room full of rabbis, "if every church and temple in America centered around encounter groups? Such a vision is possible."

Such a vision might be a fine thing to pursue.

The Plaint
of the Patriotic
Letter Writers

"... Within the sensitivity training program, however beneficent it may appear to some, there are elements that we dare not unleash upon an unsuspecting and uninformed society."
—W. S. McBirnie, in *Sensitivity Training: The Plan to Brainwash America.*

¶ Twelve red oak trees past the creek, just off the big interstate highway, there's a byroad where you turn left and go a mile and three-tenths. Then you take the left fork of that road to a big sign that says "Sinistra." Follow the driveway all the way back past the poppy fields to the main lodge, and ask for

The Plaint of the Patriotic Letter Writers

Kevin Levin. Don't be startled if whoever is at the desk isn't wearing any clothes; you'll soon feel like disrobing, too. And don't be surprised if Kevin Levin isn't around at all. He is often off spreading his ideas in other parts of the country. Whoever meets you is bound to be breathtakingly attractive. Everyone at Sinistra is. The ten males on the staff are exceptionally well-formed, the ten young ladies as shapely as they are authoritative, and the kennel of champion Labrador Retrievers (some black and some yellow) are amazingly quick to learn. There is also a defrocked swami in residence, oddly enough the only person around who habitually wears clothes. He chants, it seems incessantly, in Sanskrit. And occasionally there is a visiting expert in body awareness or political theory or both.

Unless you've applied months in advance you won't stand much chance of getting into the Creative Nonverbal Interconnection Workshops for which Sinistra is legendary. These workshops, for twenty-four people at a time, are booked until well into next year. Cancellations are unheard of.

Each group stays for four well-programmed days. Each person pays $250. That might seem a lot, but consider what you get for your money: intensely personal tutelage in Interconnection (first with only one staff member, then in groups of three and four and up to twelve). It's really marvelously liberating. Guests usually feel completely relaxed after a couple of hours on the premises. Any residual tension is quickly dispelled by the use of LSD, available on demand, or, for the more wary, the thriving patch of *cannabis* in the garden behind Kevin Levin's luxuriously rustic "cottage."

Levin shares his "cottage" with Swamba Mbote and Harriet Porterfield Bradshaw. Swamba is that arrestingly elegant Masai girl—she says she's Masai, anyway—and Harriet made her debut in Boston a few seasons back, before she gave up that sort of thing. She and Swamba keep house for Kevin, interconnecting creatively with each other when he is out of

227

Please Touch

town. They also keep track of the instructions that come via
the underground from North Korea on how most effectively
to teach Sensitive Governmental Overthrow at evening workshop sessions.

These sessions are held in a room with no furniture at all
except for an American flag used (quite amusingly, really) as
a rug. Don't be alarmed if you happen to hear yelps and
screams coming from that room. Guests in there are also
taught Improved Vocal Reaction to Group Stimuli, and sometimes things do sound as if they're getting a little out of hand.
For guests who may feel chilly, scarlet ponchos are available
to toss over their shoulders. But as I say, the climate at Sinistra is so reliably clement that hardly anybody bothers with
clothes.

Sinistra is of course an absurd fiction, but you wouldn't
think so to listen to the human potential movement's enemies.
The enemies, mobilized into shrill action by such forces as the
John Birch Society, the Voice of Americanism in Dallas, and
the Patriotic Letter Writers of Pasadena, issue propaganda that
hints of places scarcely less bizarre or menacing. They say
that the sensitivity training movement is "spreading like a cancer through every state in the Union," cajoling the innocent to
"pay for the privilege of being helped to feel like worms" and
calculated to hasten "the breakdown of all inhibitions, moral
and physical." The movement's aim, they say, is to "turn people into manipulated zombies."

These objections are paranoid, hysterical and even funny,
but not all criticism of the movement is. Some of the movement's own zealots have doubts and worries about what they
do. Here are the charges most often leveled at encounter
groups, followed by the best responses I have been able to
gather.

(1) *The groups can be run by charlatans who are corrupt*

228

or mediocre or both. True. Because sensitivity training is too amorphous to be controlled by clinical psychologists or any other professionals, anybody who feels like it can advertise "Encounter Marathons." Anybody can set up shop as a group leader, thereby gaining access to the defense mechanisms and souls of the unwary. Anybody can do harm.

"It isn't so bad that these guys don't have academic degrees," a social worker friend of mine said. "Everybody knows a lot of stupid people who have degrees. But I'll tell you one thing for sure: you can't get an advanced degree in any of the psycho-therapeutic fields without learning how easy it is to hurt people."

Ethical people in the movement retort with analogies: just because you might get electrocuted, they say, doesn't mean you shouldn't have electricity. "The atomic scientists faced the same problem we face now," said Robert Tannenbaum of UCLA. "Do you cancel any research or building because what you may learn might destroy the world?"

(2) *The groups are a hotbed of junkies and dope addicts.* Nonsense. The group movement flowered along with the hippie drug culture, to be sure, and many curious people have experimented with both, but as Rasa Gustaitis pointed out in her book *Turning On,* the whole point of the human potential movement is to expand consciousness without the use of chemicals.

"Drugs," said Robert Driver who founded Kairos, "make people into great giant sieves. Drugs take away the boundary between your skin and the rest of the world. If you don't know where that boundary is, you're lost." Synanon and several group-centered organizations patterned after it were organized expressly to fight drug addiction.

(3) *The groups invade privacy.* They do indeed. I never saw anyone in a group forced or coerced into a confession, but some I was in seemed monumental games not of "I've Got a Secret" but "I *Had* a Secret, and Here's What It Was." Person-

ally I rather like my secrets. I am disinclined to serve them up for a roomful of strangers, however congenial and well-wishing the strangers may be. George Steiner left a weekend at Esalen, where he had given a seminar, feeling the same way only more so.

"It seems to me," Steiner later said, "that there is less and less of a zone of reticence around human beings. I'm obsessed with privacy, and I was offended by their technique of embarrassing people into telling publicly about the privacies of the body and the psyche." As Theodore Roszak wrote in another but related context, ". . . it is an embarrassment to be sucked into other people's soul-searching. Do they want you to respond with praise? shock? pity? love? or disgraceful confessions of your own?" Jerry Berlin, from well within the human potential movement, admits to the same misgivings. "When I'm intimately relating to another person," he says, "I don't want the whole world or even the whole room to know about it."

(4) *The groups foster sexual promiscuity.* True, partly. Rumors of orgiastic abandon in groups are overblown, but not unfounded. In certain groups, usually those on the West Coast, the vital juices can be set astir with what to some may seem unfamiliar and undue haste. When strangers are asked, the first time they ever congregate, "Who in this room would you most like to go to bed with?" it is no wonder that those who end up retiring alone should feel forlorn. Two or three nights of such forlornness often prompt liaisons that wouldn't have happened elsewhere. And, with such a premium on honesty, it is natural that there should be morning-after group discussions along the lines of "Sleep and Tell." A woman in one Esalen group I was in confessed that she had had two sexual experiences in her five days there, "one of them fantastic."

"Was either of them with someone in this group?" the leader asked. She nodded yes. "Was that the fantastic one?" No. "Would you like to tell us who in the group it was?" The woman looked at a shy and gentle man across the room.

"Shall we tell them, Norman?" she asked. Poor Norman didn't have much choice.

"I used to think we just illuminated marital strife, not that we created it," one group leader told me. "But now I think maybe we *do* create it." Sometimes such strife arises when people rediscover their long-ignored sexuality. But many people, married and otherwise, regard that rediscovery as the human potential movement's most valuable gift. Who can mourn if a forty-one-year-old virgin suddenly feels seductive?

(5) *The groups encourage physical violence.* Nearly always false. As my Synanon tribe leader said, speaking for most of the movement, "The difference between us and Hitler is that he killed people, while we don't even let you *threaten* to hit somebody." In most groups I know of, arm-wrestling is about as far as physical struggles get. The few exceptional accounts of true violence seem to come mostly from northern California, which has more groups than any other place. Stanley Keleman, in Berkeley, says he has "acted as an emergency clinic for people who've been exposed to very extreme physical techniques by leaders who don't know where to take it next."

Esalen lore includes tales of broken toes, broken ribs, and a woman who twisted her spine so badly during a Yoga session that she had to be hospitalized. Just before I first went there one man had hurled another through an open window, in the course of an impromptu virility rite. Neither man was hurt. Schutz reports having intercepted "only once" what might have been a lethal karate chop. A technique called "psychological karate," practiced by a Bay Area therapist named Husain Chung (whose phone had been disconnected when I tried to call him), is the only one I know of that openly permits violence. Chung's forty-hour marathons, said to be among the most melodramatic in the business, are billed as providing "continuous, intensive experience in the acting out of emotions and conflicts." I doubt, however, that Chung's bravura style will take much hold elsewhere.

(6) *Groups can be fatal.* Hard to prove. Of the many thousands of people who have been to Esalen, two have died on the premises. One, a staff member, was a suicide, and the other drowned—apparently accidentally—in the bathhouse. Dr. Everett Shostrom writes of a young woman who was so depressed after an encounter group elsewhere that several weeks later she drove her car into an embankment. These three deaths might have something to do with encounter groups, but they also might have happened anyway.

(7) *Groups do psychological damage.* They can, if they are run ineptly. "Some people come home an absolute wreck, needing radical emotional surgery," said a college official who had watched many colleagues return from many groups. But Dr. Charles Seashore of the NTL estimates that the incidence of serious stress and mental disturbance is "less than one percent, nearly always in persons with a history of prior disturbances." In the twenty-odd groups I went to I saw only one instance of anything remotely approaching what professionals call a "psychotic break"—the short and happily resolved incident of the mother in the Bioenergetics workshop. A study Carl Rogers did showed there had been two such "breaks" out of 500 people. An Esalen survey showed five out of 50,000. John Weir supposes that in the fifteen years he has been leading groups, he has seen "twenty-five or thirty people dramatically, floridly disturbed." But he hastens to advance a theory popular among his colleagues: that if you're going to crack up anyway, an encounter group is the best of all possible places to do it.

"The worst thing you could do for someone who had a psychotic break," says James V. Clark, "would be to remove him from the group. The groups have an infinite capacity to heal."

"Mental hospitals," Weir told me, "only try to provide the kind of atmosphere we have here automatically."

The Plaint of the Patriotic Letter Writers

"If you want to get hurt, shook up, maybe even commit suicide," said Richard Farson, "go to college—any college. The risk of injury and damage in groups is really minimal. We may have *less* psychosis than there is outside."

"I know of no laboratory program," says Chris Argyris of Yale, "that has, or could, hurt people as much as they are hurt during their everyday work relationships."

"We go in deeper, quicker, faster," admits Schutz, "but people are safer with us than they might be elsewhere. We don't just leave them after we've opened up, and say 'Whee! You're open! Bye now!' We work them through." (Esalen, incidentally, has a professional interest in madness and psychosis. A month-long seminar in the summer of 1968, taught by psychiatrists from six countries, was called "The Value of Psychotic Experience.")

(8) *Groups hypnotize their members.* True, on occasion. I described the "body trip" Schutz gave me to Dr. Milton Kline, a New York psychiatrist who specializes in hypnotherapy. He said it sounded very much like hypnosis, "susceptibility to which is enhanced in group settings. Sometimes," he said, "people can be hypnotized into a state of *manic* euphoria, requiring hospitalization or medication. Sometimes they experience extreme anxiety, or act out intense sexual responses."

Some analysts, Kline told me, use "sensory hypnoplasty," which means having their patients work with clay "to intensify experience and help them go back to painfully repressed episodes. There are many inherent dangers in this very rapid regression." I thought of the clay session John Weir led in his lab. I don't doubt at all that he and Schutz know what they're doing, and I wouldn't hesitate to entrust myself to either of them again. But what if somebody a shade less stable than I fell into the power of group leaders a shade less principled and skillful than they?

(9) *Groups are anti-intellectual.* Frequently, dismayingly true. In their zeal to reconnect the intellect with what they call

233

"gut-level feelings" some groups dismiss all abstractions as "headshit" and "mindfucking." In an Atlanta T-group my heart went out to the schoolteacher who, when he exclaimed, "I think this is a lot of weird crap!" was instantly reprimanded, "don't say think, say *feel!*" I felt sorry too, for a girl named Elaine when someone said, "There's Elaine over in her corner *thinking* again. That thinking! It'll get you in trouble every time!"

Polysyllables are pounced on like danger signals of cancer. I was scolded at different times for using "nuance," "gregarious," "touché" and "verbosity."

"Logic," one group member said hesitantly, "can be a real turn-on. Some of my best friends are logical."

"I hope you won't take offense," I heard someone tell a group leader in San Francisco, "but I think you're well-educated." He didn't take offense.

I thought George Steiner was overdoing it a bit when he told his Esalen audience that "no great innovative thinkers have *ever* sat on the floor," but he had a point when he later asked, "What's the point of self-discovery if there's nothing, or very little, there to discover? Having them go even deeper inside themselves only shows them what *bores* they are. It would be better if they would memorize poetry, or learn a language, or play chess, or listen to music, or study butterflies." The New York psychonanalyst Dr. Silvano Arieti told me that "only the most primitive of emotions do not need a cognitive counterpart. Only with full understanding can we get to the emotional core of things."

(10) *The groups cheapen real emotion.* Sometimes true. "The techniques that are supposed to foster real intimacy sometimes destroy it," Frederick Stoller said. "Some of our new colleagues who try to gimmick it through in the area of 'instant intimacy' are guilty of this. What they do may not be *dangerous,* but it isn't more than entertaining. It doesn't expand the mind or soul."

The Plaint of the Patriotic Letter Writers

"It's too bad," said Jerry Berlin, "that some people feel obliged to hug and be affectionate when they don't really want to, and that others can't unless they're given official permission."

A nervous young man in one group I was in went around the room asking several people, including me, if we loved him. I said I did, but later regretted not having answered "*Love* you? How could I? We've just met. I wish you well, sure, and I have sympathy for you, but don't mix that up with love."

(11) *The groups themselves are guilty of the failing they most chastise in their members—phoniness.* This can be true. Dr. Ross Snyder of the Chicago Theological Seminary said in a newspaper interview that all some people learn in groups is "new ways to be impersonal—a new bag of tricks, new ways to be hostile and yet appear friendly."

"Touching," said Dr. James Bugental, "can be a way of *not* relating."

Some critics think the growth centers operate under false pretenses. "Esalen," one said, "cures under false pretenses. It's a magnificent lab for the development of new forms of therapy, but it lacks authenticity."

"It's a psychological and spiritual supermarket," agreed Alexander Lowen. "Naivete would be a mild word for the attitude prevailing there, much as I like to go there. 'Foolish' might be more like it."

(12) *The groups lead to emotional elitism.* They can indeed. A lady at a human potential party in New York announced "I'm the only person in this room who can actually feel." When I removed my shoes during one California encounter session, somebody said, "*Well!* What would the people in your office think if they could see you *now?*" as if nobody in my office or elsewhere east of the Donner Pass ever went barefoot, admired a sunset, or stopped to pick up a pebble.

Sometimes group people can be insufferably condescending. "I know where *you're* at," they might say. "You're where I was two years ago. Don't worry, you'll come out of it." And some attach grand significance to trivia—"you *say* pass the salt, but I *hear* you saying you feel neglected"—or dwell with relentless tedium on minor skirmishes of sibling rivalry and tortured adolescence.

(13) *The groups have ridiculous jargon.* Oh wow, there's a certain amount of holistic, heuristic truth in that, man. It's out of sight the way they rap on in their lecturettes and all, about how you should get in touch with yourself. When I get some air time I'm going to lay on you my story about a group that was nurturant—*very* nurturant, and growthful, too. When you like get down to Nomenclature Gulch, and integrate all your connects, when you ask where someone is, you don't mean what city or what room. Cognitively speaking, you've got to get your top dog and your underdog together.

Fishbowling through the golden glow period, using approaches we got through *FIRO* at *COPE, CRUSK, PLUNGE, PACE* and *SPRED,* we worked through our *LALI* and got into the inputs. We clinicked and critiqued about process, and shared. I'm glad I shared that with you, Bambi, I feel comfortable about your being here. I'm like glad you're part of our multidisciplinary, task-oriented, in-service training, and my level of unconditional positive regard for you is high. I think you're reely together. I reely resonated when you said that about the change agent winging it in the cousin lab. Let's try to be alive and find out where it's at and actualize. Let's have a triad about the *zeitgeist.* Let's work it through and have a lecturette about feedback. And above all, after we've dumped, let's stay in touch with the feeling.

(14) *The groups may get to be a cult.* Get to be? Few deny that they already are. "A fanaticism," says the Chilean therapist Claudio Naranjo, "could develop around the goodness in this movement. An authoritarian preaching environment could develop around the perfectly defensible enthusiasm."

The Plaint of the Patriotic Letter Writers

"We can't let it be just an emotional Maine Chance," says Robert Schwartz, at whose Tarrytown House, outside New York City, many groups are held. "Unless it's kept in the mainstream it's sure to get cultish and faddish."

(15) *The groups are pointless.* This is the harsh judgment of the San Diego Gestalt therapist Thomas Munson. "I get tired of hearing them moan 'we're not a *group* yet,' " Munson says. "What they don't seem to know is that every man damn well *is* an island, and every man's problem is to find his own way by communicating with other islands, sometimes by submarine and sometimes by causeway. If he tries to do it by subjugating himself to the group, he'll relinquish his personal identity."

"Human relations training that mucks around with emotion," says Robert Blake, "gives people a wallowing good cathartic time, but it isn't worth a tinker's damn. It isn't even a means to an end."

(16) *The groups may indeed cause stirring and wonderful things to happen, but these effects aren't valid because they don't last.* This criticism is debated so often that it is the subject of the entire next chapter.

Back Home

¶ At the Boston airport the reservations clerks seemed impersonal as robots, the skycaps avaricious and the newsstand lady grouchy. My fellow transients looked harried, with hunched shoulders and furrowed brows. I'd have looked that way too had I not just emerged from eight days of exquisitely heightened sensitivity. As it was, I was absurdly aware of the humanity of all these strangers. I had to restrain myself from gazing with what would have seemed awful intensity into their eyes, and administering unsolicited backrubs to the ones who looked tired and tight. If I had yielded to these impulses I would likely have been carted away to some institution, as they say a girl once was from the San Jose bus station after a workshop at Esalen.

Back Home

Soon afterward I joined some of my oldest, closest friends for Thanksgiving weekend at a tranquil farmhouse on the coast of Maine. Maine sounded far enough away from New York City, which afflicted them, and encounter groups, which afflicted me, to be a perfect haven for us all. But we had some tense moments.

"Don't you feel like *dancing?*" I asked them. They didn't. They didn't want to fingerpaint, either, or to walk around blindfolded. They wanted to sit before the fire and talk and read. They did just that, while I, lonely in my liberation from verbalism, danced by myself to a Doors record in the other room, feeling foolish.

Just as it is hard to be sober when nobody else is, I found what thousands of other veterans of groups have found: that it is hard to re-enter "back home" reality after the intoxicating communion of a successful encounter or T-group. "Real people," with their buttoned jackets, folded newspapers and legitimate worries about purse snatchers and rent control, are seldom prepared for all that exaggerated candor and high-voltage warmth. So much spontaneity threatens them. Among them, away from the rarefied milieu in which my feelings so tenderly and expertly had been laid bare, I felt lonelier than ever. The polite deceits of usual life left me cynical and deflated. My Loved Ones, Congenials and Higher-Ups, as the horoscope columnists like to classify people, had not been where I had been, and the difference was pronounced enough to trouble us all. I was further troubled by a new awareness of, among other things, my own shortcomings. Failings I scarcely knew I had now emerged in glaring high relief.

Toward the end of one group I was in, its trainer, Peter Caffentzis, gave advice on how to handle this transition.

"You'll feel like saying 'Wow! Am I sensitive! I don't know what happened to me, but boy, do *you* need it!' But don't do that. If you really have become all that sensitive, visualize on your way home what's been going on with the people who've been doing the rinkydink home-base stuff. Let *them* talk to *you*. See if you can hold off for a couple of days before you tell them about the group."

The re-entry from encounter groups to reality, and the business of keeping alive the elusive benefits of sensitivity training, are problems that preoccupy every student of the human potential movement. In group dynamics, however, as in psychotherapy and in all the so-called "healing professions," theory and research lag far behind practice. Plenty of research exists, but much of it is inconclusive, contradictory and written in lamentable style. One well-meaning social scientist tells of having analyzed "12,500 units of behavior." I'm not sure I even want to know what a "unit of behavior" is, but I do know that much more, much plainer research would be welcome.

Reports say that T-groups can and frequently do have a "powerful and positive impact on individuals," causing two-thirds of their members to "increase their skills." Sensitivity training, other monographs and dissertations say, has been shown to make people better managers, abler than they were before to "listen accurately, perceive the complexities of relationships, and tolerate pressures and differences."

Scientific Resources, Inc. has begun a program, financed by Coca-Cola and involving twenty other companies, which is designed to "establish norms in organizations that will be supportive of individual personal growth and change." By so doing, SRI's president Robert Allen told me, "We hope to learn how to keep alive this ephemeral whatever-it-is that people get from groups."

Whatever it is, one thing sure is that people will keep clamoring for more of it. "The most predictable behavioral change," said Dr. Kurt Back of the Duke University sociology department, "is that they'll be back next year." As one man I talked to said, "It's a pretty safe $300-a-year 'habit.' " Dr.

Back Home

Morton Lieberman, presently of Stanford University, is also at work on a long-term study of the aftereffects of groups. Esalen and Kairos have sent out questionnaires to evaluate their groups to everybody on their mailing lists.

"But the only data that really counts," one group leader told me, "is if the guy liked it or not." Most of the guys, in fact, do. Only a very few report that they regret their T-groups and labs and encounters.

"Even if it doesn't last," one T-group veteran said, "the miraculous thing is that it can happen at all."

"I've made a whole 180-degree leap from where I was before," another claimed. "I always thought I'd have to be lonely, the way I used to be all the time. I never knew that living could be this much *fun*."

"Not only did the group you and I were in cause me to revamp my whole business," an executive told me seven months after we had encountered, "but it's made me *literally* a warmer person. I don't wear undershirts or wool suits any more, even in the northern winters, because I don't need to."

Not all reports, of course, are so upbeat. As one man told me, "I went to the group, got turned on, found I was able to be intimate, fell in love with the group and the people in it, went home, and then got shot down by everybody there. Before I knew it I was back to chewing out my wife about the burnt toast, yelling at the kids to empty the garbage, and bitching as much as I ever did about my boss."

But such relapses may not be as discouraging as they seem. One study I read told of a "delayed-reaction phenomenon," meaning that the process of "refreezing" new behavior patterns to replace thawed and outmoded old ones depends among other things on the passage of a fair amount of time.

"Everybody wants to be open," I heard Kenneth Benne tell a roomful of people at Bethel. "If you know what openness means, you'll want to be open all the time, not just to people but to the sun or the subway or whatever. But most people close up when they get home, instead of staying open. They may not open again until six or eight months later."

The most hopeful study I saw suggested that these groups can be a universal panacea, serving to embolden the timid, soften the brash, and make everybody more understanding, aware, competent, honest, flexible and open. But flexibility and openness, like humor, are defyingly hard to codify. Platoons of skeptics are always lying in wait to attack whatever data do emerge from research. Some of the skepticism comes from within the movement. Many wonder, with Sheldon Davis of TRW, "what would happen if in the next five days everyone in the world went to a T-group? We might all be authentic and congruent and Rogerian, but what would we have on the sixth day?"

What we might hope to have, one wise social scientist told me, is "a reservoir of commitment to change"—the new knowledge that change for the better is, after all, possible. Systems that earnestly seek to change, whether they are as small as a marriage or as big as American Airlines, have been making several discoveries about encounters and T-groups. One is that heterogeneous labs are more effective than homogeneous ones—that you will benefit more if your group includes some people unlike yourself: of a different color or from a different tax bracket or a different level of management. Longer labs, it has also been found, produce more changes in behavior than shorter ones. Groups held in residential seclusion, at "cultural islands" like Bethel or Esalen or Lake Arrowhead, are usually more effective than those on home ground. And it is generally wasteful—"merely entertaining," as somebody said—for a system of any kind to send only one person to a lab or workshop. It is much riskier and more threatening to reveal your weaknesses in a group that includes somebody you already live with or sleep with or work with, but it is also more committing.

Back Home

I never went to a group with anyone from my real life. Probably I should have. But as my own life is far more fragmented than most, and atypical, so was my zigzag odyssey through the human potential movement—an odyssey I would emphatically discourage anyone from imitating. Nobody should follow the odd trail I blazed. My friend with the advice about wine-tasting was right. Going from one encounter or T-group to another without doing some plain, regular living in between can be as pointless as having your hair set twice in the same day. I would advise waiting a month, preferably several, between groups, and shying away from any group whose leader has not been personally and authoritatively recommended. Anybody with doubts should check with a psychologist or psychiatrist before joining a group.

I would also advise group members to prepare themselves for barrages of questions from their friends, who in time may confide, as at least two of mine did, that "you don't seem any different to *me*—a little more nervous, maybe, is all." People are always coming up to me at parties and wanting to know what my year of encounters did for me.

"*Well?*" they demand. "Did it work? Did you experience Joy? Did you Peak? How was it? What happened? Are you changed?"

These questions seem as heavy and futile as requests to "sit down and tell me *all* about your trip to Europe, *right now,*" but I guess I can't blame people for asking. By rights, after all, I ought to be the most sensitive, aware, together, congruent, straight, up-front, honest, spontaneous, authentic, self-actualizing, peaking, centered, integrated person in the western world. The recipient of what must be a record amount of feedback, I ought to know myself as no self has ever been known.

I don't, of course. Sure, I have changed since January 1968, when I went to my first encounter, but who has not? And how can I say which changes in me are traceable to the groups and which ones would have happened anyway? I would rather report on the progress of my broken foot, which is better now, thank you, although I still limp some and can't walk as far as I'd like to. As to my psyche, I am both better and worse than I used to think I was. It is easier for me now to accept my own and other people's shortcomings. (As the mother of a friend of mine says, we should all automatically forgive one another three failings. But she didn't learn that from any T-group.)

I have shed a little, at least, of my burdensome free-floating Protestant guilt, for which relief alone much thanks. I can say no a little more easily than before, though still not with the ready reasonance to which I aspire. I can let the phone ring unanswered, sometimes, and not go to parties, sometimes. With modest, erratic success and many setbacks I have tried to "act as if" I possessed such virtues as tidiness and punctuality.

I am vividly aware of, if hardly pleased by, the impression I make on others. I am still far more cryptic and oblique and glib and brittle than I would like to be. It is still true that the more helpless I feel the more brusque I seem. Without wanting to, I scare people away. When I feel most like crying, Midwestern stoicism or something compels me to insist that everything is just fine. I am still evasive; I still avoid collisions. I am still looking for the middle ground between seeming a brash, managerial mistress of ceremonies one day and a timid, blushing seventh-grader the next.

I still yearn, impossible though I know it is, to do everything and be everywhere. I still press my nose to other people's windows without doing much to locate windows of my own. I am still guilty of trading phony cocktail-party kisses with people I don't much care for, and of failing to hug some whom I really love.

My peak experiences, if anyone wants to call them that, tend to occur not *en masse* or on schedule but at quieter times —watching a blueberry ripple winter sunset, sharing a bottle

244

of wickedly good Chablis, smelling the air of the country, or finding somebody else who savors for its own sake a phrase like "Rosecrans and Sepulveda" or "pleni sunt coeli." I am more aware than I used to be of all that might go on and doesn't below my neck, but I am incorrigibly a child of the Gutenbergian print-freak heritage, and so are most of my friends.

The values of the human potential movement, for my taste, are better embodied outside encounter groups than in them. In groups I found nobody more "interpersonally competent" than Jordan Bonfante, more bent on "doing his own thing" than Paul Ryan, more adept at "living in the here and now" than Terry Spencer, more "together" than Chris Hubbard. None of these people owes the virtues I esteem in them to behavioral science. Fond though I often felt of people I encountered in groups, none of them has come to be really important to me, nor have I to any of them. There are many who would be welcome, as my Cousin Mary Louise might say, to "put their feet under my table," but most of them I have not even seen again, and probably won't. Encounter groups don't work that way. They are organized to show all their members how they come across to the world at large. Their purpose is not to spark enduring friendships but to provide a finite microcosm. The NTL people knew what they were doing when they called their groups "laboratories." It would be sad and futile, I think, to confuse the feelings born in these laboratories with genuine friendship, but people do. For a time I did myself. As a life style, I can say with authority, encounter groups are at the very least unsettling.

Exposure to so bewilderingly many strangers, in encounters that tantalized more often than they nourished, had pronounced effects on me. For a while, as I tapered off from groups, I could not bear the sight of an egg-timer or the company of more than two or three other human beings. I came to cherish as I never had the luxury of quiet tête-à-têtes

Please Touch

(known to some as "dyads" or "raps") with proven friends,
    one
    at
    a
    time.
I have come to esteem history as a component of friendships.
In my case at least friendships are not igneous but sedimen-
tary. Mine usually take a year, sometimes several, before they
ripen, and I am not persuaded that behavioral science can
hasten this process. Behavioral science can enrich the flavors
and enlarge the menu of hors d'oeuvres, but I have not known
it to supply the meat.

I had some physical symptoms in the course of this odd
year, too. Along with the newfound blessings of feeling more
at ease (if not conspicuously more lithe) on the dance floor,
and "staying with" all sorts of feelings I hadn't even known
were there, I developed a slight but perceptible facial twitch.
It lasted several weeks. Having been off cigarettes for eight or
nine years I resumed smoking, quit again, resumed again, and
am now, so help me, about to stop. My case of Hong Kong flu
at Christmastime 1968 was so florid and operatic I really
thought it would be terminal.

I also acquired, and retain, a stare I am often told is too
penetrating. This is because back in the days before I ever
heard of encounter groups I used to be accused of seeming
evasive and shifty-eyed. All those Eyeballing exercises more
than took care of that problem. I would often think, during
Eyeballing, of my Auntie Grace, who used to say she had a
trick of focusing on the space between the eyes, just above the
bridge of the nose, when she looked at people. So, I'm told,
have the Tibetans, who think we all have invisible third eyes
in that vicinity. Maybe she and they are right.

During my Bioenergetics workshop I was advised to quit

keeping my mouth shut when not in use, as for years had been my wont, but slackly open.

"You have pretty teeth," said a man named Ben. "Why don't you let them show?"

"Because I'm trying to avoid having a fake, hypocritical smile," I explained. "Wouldn't it look simian and stupid for me to go around with my mouth open?"

"Better that than looking like some uptight librarian," he said. So I took to baring my pretty teeth, fancying I might thereby resemble some provocative French starlet. But this little illusion was shot down the next time I saw my mother.

"What's the matter with your *mouth?*" she wanted to know. "Can't you breathe through your nose?"

I never developed much patience with sly inquiries about the "nudie group gropes" and "touchie-feelie encounters" that people liked to assume had become my new habitat. What perturbed me more, however, was my own inability to explain these matters. But I know now what I wish I had said to all those people at all those dinner tables who asked, in effect, "Now just what *is* all this ridiculous nonsense? What kind of a world would we *have* if everyone did what these 'groups' of yours say, and expressed everything that occurred to him? That's anarchy! What about civilization? What if what I felt like doing right this minute was shooting you dead?"

The answer, I think, is not to express feeling so much as to recognize it. Group philosophy—wise group philosophy, anyway—does not prescribe that you run to inform your old landlord that everyone secretly thinks he's effeminate, or your boss that you've always thought he was a stupid tyrant. The aim is first to know, in your head and below it, what you think and feel, and then to reflect on newly unearthed alternatives to your accustomed ways of being. Once it is unlocked, the door between your feelings and the cosmos need not be kept yawning open. It can be left ajar.

Please Touch

Meanwhile, hope for all the Sherris and Marcs and Kevins and Jennifers who now ride tricycles may lie in risking more emphasis on warmth, even at the expense of light. Maybe we have plenty of light already.

Appendix

I. *SOME PLACES I DIDN'T GO*

The human potential movement is a tempting target for cynics and iconoclasts. The good it does is indeed ephemeral. Some of its practitioners are indeed charlatans, or humorless egomaniacs, or both. Some of their programs, along the lines of "An $85 Weekend for People with Prehensile Toes," are indeed frivolous. A few are downright salacious. If the movement holds to these courses it will deserve the oblivion some hope will be its fate.

But cynicism is too easy a stance, and too myopic. Cynics overlook the promise generated within the movement by bright and informed idealists with the highest of motives. These idealists are working to design and lead encounter groups and workshops not for pampered borderline neurotics but for people in real trouble. Their programs are not sensational, and don't make big headlines. They deserve more attention, more money and more influence than they have yet managed to attract. Part of their obscurity, however, is their own fault. When I asked to sit in on several such programs, I found the idealists elusive and skittish.

249

Please Touch

"Can't you wait six months until our next grant comes through?" I was asked once.

"You'll understand," someone else told me, "that we can't have anyone here from the *media*—that would ruin everything."

"Too bad you weren't here last Thursday," a lot of others said. But I only had just so many Thursdays. Given a good many more, I would like to have told firsthand of several programs that sounded constructive, socially conscious and promising. Here, in brief, are some examples:

\# The Riverside Community, a New York City organization with a mailing list of 500, ranging from residents of Spanish Harlem and Jersey City to bluestocking alumnae of Bryn Mawr. Loosely connected to the National YMCA, Riverside charges very little for its day-long encounter workshops and weekend T-group retreats. Social action is emphasized as well as personal growth.

\# A Middletown, Connecticut, program has held weekend training laboratories in which representatives of hospitals, schools, the police force, the YMCA, the Red Cross, the Chamber of Commerce, real estate firms, churches and black militant groups have all taken part. Herbert Shepard of Yale University has been in charge. Funds have come from the state government and from a private profit-making foundation. For the weekend encounters employed adults are charged $25, unemployed ones $10. A few get free scholarships.

\# TRW Systems, in Redondo Beach, California, is as committed as any firm to the uses of applied behavioral science. In early 1969 TRW began a program involving 100 people from a section of Los Angeles called Harbor City, where nearly 100 percent of the population are on welfare and the median age is eighteen. Using T-groups, problem-solving work groups and many other techniques, TRW found jobs for its recruits. Eight months later all but 7 of the 100 were still employed—five had been fired, one was in jail, and one had gone to school. TRW visionaries also talk of someday establishing a "floating T-group"—to meet in pool halls or rooming houses—to introduce other Harbor City people to their corporation.

\# In the impoverished and crime-prone 30th Precinct of New York City, eighteen policemen were chosen for a "Family Crisis

250

Appendix

Intervention Unit." Psychologists and graduate students at the City College of New York worked with the policemen over a two-year period, in a program that included Spanish lessons, T-groups and role-playing. In patrol car teams of two, the policemen answered all radio calls within the precinct that had to do with domestic trouble. On the average they had two calls per team per night. During the time of the experiment the precinct had no homicides, no suicides, and no charges of police brutality. "The big idea," said Dr. Wilson Meaders who helped train the policemen, "was to talk to the people who were having the fights *separately, and then* bring them together."

"Yeah," said one of the patrolmen in the experiment. "What a lot of people need is just to be *listened* to. A lot of these people never had anybody hear their side of the story before. They're very afraid, not just of each other but of the whole world."

Other programs designed to establish rapport between policemen and ghetto people have flourished in many places, including Grand Rapids, Michigan; Houston, Texas; Sausalito, California; and Buffalo, New York.

In many cities T-groups are being used on a wide scale for nurses, orderlies and other hospital personnel, with the result that they get on much better with one another and with their patients.

Dr. Eva Schindler-Rainman, a Los Angeles trainer who specializes in nonverbal communication and the problems of schools, spent one of the hottest weeks of the summer of 1968 in Wichita, Kansas. There she trained teachers who were to be assigned that fall to classrooms of "inner-city" schoolchildren. A few summers before she designed an elaborate T-group program for the newly-integrated school system of Riverside, California. Her design involved not only students, teachers and parents but also the superintendent, nurses, secretaries and custodians, meeting in groups of fifteen.

"I have a whole theory of training," Dr. Rainman said. "I don't cut people off. I believe in support. That's how people learn. I always invite the opposition in. There's no hope of changing their minds if you don't give them a hearing. If we're going to change a piece of society, we have to seek out those who are most resistant to the change, as well as those who want it. Junior League types, with whom I've worked a lot, are beautiful, but they're every bit as crippled as the blacks."

Junior Leaguers have applied to the NTL for a nationwide program (sponsored by the Sears, Roebuck Foundation) to learn more effective ways to work in their communities. In laboratory seminars they confront ghetto people. The YMCA, the Campfire Girls, and several other social agencies have become committed to similar programs. The National YMCA has led some 6,000 teenagers through different sensitivity groups, ranging from three-day weekends to ten-day laboratories, with dramatically positive results.

Esoteric veterans of the human potential movement talk of founding communes and kibbutzim—isolated country retreats where honesty and openness can prevail. (Dr. Frederick Perls has founded a commune in British Columbia; Philip Slater of Brandeis University said he hoped to start one of his own.) A less exotic manifestation of the widespread longing for "community" is the neighborhood T-group. Robert Allen, the New Jersey trainer, would like to pioneer with such groups. "We have to get to know each other as people," Allen says. "There ought to be T-groups in neighborhoods and communities, financed first by foundations and the federal government, and later by municipalities. I started a T-group in my own neighborhood, where I'd lived for nine years without knowing a thing about most people, or they about me. It turned out that an old guy everybody thought was mean and hostile had a hearing problem. It turned out the neighbors thought something was funny about me, too, because on my days off I'd sit outside and read instead of chatting or beating rugs. But once we explained ourselves we all got along better.

"Maybe such groups could be organized in big city apartment buildings as well as in the suburbs. Maybe someday there will be neighborhood health centers for normal people. Maybe someday heads of state can meet in the same open spirit. Maybe this could alter the course of history. It would be hard to napalm a man if you knew his wife and children."

II. *SOME OTHER DREAMS*

"We must build environments," Betty Berzon told a convention of fellow psychologists, "that will foster growth and develop more loving, nurturing individuals. We have to get into whole systems, to fight climates that inhibit change. We really need to change our whole life style, so that our world can come into tangency and I can know, even if only for a little while, what it's like to be you."

"In the next 100 years," said Warren Bennis, "we're going to be learning mostly about ourselves, and how we relate to each other and to the technology it's taken us the last 100 years to understand. This time there'll be a new Manhattan Project in the social sciences. As social technology evolves and matures, we will learn how to become more aware of ourselves and our impact on other people."

NTL Institute officials, who for twenty-two years have used sensitivity training, T-groups and other techniques to solve human and social problems, continue to have grand hopes and plans. In late 1971 the NTL will establish, on a 375-acre site in Virginia, "the world's first university devoted entirely to applied behavioral science." Postdoctoral master's degrees in applied behavioral science and in humanistic psychology will be offered. So will experimental new curricula, and a "Think Tank" where resident and visiting social scientists can contemplate, and attempt to bridge, the gaps that separate knowledge from action.

Visions of Think Tanks also dance in the heads of the leaders of Esalen, a continent away, who hope to raise enough money to establish an "Alternate University Model," where they might "gather together a dozen professionals from every branch of the human potential movement—from encounter groups to astrology to computer research—with the aim of setting up a program leading to a Master's Degree in Awareness." (O brave new world! O gaudeamus igitur! Imagine: a graduation procession, filled with pomp and circumstance, of academics so quiveringly sensitive that their very caps and gowns would have raw nerve ends.)

Every zealot of the movement has his private fantasy of awak-

253

ening a numbed and sluggish populace. Some talk of setting up microlabs or Encountertapes in airports, for the diversion of bored and exasperated people waiting for planes. Bernard Gunther, Esalen's chief evangelist of sensory fulfillment, dreams of replacing the "seventh inning stretch" at baseball games with a "seventh inning awareness break." Others suggest that people summoned for jury duty, waiting outside courtrooms for their names to be called, might pass the tedious time by forming *ad hoc* encounter groups—or that factory workers on coffee breaks might be led in similar exercises, designed to make them feel less like machines.

Television and radio will probably do more than they so far have to show real people engaged in real encounters. Synanon officials talk of televising their Games. "T-Group 15," the interracial Boston radio experiment, deserves to be imitated. So does "Some of My Best Friends," a similar confrontation produced for educational television by Dr. Charles Seashore of NTL. Esalen, already parodied in the commercially successful movie "Bob & Carol & Ted & Alice," plans its own series of films.

Another whole chapter of this book could have been written, time permitting, on the influence the movement has had on the theatre and vice versa. This influence is sure to grow. Casts of several recent plays have been led through specially tailored versions of encounter groups and sensitivity training. (Actors and actresses in the celebrated nude revue *Oh! Calcutta!* did not begin rehearsal until they had experienced a number of "trust exercises".) "Method acting," a technique devised by Konstantin Stanislavski and perpetuated at Lee Strasberg's Actors Studio in New York, relies in part on exercises well known to habitues of the human potential movement. All the world is indeed a stage.

Growth Centers themselves can be depended upon to grow, in real estate, in renown and in the sophistication of their facilities. Joyce Weir described to me the idea room she and her husband John have in mind for their Advanced Personal Growth laboratories: "a mink-lined salad bowl with controllable lighting and ventilation, furnished with bodies instead of tables and chairs."

Independent group leaders like James and Elizabeth Bugental will continue to blend encounter groups with trips to art galleries, plays and concerts. Bill and Audrey McGaw have already shepherded encounter groups on camping trips and boating excursions outside San Diego. Dr. Harvey Wasserman, a Connecticut psychiatrist, plans a raft trip to shoot the rapids on the Colorado River in the Grand Canyon. That trip will also be an encounter group, with Betty Fuller of Esalen as co-therapist.

Encounter groups and T-groups as we know them now, in short, are sure to evolve and change. They are also sure to be savagely attacked, and vigorously defended, as the human potential movement collides with more conventional sectors of society. "Right now," as Dr. Moreno says, "we're going through a transitional period of anarchy and chaos. The giants are dead" (himself excluded, presumably) "and 200 million midgets are in charge. We have to wait for the Psychonauts to take over from the Astronauts before we get to what we need: a psychiatry and sociatry for all mankind."

Even Michael Murphy, who at five feet eleven inches is one of the more imposing of the "midgets" now in command, concedes that the movement is "still in its infancy. We have to go through our gangly, pimply adolescence before we get where we want to go." His colleague Robert Driver, who founded Kairos, agrees.

"What allures people," Driver says, "is the idea of a new kind of learning environment. We have to keep working toward that."

Driver's father, an insurance executive, is said to have been dismayed when his son decided not to follow the same profession.

"But I told him," the younger man said, "that this *is* a form of insurance."

III. *THE EXTENT OF THE MOVEMENT*

I first began to realize the extent of the human potential movement one morning on the campus of UCLA. I was on the voyeur's side of a one-way window, watching a session of Business Administration 182, a sensitivity training course that has far more applicants (from many unrelated schools of the university) than openings.* Also observing, with a quizzical look on his smooth features, was a polite visitor who told me his name was Morio Kure. Like the *I Ching,* Hatha Yoga, Zen Koans, the word "OM" and many forms of meditation, Mr. Kure had come to the human potential movement from the Orient. Specifically he came from the Mitsubishi Bank in Tokyo.

When I met him he was just finishing a four-month pilgrimage of the high points and shrines of the American training circuit. He had been to Bethel and the WBSI in La Jolla and many places in between. He was soon to take the knowledge he had gained back to his bank's training program. T-groups, he told me, had already affected 3,000 Japanese.

"Mostly in businesses," he explained. "Also priests and monks. Also nurses. There are usually twelve in a group, and the groups last four or five days. In Japan we call sensitivity training 'Western Zen,' because like Zen it is a way to pursue the truth. Like Zen it is painful when it is over, but worthwhile.

"We in Japan are much more open about business than you are, but less open about private problems. Japanese women very rarely have a chance to express their feelings. But we have a saying: there are two bad postwar trends in Japan, nylon socks and women getting stronger."

Australia has its own sixty-member Institute for Human Relations, analagous roughly to the NTL. Labs have been tried in Nigeria, Togo, Zambia and Kathmandu. India has an association of trainers. South Vietnamese educators have been exposed to NTL laboratories, and so have Peace Corps people in Guatemala and Chile. Chile also has an outpost of Esalen, organized by the Gestalt therapist Claudio Naranjo with the help of the Pan-American Health Organization. Sensitivity training methods are said to be extremely popular with Colombian businessmen, and with medical schools in all South American countries except Ecuador, Bolivia and Paraguay. Engineering and education schools in South America also use such groups.

Europe is smitten too. As the French speak of such evidently untranslatable Yankeeisms as *le sweater* and *le drugstore,* so have

* Social Relations 120, at Harvard, is even more legendary among academics on the encounter circuit.

Appendix

they also come to refer to *le T-group,* which one Frenchman told me he preferred to the alternate form *le groupe diagnostique.* French prisoners—at least some in Lyons—have also been subjected to group techniques, as have convicts at such an unrelated place as the Colorado State Penitentiary.

Holland has thirty sensitivity trainers of its own. Fleets of Norwegian fishermen have had fewer union problems, it is said, since their exposure to group techniques. Dr. Traugott Lindner, who runs the European Institute for Trans-National Studies and Group and Organizational Development, told me at Bethel that he gets many requests for information about training from Iron Curtain countries. "Once," he said, "there was a lab in Poland, where openness is enormous. But everything connected with sociology is a hot potato in totalitarian countries. All the universities had to stop teaching it in East Germany."

Dr. Lindner hopes to conduct "Ski Labs" in the Tyrolean Alps, for people from both sides of the ocean. "Transatlantic labs," he says, "are a good idea. The sports atmosphere is very beneficial. People really need more exercise than they usually get in groups. It's not good to just sit there all day long."

In a similarly adventurous spirit the Santa Barbara branch of the University of California last summer dispatched a class called "Intellectual and Intercultural Relations X312" to Denmark for three weeks. Along with smorrebrod and visits to Tivoli, students get credit for ninety-six quarter hours of dyads, feedbacks, encounters, sensitivity and awareness training.

Canada begins to teem with sensitivity training. Vancouver has a Growth Center called Shalal, reported to be one of the more promising, and the University of Montreal puts 3,000 people through T-groups every year. The movement's breadth in the United States seems so vast that until now nobody, to my knowledge, has attempted any directory of its outposts. For the benefit of people who want to find some avenue to an encounter or laboratory training group near them, here is a list I am sure is incomplete but which I hope may help.

GROWTH CENTERS AND
KINDRED ESTABLISHMENTS

SOUTHERN CALIFORNIA
   Paul Bindrim—Los Angeles
   Center for the Study of the Person—La Jolla
   Dialogue House Associates, Inc.—San Jacinto
   Gestalt Therapy Institute of San Diego—San Diego
   Gestalt Therapy Institute of Southern California—Santa Monica
   Human Development Institute—Los Angeles
   Human Potential Institute—Palos Verdes Estates
   Human Resources Institute—La Jolla
   Institute of Group Psychotherapy (Dr. George R. Bach)—
      Beverly Hills
   Institute of Therapeutic Psychology (Dr. Everett Shostrom)—
      Santa Ana
   Kairos (The Ranch)—Rancho Santa Fe
   Kairos (Town House)—San Diego
   National Center for the Exploration of Human Potential (Dr.
      Herbert Otto)—La Jolla
   Nexus—El Cajon
   The Openings—Goleta
   Topanga Center for Human Development—Reseda
   Synanon—Santa Monica
   Western Behavioral Science Institute—La Jolla

258

Appendix

Mary Whitehouse Studio—Santa Monica
Yokefellows—Burlingame

NORTHERN CALIFORNIA
American Association for Humanistic Psychology—San
    Francisco
Berkeley Center for Human Interaction—Berkeley
Blue Mountain Center of Meditation—Berkeley
Bridge Mountain Foundation—Ben Lomond
Casaelya—San Francisco
The Center—Stanford
Center for Human Communication—Los Gatos
Esalen Institute—Big Sur
Esalen Institute—San Francisco
Ann Halprin Studios—San Francisco
Humanist Institute—San Francisco
Explorations Institute—Berkeley
Institute for Multiple Psychotherapy—San Francisco
New Horizons—Los Gatos
San Francisco Gestalt Therapy Institute—
    San Francisco
San Francisco Venture—San Francisco
Institute for Creative and Artistic Development—
    Oakland
Institute for Group and Family Studies—Palo Alto
S.E.L.F. Institute—Los Altos
Society for Comparative Philosophy Inc. (Alan Watts)—
    Sausalito
Still Point Foundation—Los Gatos
Synanon—Oakland
Tahoe Institute—South Lake Tahoe
Transpersonal Institute—Palo Alto

NORTHWEST
Northwest Family Therapy Institute—Tacoma, Washington
Seminars in Group Process—Portland, Oregon
Senoi Counseling and Growth Center—Eugene, Oregon

259

Please Touch

SOUTH

Adanta—Decatur, Georgia
Center of Man (Sidney Jourard) Mincanopy, Florida
Family Relations Institute—Annandale, Virginia
Han Institute—Boca Raton, Florida
Hara, Inc.—Dallas, Texas
Laos House: Southwest Center for Human Potential—Austin, Texas

NORTHEAST

Association of Community Trainers—New York, New York
Anthos—New York, New York
Aureon Institute—New York, New York
Cumbres—Dublin, New Hampshire
Dialogue House Association—New York, New York
Encounter (addict rehabilitation)—New York, New York
G.R.O.W.—New York, New York
Human Dimensions Institute—Buffalo, New York
Human Resource Center of Connecticut—c/o Norman Lifton, Mansfield, Connecticut
Human Resources Development—South Acworth, New Hampshire
Institute for Experimental Education—Lexington, Massachusetts
Institute for Rational Living—Philadelphia, Pennsylvania
Moreno Institute of Psychodrama—New York City
Moreno Institute of Psychodrama—Beacon, New York
Orizon Institute—Washington, D.C.
National Council of Churches (Training Office, Department of Educational Development)—New York City
Personal Growth Center—Great Neck, New York
Plainfield Consultation Center—Plainfield, New Jersey
Psychosynthetic Research Foundation—New York City
Riverside Community (c/o Carmen McBean, National YMCA) —New York City
Alec Rubin Theatre of Encounter—New York City
St. Clement's Church—New York City
Sky Farm Institute—Calais, Vermont

Appendix

Synanon—New York City
Tarrytown House—Tarrytown, New York
Wainwright House—Rye, New York

CANADA
Cold Mountain Institute—Edmonton, Alberta
Evering Consultants—Toronto, Ontario
Gestalt Training Institute of Canada (Dr. Frederick Perls)—
    Lake Cowichan, Vancouver, British Columbia
Shalal—Vancouver, British Columbia
Strathemere—North Gower, Ontario
Synergia—Montreal, Quebec

MEXICO
Yolotli—Mexico City

PUERTO RICO
Synanon—San Juan

NATIONAL TRAINING
LABORATORIES DIVISIONS

NTL Institute for Applied Behavioral Science—Washington,
    D.C.
Midwest Group for Human Resources—Kansas City, Missouri
NTL Institute—Portland, Oregon
NTL Institute—Salt Lake City, Utah
NTL Laboratory locations—Bethel, Maine; Cedar City, Utah;
    Lake Arrowhead, California
Western Training Laboratories—c/o UCLA, Los Angeles

OTHER ORGANIZATIONS THAT SELL OR OFFER LABORATORY OR SENSITIVITY TRAINING

Adult Education Council—Denver, Colorado
Atkins-Katcher Associates—Los Angeles, California
Richard Beckhard Associates—New York, N.Y.
Blansfield, Smith & Co., Inc.—Carmel, California
Human Development Institute (a Bell & Howell firm)—
    Atlanta, Georgia, and Los Angeles, California
Leadership Resources, Inc.—Washington, D.C.
PACE (Personal And Company Effectiveness)—Los Angeles,
    California
Personnel Research & Development Corp.—Cleveland, Ohio
Scientific Methods, Inc.—Austin, Texas
Scientific Resources, Inc.—Union, New Jersey
Social Dynamics, Inc.—Boston, Massachusetts
Training Consultants International—Minneapolis, Minnesota

SOME CORPORATIONS THAT HAVE USED VARIOUS FORMS OF LABORATORY TRAINING

Alcan
American Airlines
Applied Power Industries
Atlantic Refining
Bell Telephone of Canada
Bell Telephone of Pennsylvania
Boeing
Celanese

Appendix

Curtiss Wright
Corning Glassworks
Dow Chemical
E G & G
Esso
Esso Research and Engineering
Federated Department Stores
General Aniline and Film
General Electric
General Foods
Hotel Corporation of America
Humble Oil
International Business Machines
Kaiser Aluminum
Eli Lilly
Arthur D. Little
Maytag
Midas Mufflers
Monsanto
Moog Servo
Ortho Pharmaceuticals
Polaroid
Port of New York Authority
Procter & Gamble
Saga Foods
Standard Oil
Sun Oil
Texas Instruments
TRW Systems
Trans-Canada Airlines
Union Carbide
West Virginia Pulp & Paper
Illinois Central Rail Road

Please Touch

COLLEGES AND UNIVERSITIES INVOLVED, OFFICIALLY OR OTHERWISE, WITH ENCOUNTER GROUPS OR LABORATORY TRAINING

CALIFORNIA
Diablo Valley College—Pleasant Hill
Immaculate Heart of Mary College—Los Angeles
John F. Kennedy University—Martinez
Sacramento State College (c/o Associate Dean of Students)—Sacramento
San Diego State College (Department of Psychology)—San Diego
San Francisco State College (Downtown Center)—San Francisco
Sonoma State College (Department of Psychology)—Sonoma
Stanford University (Research Institute)—Menlo Park
United States International University—San Diego
University of California at Berkeley (Department of Psychology)
University of California Extension Division—San Francisco
University of California at Los Angeles (Institute for Industrial Relations; Graduate School of Business Administration; UCLA Extension)
University of California Medical Center (Division of Community Psychiatry)—Los Angeles
University of California at Santa Barbara (Department of Psychology)
University of Redlands (Johnston College)—Redlands
University of Southern California (Youth Studies Center)—Los Angeles

WEST
Brigham Young University (Department of Psychology)—Provo, Utah

264

Appendix

Central Washington State College (Research and Development Center)—Ellenburg, Washington

Colorado State College (c/o Dean of Students)—Fort Collins

Gonzaga University (School of Business Administration)— Spokane, Washington

Portland State College (School of Social Work)—Portland, Oregon

University of Oregon (Department of Psychology)—Eugene, Oregon

University of Utah (Division of Community and Urban Development)—Salt Lake City, Utah

SOUTH

Duke University (Departments of Psychology and Psychiatry) —Durham, North Carolina

Georgia State College (Community and Group Laboratory)— Atlanta, Georgia

University of Florida (Department of Psychology)—Gainesville, Florida

University of Tennessee (Department of Psychiatry)—Memphis, Tennessee

University of Texas (Department of Psychology)—Austin, Texas

MIDWEST

Antioch College—Yellow Springs, Ohio

Case-Western Reserve University (Division of Organizational Studies)—Cleveland, Ohio

George Williams College (Center for Human Relations & Community Studies)—Chicago, Illinois

Michigan State University (State Training Laboratory)— Lansing, Michigan

Ohio State University (Department of Psychology)—Columbus, Ohio

Purdue University (Graduate School of Industrial Administration)—Lafayette, Indiana

St. Louis University—St. Louis, Missouri

St. Mary's College—Notre Dame, Indiana

265

University of Cincinnati (Human Relations Center)—Cincinnati, Ohio

University of Kansas (Department of Psychology)—Lawrence, Kansas

University of Michigan (Survey Research Center, Center for Research and Utilization of Scientific Knowledge)—Ann Arbor, Michigan

University of Notre Dame—Notre Dame, Indiana

University of Wisconsin (Research and Development Center; Department of Psychology)—Madison, Wisconsin

EAST

Boston College (Institute for Human Resources, Department of Psychology)—Boston, Massachusetts

Boston School for Human Resources—Boston, Massachusetts

City College of New York (Graduate Department of Psychology)—New York, New York

Duquesne University—Pittsburgh, Pennsylvania

Fairleigh Dickinson University (The Center for Human Development)—Rutherford, New Jersey

George Washington University (Group Relations Conference)—Washington, D.C.

Goddard College—Plainfield, Vermont

Harvard University (Graduate School of Business Administration)—Boston, Massachusetts

Lesley College (c/o Dean of General Education)—Boston, Massachusetts

Massachusetts Institute of Technology (Sloan School of Industrial Management)—Cambridge, Massachusetts

The New School for Social Research—New York, New York

New York University (Graduate School of Business Administration)—New York, New York

Newark State College (Laboratory for Applied Behavioral Science)—Union, New Jersey

Postgraduate Center for Mental Health—New York, New York

Appendix

State University of New York (Department of Psychology)—
Buffalo, New York

State University of New York at Albany—Albany, New York

Syracuse University (School of Education)—Syracuse, New
York

Teachers College of Columbia University—New York, New
York

Temple University (Group Dynamics Center)—Philadelphia,
Pennsylvania

University of Maryland (Human Development)—College Park,
Maryland

University of Rochester (Management Research Center)—
Rochester, New York

University of Vermont—Burlington, Vermont

Washington School of Psychiatry (Group Relations Conference)
—Washington, D.C.

Yeshiva University (Graduate School of Humanities and Social
Studies)—New York, New York

Index

269

Index